大学商务英语综合教程 2

第二版
SECOND EDITION

学生用书

主编
杨翠萍
蔡　莉

陈洁倩　吴　朋　江小娣
成矫林　朱　青　孔燕平　编
薛初晴　刘鸣放

清华大学出版社
北京

内 容 简 介

本教程选材涵盖当今国际经济贸易和商务的重要领域，时效性强、典型性高、语言地道。

教程板块设计突出国际商务知识的传授与英语技能提高的有机结合，注重培养学生的实际应用能力。每个单元重点讨论、分析一个商务专题，由"导入活动""阅读活动""商务实践"和"专业扩展"四部分组成。各部分内容的设计与编写坚持了操作性与挑战性并重的原则，以保持学生的学习热情和自觉实践的积极性。其中的"商务实践"板块围绕单元主题，参照各种真实的商务交际情景，为学生设计了灵活多样的商务英语口头与书面交际的任务，是本教程的一大特色。本教程配套精美教学课件，为教师课堂教学提供帮助。课件下载路径：ftp://ftp.tup.tsinghua.edu.cn。

本教程适合大学商务英语专业的学生及BEC（Business English Certificates）等商务英语考试的备考人员使用。

版权所有，侵权必究。举报：010-62782989，beiqinquan@tup.tsinghua.edu.cn。

图书在版编目（CIP）数据

大学商务英语综合教程学生用书.2/杨翠萍，蔡莉主编.—2版.—北京：清华大学出版社，2016（2021.8重印）

ISBN 978-7-302-44452-7

Ⅰ.①大… Ⅱ.①杨… ②蔡… Ⅲ.①商务-英语-高等学校-教材 Ⅳ.①H31

中国版本图书馆CIP数据核字（2016）第169631号

责任编辑：蔡心奕
封面设计：平　原
责任校对：王凤芝
责任印制：刘海龙

出版发行：清华大学出版社
　　网　　址：http://www.tup.com.cn, http://www.wqbook.com
　　地　　址：北京清华大学学研大厦A座　　邮编：100084
　　社 总 机：010-62770175　　邮购：010-62786544
　　投稿与读者服务：010-62776969, c-service@tup.tsinghua.edu.cn
　　质量反馈：010-62772015, zhiliang@tup.tsinghua.edu.cn

印 装 者：三河市铭诚印务有限公司

经　　销：全国新华书店

开　　本：185mm×260mm　　印张：18.75　　字数：367千字

版　　次：2009年8月第1版　　2016年8月第2版　　印次：2021年8月第5次印刷

定　　价：76.00元

产品编号：065960-04

第二版前言 Preface

《大学商务英语综合教程》（第2版）是一套依据现代外语教育对教材意义及功能的要求，结合应用语言学专门用途英语的最新研究成果设计和编写的、融英语语言知识及技能和国际商务知识及技能于一体的复合型英语教材。

本教材既可供高校英语专业或商务英语专业的本、专科学生使用，也可供国际经济贸易、金融、财会、工商管理等专业的学生作为复合型专业英语教材使用，还可作为大学英语选修课教材及相关行业的培训教材。

本教材的编写宗旨是：遵循现代外语教学理念和应用语言学专门用途英语的教学原则；充分考虑学习者在经济、贸易、金融、管理等方面的专业需求，力求以人为本，将英语技能的培养和专业知识的学习有机地结合起来，满足学生在专业和英语两方面的需求；提高学生的商务英语交际能力；拓宽学生的知识领域，全面提高学生的综合素质。

本教材是一套培养复合型、应用型人才的语言实践课教材，其设计和编写完全是从提高学生的综合语言应用能力出发，针对中国学生在商务英语方面的薄弱环节和实际需要，做到了有的放矢。教材的主要特点体现在以下几个方面：

一、选材新颖，内容丰富。本教材在选材上注重内容的知识性、趣味性、可思性、时效性和前瞻性，同时也注重语言的规范性和致用性。教材中专业知识覆盖面广，涉及了商务活动的各个方面，如市场竞争、营销策略、经营风险、企业管理、财税管理、商业文化、电子商务、国际化等。所用材料全部摘自国外主要经济、金融、管理等方面近年来的报刊、专业书籍以及因特网上的最新信息。而且，许多资料，如商务文件、信函、广告、产品说明书等都是来自某些企业、公司或公共场所的全真语料，旨在为学习者创造一个真实、生动的交际环境，有效地激发他们的学习欲望，使他们能自觉地提高自己用英语进行商务活动的能力。

二、以任务为路径，以交际为目的。本教材注重吸收国外商务英语教学及研究领域的成果，努力实现理论和实践的有机统一。教材遵循任务型编写原则，强调教学过程中的互动性，突出对学生交际能力的培养，通过灵活多样的商务活动情景或场合，为学习者设计了形式各异的交际任务，如双人讨论、小组讨论、角色扮演、情景模拟等，鼓励学生在完成任务的过程中发挥主动性，积极合作，将课堂所学用于实践，并将自己生活中的经历和观点融入交际活动中，以实现学以致用，提高交际能力的目的。

三、内容设计严谨，综合应用性强。本教材的每个单元由"导入活动（Lead-in）""阅读活动（Reading）""商务实践（Business Practice）"和"专业扩展（Relevant Extension）"四部分组成。各部分内容的设计与编写坚持了操作性与挑战性并重的原则，以保持学生的学习热情和自觉实践的积极性。

1. **导入活动** 以各种贴近学生生活、易于学生交流、与单元主题相关的内容为素材，设计了双人讨论和小组讨论等互动练习，旨在引发学生思考，激发他们对本单元内容的学习欲望。

2. **阅读活动** 主要围绕一篇与单元主题相关的文章进行。文章的长度适中，难易度由浅入深，其中的生词、习语、专有名词和有关表达等均有中英文注释，以帮助学生提高阅读效率。本教材注重提高学生分析问题的能力。每篇文章后面除了针对文中的观点、要点以及具体细节的理解设计讨论问题之外，还要求学生对文章的篇章结构和文体风格等进行分析、归纳，使他们在了解商务英语语言特色的基础上，明白文章形式与内容之间的关系，懂得观点的逻辑组织和清楚表达的重要性，从而对提高其写作能力提供一定的帮助。针对文章中重要的词或词组所设计的练习都以商务、经济等方面的内容为素材，而且形式多种多样，尽量避免重复，从而引发学生的新奇感，令其自觉参与活动。此外，这部分还设计了英汉互译练习，以增强学生的翻译技能，并提高其活学活用的能力。

3. **商务实践** 是本教材的重要特色。这部分围绕单元主题，参照各种真实的商务交际情景，为学习者设计了灵活多样的口头与书面交际的任务。在口头任务设计中，不仅注重培养学生的自主学习能力，同时还强调了研究性学习与合作性学习的重要性。多数活动要求学生以小组为单位，根据提示与指导，通过因特网和图书馆等途径获取有关资料，在小组研究与合作的基础上，规划实施各个步骤，最终实现交际目标。为了丰富输出内容和规范口语表达，这部分还给出了相关信息提示和常用表达范式。结合单元主题或口语练习，该板块还设计了关于各种商务应用文的写作练习，其中包括公司介绍、产品说明书、插页广告、备忘录、公司业务通信以及常见的贸易信函等，同时，提供了某些公司真实而优秀的商务文件作为范例，并对其构架及主要内容或表述方式进行了分析，以便于学生进行实践性写作练习。

4. **专业扩展** 是本教材的另一个重要特色。为了进一步满足学生对专业知识的需求，这部分根据单元主题设计了相关专业术语的巩固性练习和专业阅读练习。

鉴于学生在高年级还需分门别类、系统地学习专业课程，此处的练习避免过深过专，旨在使学生学习一些常用的专业术语，掌握一定的专业基础知识，提高他们在专业英语方面的阅读能力。另外，考虑到不少学生日后可能会参加BEC（Business English Certificates）等商务英语考试，此处的练习从内容到形式都兼顾了这类考试的要求。所以，本教材也可以为学习者通过BEC或TOEIC（托业）等国际商务英语考试提供很大的帮助。

四、学生配套用书各单元包括主题简介、课文相关信息注解、课文难句解释、常用词或词组学习、商务实践活动补充信息、课文参考译文，为教师的课堂教学实践和学习者的自主学习提供了有力的帮助和极大的方便。

五、本教程配套精美教学课件*，为教师课堂教学提供帮助。

《大学商务英语综合教程》（第2版）的编写立足本国，博采众长，力求新颖。教材宜采用糅合中外多种教学法之长的折中主义（eclecticism）教学法。教程每册由10个单元组成。建议每6个课时完成一个单元。但使用时，各校可根据情况灵活处理。

《大学商务英语综合教程》（第2版）为上海市教委第五期重点学科（外国语言学及应用语言学）资助项目（项目编号：A-3102-06-000），主要由上海对外经贸大学主持编写，邀请复旦大学、上海外国语大学、上海师范大学等院校多名具有丰富的商务英语教学经验的教师参与，由大家共同努力完成。此外，本教程还邀请国内商务英语教学领域的资深专家、上海对外经贸大学副校长叶兴国教授和美国达科他州立大学英语学院教授John Nelson博士对书稿进行了审阅。从教材编写体系的形成到文字内容的修改及润色，他们都提出了许多宝贵的建议，并给予热情的指导和帮助。清华大学出版社对此教程的编写提供了大力的支持。在此，我们教材编写组对所有关心、支持和帮助过该教材编写工作的领导、专家、教授以及有关同志一并表示衷心的感谢。

本教材从内容到形式有许多大胆的尝试，但由于编者的水平所限，书中难免有不妥或疏漏之处。欢迎外语界专家、同仁以及本教材的所有使用者批评指正。

编　者
2016年6月

---

* 与本教程配套的教学课件，可以从清华大学出版社的资源库中免费下载。请访问ftp://ftp.tup.tsinghua.edu.cn/，进入"外语分社"目录下，选择所需的课件。

目录 Contents

Unit 1 Competition 1
  Lead-in 2
  Reading: **Head-to-head in the Clouds** 3
  Business Practice 14
  Relevant Extension 21

Unit 2 Retailing 27
  Lead-in 28
  Reading: **Retail's Little Guys Come Back** 29
  Business Practice 40
  Relevant Extension 46

Unit 3 E-Commerce 53
  Lead-in 54
  Reading: **Taking E-Commerce to the Next Level** 55
  Business Practice 65
  Relevant Extension 69

Unit 4 Communication 75
  Lead-in 76
  Reading: **Employees Want to Hear It "Straight" from the Boss's Mouth** 77
  Business Practice 88
  Relevant Extension 95

Unit 5 Customer Service 103

Lead-in 104
Reading: **Customer Service Champs** 105
Business Practice 116
Relevant Extension 125

Unit 6 Human Resources 131

Lead-in 132
Reading: **The Search for Talent** 133
Business Practice 145
Relevant Extension 156

Unit 7 Business Crisis 163

Lead-in 164
Reading: **Why Good Times Are the Most Dangerous** . 165
Business Practice 176
Relevant Extension 181

Unit 8 Business Ethics 189

Lead-in 190
Reading: **Integrating Ethics at the Core** 191
Business Practice 202
Relevant Extension 208

目 录

Unit 9 International Trade 215

    Lead-in..216
    Reading: **Exports Are Giving the Economy a Surprise
                 Lift**..216
    Business Practice..228
    Relevant Extension 233

Unit 10 Globalization 239

    Lead-in..240
    Reading: **Emerging Giants** 241
    Business Practice..251
    Relevant Extension 261

附录 1   Glossary 269
附录 2   Phrases & Expressions 281
附录 3   Activity File................................... 287

UNIT 1
Competition

1. Work with a partner. Try to name the leading companies and their competitors of the following business sectors in the Chinese market, and discuss their advantages and disadvantages.

Business sectors	Leading companies	Competitors
Mobile telephone service		
Airline		
Luxury car		
Word processing program		
Web search engine		
MP3 player		
Kitchen cleaner		
Bank		

2. Work in groups. Read the brief introduction to Airbus A-380 and Boeing B-787, two broad-bodied aircrafts, consider their different qualities, and discuss the following questions.

Airbus A-380

- *Airbus' double-decker passenger jet;*
- *The largest airliner ever built, it nearly stretches from goal line to goal line of a football field;*
- *Three full decks with large space for passengers;*
- *Capable of carrying 840 passengers;*
- *Big and fat with all the polish of a portly dowager.*

UNIT 1 Competition

Boeing B-787

- *Boeing's super-efficient airplane with new passenger-pleasing features;*
- *Uses 20 percent less fuel than any other airplane of its size;*

- *Offers forty to sixty percent more cargo revenue capacity;*
- *Computational fluid dynamics and wind tunnel testing sleek and quick, and capable of long outings.*

1) Which airplane would you pick for a trans-Pacific flight? Why?
2) Which company do you think is more competitive in the market from the angle of customers? Give the possible reasons.
3) What is the target market of the two leading aircraft manufacturers for their latest products? Point out phrases in the descriptions that help you determine your position.
4) How can consumers — in this case, air travelers — as well as companies be affected by competition?

Preview: Many consider competition as a negative factor, but is it? In this article on the competition between two companies described in a new book by John Newhouse, the writer presents the fierce rivalry between Boeing and Airbus, the world's two leading civil aircraft manufacturers. Compared to the competition in other fields, their competition is fiercer by involving much more money, and their battle encourages the government's interference. Generally speaking, Boeing and Airbus have each enjoyed an advantage over the other during the last decades. Both Boeing and Airbus are facing problems, but John Newhouse predicts that they will continue their competition in the long run.

Head-to-head in the Clouds

By John Newhouse

[1] The struggle over the world market for big jet aircraft makes for **epic narrative**.

Involving billions of dollars and a great deal of national pride, the story of two industrial giants fighting each other — from the new world, from the old—is so **gripping** that there is nothing quite like it in global business. The cost of developing the product is **astronomical**, and it takes years to come to market and is then in the air for just a generation. Coke **versus** Pepsi[1], Sony[2] versus Samsung, Unilever[3] versus Procter & Gamble[4]— none of those battles has quite either the same **grandeur** or the same high **stakes**. Only Big Oil[5] in its desperate search for new reserves comes close, but in that business there are several players, and the rules are mostly set by a producers' **cartel**.

[2] In the civil aircraft business the market rules, though governments are more than keen spectators, pouring in hundreds of millions of dollars of support (openly) in Europe, less directly in America. In this business make one bad bet, or suffer a single **flop**, and you have to live with the consequences for years. Both companies have had that experience in the past decade. The reality of a global **duopoly** is that each company is forced to press ahead with difficult and risky technology, **bombarding** the market with new products that should make the life of ordinary people better, whether they are flying the Pacific on business or enjoying a cheap weekend in Prague[6], borne there by a budget airline.

[3] Boeing[7] is America's biggest exporter, while Airbus[8] is a **potent** symbol of European industrial **prowess**. There is no better **commentator** on this sporting struggle than John Newhouse, a journalist-**cum**-foreign-policy adviser, who made his name back in 1982 with a book on big jets, called "The Sporty Game". A quarter-century on, he revisits the **aerial** field of dreams to catch up on the latest play. An American who has studied and written extensively about Europe and advised the Clinton[9] administration on it, for he knows both sides of the Atlantic well enough to have a **wry**, disinterested attachment.

---

1 Pepsi /ˈpepsɪ/　百事饮料国际集团，是美国一家享誉全球的跨国公司
2 Sony /ˈsəʊnɪ/　日本索尼公司，是世界上民用 / 专业视听产品、通信产品和信息技术等领域的先导之一
3 Unilever /ˈjuːnɪˈlevə/　联合利华，是全球最知名的日用消费品公司之一，1930 年由荷兰人造黄油公司与英国利华兄弟制皂公司合并成立
4 Procter & Gamble /ˈprɒktə ænd ˈɡæmbl/　美国宝洁公司 (P&G)，是世界最大的日用消费品公司之一
5 Big Oil 石油巨头，指对石油生产和销售垄断的美孚、壳牌等大公司
6 Prague /prɑːɡ/　布拉格（捷克首都）
7 Boeing /ˈbəʊɪŋ/　美国波音公司，是世界最大的航空航天公司
8 Airbus /ˈeəbʌs/　空中客车，欧洲著名的飞机制造商，由英、法、德合作成立
9 Clinton /ˈklɪntən/　克林顿，美国前总统

[4] For most of the 1990s the story was Airbus, the European underdog, **relentlessly** pursuing Boeing, the world leader. The European group made a **sustained sprint** to go from 20% of the market to snatching the lead from Boeing in 2001. Then, after five years on top, Airbus's world started falling apart, or so it seemed. Last year Boeing regained the lead, selling more planes than the European company for the first time since 2000. Now Airbus is in decline.

[5] In less than three years Boeing has won a record-breaking 500 orders for its new middle-sized **long-haul** aircraft, the 787. By contrast, Airbus's **super-jumbo**, the A-380, is running late and its new A-350 is being re-designed after heavy criticism from potential customers. Airbus has had four different bosses in the past two years, as production delays led to boardroom **squabbling** between its German and French shareholders. The British, in the shape of BAE Systems[1], which used to own a fifth of Airbus, quickly sold up and slipped away, turning their back on European civil **aerospace** to concentrate on America.

[6] Boeing now has a **decisive** lead in the most **lucrative** part of the market — for wide-bodied long-haul jets — with one established product, the **ubiquitous** 777, and the hugely successful new 787. Airbus's competing product is several years away and orders are only **trickling** in for its huge gamble, the super-jumbo that will be capable of carrying 555 passengers. So is Airbus **doomed**, as some commentators suggest? Not at all: the reality is that both companies have record order books and overworked factories, and they face a market that is set to keep growing, **albeit** with **cyclical** ups and downs.

[7] Boeing executives are careful to avoid crowing over their latest **triumphs**; ten years ago Boeing's planes were losing height as Airbus rose. Its factories around Seattle[2] ground to a halt for a month as production delays **accumulated**. In the past three years Boeing's top management has been **rocked** by **corruption** and sex **scandals** that cost the jobs of two chief executives and one potential **successor**. To this day Boeing is seen with **suspicion** in some parts of the Pentagon[3], as a result of the industrial **espionage** and contract rigging that were **rife** a few years ago.

[8] But, as Mr. Newhouse's **clinical dissection** of Airbus's latest problems makes clear, the most serious issue the European champion faces is its internal divisions. The French suspect the Germans of wanting to grab a bigger share of the high-tech work and the jobs that go with it. The Germans (and the British in their time) were happy to give

---

1 BAE Systems　BAE 系统公司，英国著名的全球防务和航空公司
2 Seattle /sɪˈætl/　西雅图，美国西北部城市
3 Pentagon /ˈpentəɡən/　五角大楼，美国国防部

up the soft loans from government — to settle a long and **acrimonious** trade dispute with America — but both suspected that the French would keep doing out money to **secure** more Airbus work for France. Airbus should soon bounce back in the market, if only because airlines — the manufacturers' customers — would never **tolerate** an American **monopoly**. But how long that will take is anyone's guess.

(860 words)
From *The Economist*

New Words

head-to-head
a. in which two people or groups face each other directly in order to settle a dispute or competition 短兵相接的；正面交锋的
n. 白刃战；势均力敌的比赛

epic /ˈepɪk/
n. poetic account of the deeds of one or more great heroes, or a nation's past history 描写英雄事迹的诗，史诗
a. having the feature of an epic 具有史诗性质的，史诗般的

narrative /ˈnærətɪv/
n. story or tale; orderly account of events 故事；叙述

gripping /ˈɡrɪpɪŋ/
a. exciting or interesting in a way that keeps your attention 激动人心的；吸引人的；扣人心弦的

astronomical /ˌæstrəˈnɒmɪk(ə)l/
a. of enormous magnitude; immense 巨大的；庞大的

versus /ˈvɜːsəs/
prep. (in law or sport) against 对；对抗

grandeur /ˈɡrændʒə/
n. impressive beauty, power, or size 伟大；壮丽；雄伟

stake /steɪk/
n. sum of money risked on the unknown result of a future event 投资；赌注

cartel /kɑːˈtel/
n. a combination of independent companies in order to limit competition and increase profit 卡特尔（各公司为了减少竞争、增加利润而组成的联盟），企业联盟

flop /flɒp/
n. a failure 失败

duopoly /djuˈɒpəli/
n. a situation in which two suppliers dominate the market for a commodity or service 两家卖主垄断市场（的局面）

bombard /bɒmˈbɑːd/
v. keep attacking (as if) with gunfire 轰击，不断攻击

potent /ˈpəʊtənt/
a. powerful and effective 有力的；有效的

prowess /ˈpraʊɪs/
n. usual skill or ability 不凡的技能

commentator /ˈkɒmenteɪtə/
n. a broadcaster or writer who reports and analyzes events in the news 评论员；在新闻中报告和分析事件的广播员或作家

cum /kʌm/
prep. used between two nouns to show that something has two purposes; as well as 兼作；和

aerial /ˈeərɪəl/
a. of, for, or by means of aircraft 航空的；飞机的；由飞机进行的

wry /raɪ/
a. dryly humous, often with a touch of irony showing dislike, lack of pleasure 嘲弄的，用反语表达幽默的；不高兴的；不屑的

relentlessly /rɪˈlentlɪsli/
ad. without stopping, determinedly; strictly, cruelly 不停地，不松懈地；无情地，残酷地

sustained /səˈsteɪnd/
a. continuing at the same level or rate for a

UNIT 1 Competition

long time 持续的，持久的

sprint /sprɪnt/
n. a burst of speed or activity; a short period of running 速度或活动的突然爆发；全速疾跑；短距离赛跑

long-haul /ˈlɒŋhɔːl/
a. involving the transport of goods or passengers over long distance（运送货物或旅客）长途的；远距离的

super-jumbo /ˈsjuːpəˈdʒʌmbəʊ/
n. 特大型客机

squabble /ˈskwɒbl/
v. quarrel, esp. noisily and unreasonably 口角；争吵

aerospace /ˈeərəʊspeɪs/
n. the industry of building aircraft and vehicles and equipment to be sent into space 航空航天工业；航空航天技术

decisive /dɪˈsaɪsɪv/
a. having a decided or definite outcome or result 决定性的；有明确结果的

lucrative /ˈluːkrətɪv/
a. profitable; bringing in money 可获利的，赚钱的

ubiquitous /juːˈbɪkwɪtəs/
a. appearing, happening everywhere 无处不在的；十分普遍的

trickle /ˈtrɪkl/
v. flow in drops or in a thin stream 缓缓地流；细流

doom /duːm/
v. make sb./sth. certain to fail, suffer, die, etc. 使……在劫难逃；注定失败

albeit /ɔːlˈbɪːɪt/
conj. even though; although; notwithstanding 即使；虽然；尽管

cyclical /ˈsɪklɪk(ə)l/
a. recurring in cycles 循环的；周期性的

triumph /ˈtraɪəmf/
n. (joy or satisfaction at a) success or victory 成功；胜利；得意洋洋

accumulate /əˈkjuːmjuleɪt/
v. gradually increase in number or quality over a period of time（数量）逐渐增加；（质量）渐渐提高

rock /rɒk/
v. (fig.) disturb or shock (sb./sth.) greatly〈喻〉使（某人/某事物）极为不安或震惊

corruption /kəˈrʌpʃən/
n. dishonest or illegal behavior, especially by people in authority 腐败；贪污；贿赂；受贿

scandal /ˈskændl/
n. behavior or an event that people think is morally or legally wrong and causes public feelings of shock or anger 丑行；使人震惊的丑恶事；丑闻

successor /səkˈsesə/
n. person or thing that goes after another 继任者；接替的事物

suspicion /səsˈpɪʃən/
n. feeling that sb. has done sth. wrong, illegal or dishonest, even though you have no proof 怀疑；嫌疑

espionage /ˈespɪənɑːʒ/
n. practice of spying or using spies 侦探；间谍活动

rife /raɪf/
a. (of bad things) widespread; common 流行的；普遍的

clinical /ˈklɪnɪkl/
a. very objective and devoid of emotion; analytical 十分客观且不带个人情感的；分析的

dissection /dɪˈsekʃən/
n. careful examination or analysis 剖析；仔细研究或分析

acrimonious /ˌækrɪˈməʊnjəs/
a. (of an argument, etc.) angry and full of strong bitter feelings and words 尖刻的；讥讽的；激烈的

secure /sɪˈkjʊə/
v. succeed in getting (sth. for which there is a great demand) 获得

tolerate /ˈtɒləreɪt/
v. put up with; endure 容忍，忍受

monopoly /məˈnɒpəlɪ/
n. complete control of trade in particular goods or the supply of a particular service 垄断；专营服务

Phrases & Expressions

make for
    be likely to have a particular result or help to make sth. possible 促成；有利于

come close to sth./to doing sth.
    almost reach or do sth. 几乎达到；差不多

press ahead (with sth.)
    continue doing sth. in a determined way 加紧（努力）；坚决继续进行

make one's name
    become famous 成名

catch up on
    find about things that have happened 了解（已发生的事情）

fall apart
    have so many problems that it is no longer possible to exist or function, collapse 崩溃；破裂

in the shape of sb. /sth.
    appearing specially as sb./sth. 以某人 / 某事物的形式

turn one's back on
    reject sb./sth. that you have previously been connected with；turn away from sb. in an impolite way 背弃；掉头不理睬某人

ups and downs
    alternation of good and bad fortune 盛衰；浮沉

crow over
    talk too proudly about sth. you have achieved, especially when sb. else has been unsuccessful 自鸣得意，扬扬得意

lose height
    lose the leading position 失去领先地位

grind to a halt
    (of process) stop slowly （指过程）慢慢停止

contract rigging
    cheating in contract 合同欺诈

to this day
    even now, when a lot of time has passed 直到如今；甚至现在

go with
    exist at the same time or in the same place as sth.; be found together 与某事同时（或同地）存在；与某事相伴而生

soft loan
    无条件长期低息贷款；优惠贷款

dole out
    distribute food or money in small amounts 布施；少量分配

bounce back
    recover jauntily from a setback （受挫折后）恢复元气

UNIT **1** Competition

Exercises

Comprehension

1. Mark the following statements true (T) or false (F) or not mentioned (NM) in the passage. Discuss with your partner about the supporting points for each statement.

    1) _____ Billions of dollars are invested in the civil aircraft business in part because this business can reflect national pride.

    2) _____ Competition is unavoidable for each company no matter which industry it specializes in.

    3) _____ Government plays a role of an onlooker, so it cannot interfere in the companies' operation especially in civil aircraft business.

    4) _____ In the past, Boeing had been the leading company in civil aircraft business until 2001 when Airbus took over.

    5) _____ It can be inferred that the shareholders of Airbus are displeased and there are disputes among them.

    6) _____ In civil aircraft business, if a company makes a wrong decision, it will take a long time to recover from the error.

    7) _____ Both Boeing and Airbus have to work overtime to succeed under the fierce competition between them.

    8) _____ The management of Boeing voices great pride in their latest victory over Airbus.

    9) _____ One reason Airbus has declined in recent years is that its shareholders are not in agreement with each other on its developing strategy.

    10) _____ It is predicted that the Airbus will be likely to go out of business soon if current trends continue.

2. Match the headings on the right column with their equivalent numbered paragraphs on the left column, and compare your answers with your partner's.

    Para. 1   A. The unfavorable situation of Airbus

    Para. 2   B. An American commentator's study of Boeing and Airbus

    Para. 3   C. The benefit of growing market and its effect on both companies

    Para. 4   D. Brief introduction of the competition in recent years

9

Para. 5	E. Both companies' continuous efforts driven by a global duopoly
Para. 6	F. Unstable management in Boeing
Para. 7	G. The hope for Airbus' recovery
Para. 8	H. The fierce competition between two leading aircraft manufacturers

Critical Thinking

Work in group to discuss the following questions.

1) It is said fishermen never worry about their crabs running away, once caught. They simply place crabs inside a basket, never finding a single crab crawling its way outside. And if one were to peep-in, it is easy to know why: if a crab tries to climb to the top, the others pull it back. How can you relate this 'crab mentality' to the corporate rivalry between Boeing and Airbus, or between some other companies of the same line? Support your ideas with some examples.

2) In China today, what do markets see the fiercest competition, and what markets are still under inadequate competition?

3) How can Chinese companies manage to survive in the face of keen world competition?

Vocabulary

1. Which word in each group is the odd one out?

1) field	line	arena	trade
2) gamble	stake	risk	bet
3) scandal	bribery	corruption	espionage
4) aircraft	aerospace	airship	airliner
5) allowance	perk	budget	bonus
6) empowerment	executives	administration	management
7) analysis	investigation	inspection	dissection
8) discussion	dispute	squabble	conflict
9) shareholder	shareout	stockbroker	stockholder
10) cartel	alliance	duopoly	monopoly

UNIT 1 Competition

2. **Correct the sentences below using the expressions from the text, then put synonyms or definitions of the corrected expressions in the spaces provided.**

   1) The jump in oil prices will make up public awareness of renewable energy resources like wind, hydro, biomass and solar.

      correct form: _____   definition: _____

   2) The new president, in his speech, emphasized that all the staff should press for joint effort to conquer the financial crisis in the company.

      correct form: _____   definition: _____

   3) Some western financial institutions are trying to catch up with Chinese latest economy by analyzing the growth in GDP.

      correct form: _____   definition: _____

   4) Having heard the rumor that the leading company would fall down, many shareholders flooded into the stock exchange to cash their stocks.

      correct form: _____   definition: _____

   5) Being greatly interested in international markets, the company has turned back to some local markets of limited purchasing power.

      correct form: _____   definition: _____

   6) Bill Gates made his fame by establishing Microsoft Cooperation which has been the leader of the world's IT industry and has a sharp edge over all the other competitors.

      correct form: _____   definition: _____

   7) There are a growing number of CEOs giving away their swanky offices in favour of working among the people in a bid to be more approachable.

      correct form: _____   definition: _____

   8) Many fashion-conscious shoppers tend to pursue the stylish products and the high technology that goes along with them.

      correct form: _____   definition: _____

   9) Our rapid profit growth has ground to a stop on account of the fierce competition from the township enterprises.

      correct form: _____   definition: _____

   10) If a company on the verge of bankruptcy wants to come back, it should put just as much energy into the bottom of the org chart as it does at the top.

       correct form: _____   definition: _____

3. Rewrite the following sentences using the noun forms of the verbs in the box. Do not change the meanings of the sentences.

| suspect | accumulate | monopolize | concentrate | corrupt |
| tolerate | export | squabble | dissect | succeed |

Example: We will promote this product by offering customers a free gift.
Our promotion of this product will involve offering customers a free gift.

1) The shareholders suspect that the main product of TCL is likely to be deleted because it has lost market share.

2) The press reported that China exported three million tons of cotton goods in last decade.

3) In course of the years the company has been managed improperly and its debts have accumulated gradually.

4) The newspaper alleged that the general manger was badly corrupted and sentenced to ten years' imprisonment.

5) A common complaint is that some companies try to monopolize a market through "predatory" or below-cost pricing.

6) It is beyond doubt that Tom Newhouse will succeed to his father as the director of the board.

7) The public will not tolerate the monopoly of AT&T in telecommunication.

8) The conference concentrates on the current dispute between management and labors.

9) It is a shame for the executives to squabble in meeting for such a trifle thing.

10) Business analytics programs can be used to dissect business data so your clients can make informed decisions more quickly.

Translation

1. **Translate the following paragraphs into Chinese.**

    In this business make one bad bet, or suffer a single flop, and you have to live with the consequences for years. Both companies have had that experience in the past decade. The reality of a global duopoly is that each company is forced to press ahead with difficult and risky technology, bombarding the market with new products that should make the life of ordinary people better, whether they are flying the Pacific on business or enjoying a cheap weekend in Prague, borne there by a budget airline.

    Airbus's competing product is several years away and orders are only trickling in for its huge gamble, the super-jumbo that will be capable of carrying 555 passengers. So is Airbus doomed, as some commentators suggest? Not at all: the reality is that both companies have record order books and overworked factories, and they face a market that is set to keep growing, albeit with cyclical ups and downs.

2. **Put the following passage into English, using the words and phrases given in the box.**

cyclical	ups and downs	secure	triumph	establish
monopoly	lose height	ubiquitous	press ahead	tolerate

    当今世界，市场竞争无处不在，并且日益激烈。一个公司已不可能完全垄断市场，通常是几个大公司瓜分市场。实际上，每个公司都在加紧努力，提高产品质量和服务水平，以求建立自己的市场地位，获得一定的市场份额。即使如此，一个公司也经常会周期性地起起落落，有时甚至会失去原有的优势地位。原因有二：一方面是由于公司经营方面出现了问题；另一方面是由于消费者不能容忍某种产品长时间地占领市场。因此任何公司都不必因成功而得意，因失败而丧气。

Offers & Counter-offers

In business negotiation, an offer is the seller's promise to supply goods on stipulated terms. It is often a reply to an inquiry. A counter-offer is the refusal of an offer, is a new offer to the former offerer. That is to say, the former offerer now becomes an offeree, and so the former offeree now an offerer. And if the new offeree does not agree to some of the terms, he will give the new offerer a counter-counter-offer. The following are some guidelines about how to make offers and counter-offers properly.

Guidelines for Making Offers & Counter-offers Professionally

◆ Be sure you understand the offers and counter-offers, and seek clarification if needed. Stay cool when your offer or counter-offer is rejected.

◆ Let your opponent make the first offer and remember each counter-offer is an entirely new offer.

◆ Set a baseline figure and explain the basis for any offer or counter-offer. Avoid lowballing and highballing.

◆ Respond calmly to lowball or highball offers. Avoid polarization from unwise ultimatums and insert an "unless" into your ultimatums.

There should be different prices for customers from different countries or different specializations. Generally speaking, the customers from Middle East and South East Asia are more price-sensitive, so you'd better offer a competitive price the first time. As American customers care more about added value and services, you should consider these as a cost when you quote, but you should point out that the price includes the added service.

Read the following simulated negotiation in pairs and role play the situations below.

A: My name is John Lee. I've set up the appointment yesterday. I also phoned you this morning for this meeting.

B: Yes, I'm expecting your visit. Welcome to our office and please come in.

UNIT 1 Competition

A: This is my business card.

B: This is mine. Here are our catalogs and samples. Please take a look.

A: How much is this model?

B: What's your quantity? (How much quantity do you request?)

A: What's your minimum order quantity and how long is your delivery time?

B: Our minimum quantity is 1, 000pcs and the best delivery time is within 30 days after receiving your L/C.

A: Please quote the price based on 1,000pcs.

B: What price term do you want us to quote you? FOB, CFR or CIF? And what shipping method do you request?

A: Please quote us CFR price by air freight to Paris.

B: Our best CFR price by air to Paris is at US$10/pc for 1,000pcs.

A: It seems a little bit too high. (It's too expensive.) (It's far from our target price.)

B: What's your target price? What price will you place the order?

A: We need US$8/pc. Can you accept?

B: Sorry, it's under our cost. However, since this is our first deal, we would give you the best price at US$9/pc to start the business. Please understand that we use top-quality raw material and we do 100% inspection on every shipment. We can assure you the best quality products.

A: But, we don't need such high quality products as they will be sold to the middle range user. (They will be used on toys/low end products)

B: O.K. If you can accept lower quality, we can use less expensive raw material. In that case, the price can be lowered to US$8/pc. (Then, we can accept your price.)

A: That's fine. Then I'll need 3 samples for test.

B: No problem, but we have only one sample available here in our showroom. We'll ask our manufacturer to send more samples to the office by tomorrow. When are you leaving Shanghai?

A: I'm leaving early tomorrow morning.

B: Well, in that case, we'd suggest you to take this available sample back first; we'll send you the other two samples by air parcel post to your office.

A: It sounds like a good idea.

B: But, we request you to pay for the sample charge in advance as this is a high value product. However, the sample charge will be refunded when you place us the order (when offering).

A: O.K., no problem. Do you accept traveler's check?

B: Yes, of course.

A: I'll bring this sample back and please mail us the other two pieces ASAP.

B: We promise to send them out within this week. Don't worry about it. By the way, when can we expect your order?

A: We'll confirm you our order as soon as the samples are approval (upon sample approval) (as soon as your samples pass our engineering test).

B: Thank you for your interest in our products and awaiting good news from you soon and also thanks for your visit. If you have time, we'd like to invite you for dinner tonight.

A: Sorry, since the time is too short and I'm fully occupied. Maybe next time. (I still have an appointment with another supplier.)

B: O.K. Wish you have a good stay here and hope to see you again soon.

A: Thanks. I hope to come here again soon.

1) A retailer is placing an order with a wholesaler of window curtains.

Retailer:
- You hope to break into the market with the new window crutain.
- You need to order 50 sets at the quoted price for a start.
- You want to have a 10 % discount.
- You want 30 days' credit.
- You require delivery in one week.

Wholesaler:
- You set a competitive price of U.S. $52.20 per set.
- You have a bonus if the order is over 100 sets.
- You suggest an increase of quantity to 150 sets.
- You don't give a discount for orders of less than 100 sets.
- You require payment on delivery.
- You can deliver in two weeks.

UNIT **1** Competition

2) A foreign merchant is negotiating the business of black tea with a Chinese sales rep.

Foreign merchant:
- You want to place an order of 300 cases of black tea.
- You want to make a 10% reduction on the quoted price.
- You want 60 days' credit.
- You require an earlier shipment.

Chinese sales rep.:
- You require a minimum order of 300 cases.
- You don't cut the price for the orders of less than 350 cases.
- You can only accept a reduction of 5% for a big order.
- You require payment on delivery.
- You can arrange a shipment in two weeks.

Language Hints

Buyer:
- Your price seems a little bit too high.
- It's far from our target price.
- This is out of my price range.
- Please quote the price based on 1,000pcs.
- Does the price include delivery and installation charge?
- What's your minimum order quantity and how long is your delivery time?
- Could you offer us 50 sets for a start?
- True, the quantity is small, but if we can do well with it, substantial orders are sure to follow. You can bank on that.
- Well, there's something in what you say. Now what's your most favorable quotation?
- What risk do you cover and what's the insurance rate?
- Could you give me a discount?
- I wonder if you could alter the specifications.
- ...

Seller:
- What's your target price? What price will you place the order?
- What's your general price range?
- What price term do you want us to quote you? FOB, CFR or CIF?
- What's your most favorable quotation?
- Our best CFR price by air to Paris is at US$10/pc for 1,000pcs.
- What's your quantity?(How much quantity do you request?)
- You may find our price the most competitive.
- Sorry, it's under our cost. However, since this is our first deal, we would give you the best price at US$9/pc to start the business.
- Unfortunately, I can't lower my price.
- I'm afraid we can't give you any credit.
- ...

A Fax

Fax (short for facsimile, from Latin fac simile, "make similar", i.e. "make a copy") is a telecommunications technology used to transfer copies (facsimiles) of documents, especially using affordable devices to operate over the telephone network. The word telefax, short for telefacsimile, for "make a copy at a distance", is also used as a synonym. The device is known as a telecopier in certain industries.

Many business organizations have their own printed sample fax, which usually includes three parts: fax head, fax headings and body text. Fax head is the same as letterhead with a company's name, contact information at the top of a piece of letter paper. Fax headings include:

- TO (name of the receiver's company or organization)
- ATTN (name of the receiver)
- FROM (name of the sender)
- REF NO (fax No. of the receiver's company or organization)
- DATE (day/month/year or month/day/year)
- CC (copy to other relevant persons. It is optional)
- SUBJECT (main idea of the fax message)
- TOTAL NUMBER OF PAGES

Generally, business fax body is written in the form of a business letter, but sometimes it omits the salutation and complimentary close. It should use the language of a formal letter. Be clear, concise, informed, sincere and polite. Do not exaggerate.

The following sample is an offer fax based on enquiry from Bestbuy Global Corporation in London. Study it first, then reply to the offer fax on behalf of Susan Brown, the purchasing manager of Bestbuy Global Corporation. The Chinese hints of the reply fax are given below. Add anything necessary.

UNIT **1** Competition

BRILLIANCE GROUP

ADDRESS: 18 HUAIHAI ROAD, SHANGHAI 200203 CHINA

TEL: (086-21) 65845666 FAX: (086-21) 65845667

EMAIL: brilliancegroup@bailian.com

(fax head with a company's name and contact informa-tion)

TO: Bestbuy Corporation

FROM: Henry Sun, Sales Dept.

ATTN: Ms. Susan Brown, Purchasng Dept.

DATE: 6 April 2008

CC:

REF NO: BG (c)-26

SUBJECT: Offer-Reply to Reference BG/O12

Total Number of Pages: 1

(Including this cover)

(fax headings—fill it in a clear manner)

Dear Sirs,

Many thanks for the enquiry of 8 March 2008, reference BG/O12. We have pleasure in quoting as follows:

Black cotton men's shirts as per sample, label No. 306, in assorted sizes between 35 and 44, individually packed in plastic bags and boxed in 100's, no less than 50 of each size, packed in export crates of 1,000 shirts.

　　　AU $ 7.00 per shirt

　　　EXW Textiles Building Haymarket

Payment: By Irrevocable Letter of Credit opened in our favour with the National Bank of NSW, Industrial Area Branch.

Quantity: Minimum order 20,000 shirts, maximum

(fax body text)

fax tips:
* Compose fax body in short paragraphs.
* Use clear, concise, sincere and polite language.
* Proofread the fax message.
* Do not exaggerate.

19

present capacity 200,000 shirts a month.

Delivery: Within 3 months of notification of receipt of Letter of credit.

Validity: This quotation is firm for orders dispatched before 1 August 2008.

We hope that this meets with your approval. Please let us know by fax if you require any further information or samples.

Yours sincerely,
Sales Dept.
Herry Sun

> Your signature

Exercise:

Now write a fax to reply to Brilliance Group with the following Chinese hints.

感谢贵公司4月6日报价和服装样品，我公司对贵方服装的质量和价格均感满意，现提出订货如下……

关于具体交易条件，今晨我已同孙先生在电话中达成协议：

1. 价格按你公司4月6日报价中所列，包括运至最终目的地的费用的价格。
2. 货款于货物到达悉尼后一个月内，以澳元付给你方驻悉尼代表。
3. 保险由你公司通过驻悉尼代表与劳埃德（Lloyd）保险公司经纪人洽办。

希望尽快交货，并望第一批到货能证明与你方所提供的样品一致，以便今后建立定期业务关系。

UNIT **1** Competition

Business Expressions

1. Match the expressions in the box with the definitions below and translate them into Chinese.

market leader	market challenger	market follower
exclusive dealing	perfect competition	predatory pricing
oligopoly market	price discrimination	competition regulation
barriers to entry	monopoly tycoon	competition mechanism

   1) either the company that sells the most of a particular type of product, or the product itself that sells the most

      _____   _____

   2) a company content to maintain its existing market share behind an established market leader

      _____   _____

   3) a company holding a major market share and competing vigorously with the market leader for outright leadership

      _____   _____

   4) a market form in which a market or industry is dominated by a small number of sellers (oligopolists)

      _____   _____

   5) an economic model that describes a hypothetical market form in which no producer or consumer has the market power to influence prices

      _____   _____

   6) the rules usually brought into full play by the government for a better functioning and controlling of markets

      _____   _____

   7) a phenomenon that occurs when one person trading with another imposes some restrictions on the other's freedom to choose with whom, in what, or

where they deal

_____   _____

8) a means of charging different prices to different buyers whose ideal form is to charge each buyer the maximum that the buyer is willing to pay

_____   _____

9) the practice of a firm selling a product at very low price with the intent of driving competitors out of the market, which is also known as destroyer pricing

_____   _____

10) a person who acquires wealth by buying and developing the monopoly properties you know and love

_____   _____

2. Choose the proper adjectives to make word partnerships with *competition*. Match the verbs with the prepositions (where necessary) to make phrases with *competition*.

Adjectives		Verbs		
fierce		adapt		
hard		ignore		
cut-throat		win		
intense		lose	in	
dirty		enter	into	
deep		participate	off	
keen		withdraw	with	
stiff	competition	be	up to	competition
strong		face	to	
tough		go	from	
serious		beat	up	
severe		fight	against	
heavy		cope		
aggressive		welcome		
healthy		respond		
unfair		avoid		

22

3. Choose the appropriate words or expressions from the following box to complete the passage.

returns on capital	long-term advantage	staff of life
shareholders	earnings	competitive landscape
core competency	value-creating	competing
competitive advantage	brand portfolio	capital markets

Competitive advantage is a position that a firm occupies in its ___1)___ . A competitive advantage, sustainable or not, exists when a company makes economic rents, that is, their ___2)___ exceed their costs. A company's competitive advantage largely determines its ability to generate excess ___3)___ and links the business strategy with fundamental finance and ___4)___ . In the end, it is a company's competitive advantage that allows it to earn excess returns for its ___5)___ . Without a competitive advantage, a corporation has limited economic reasons to exist — its competitive advantage is its ___6)___ . Without it, the corporation will wither away.

A firm possesses a sustainable competitive advantage when it has ___7)___ processes and positions that cannot be duplicated or imitated by other firms that lead to the production of above normal rents. A sustainable ___8)___ is different from a competitive advantage in that it provides a ___9)___ that is not easily replicated. In marketing and strategic management, sustainable competitive advantage is an advantage that one firm has relative to ___10)___ firms. The source of the advantage can be something the company does that is distinctive and difficult to replicate, also known as a ___11)___ — for example Procter & Gamble's ability to derive superior consumer insights and implement them in managing its ___12)___ . It can also be an asset such as a brand (e.g. Coca Cola) or a patent, such as Viagra.

Specialized Reading

1. Read the following passage and write out the corresponding heading for each paragraph.

1) _____

Merriam-Webster defines *competition* in business as "the effort of two or more parties acting independently to secure the business of a third party by offering the most favorable terms". Seen as the pillar of capitalism in that it may stimulate innovation, encourage efficiency, or drive down prices, competition is touted as the foundation upon which capitalism is justified. According to microeconomic theory, no system of resource allocation is more efficient than pure competition. Competition, according to the theory, causes commercial firms to develop new products, services, and technologies. This gives consumers greater selection and better products. The greater selection typically causes lower prices for the products compared to what the price would be if there was no competition (monopoly) or little competition (oligopoly).

2) _____

However, competition may also lead to wasted (duplicated) effort and to increased costs (and prices) in some circumstances. For example, the intense competition for the small number of top jobs in music and movie acting leads many aspiring musicians and actors to make substantial investments in training that are not recouped, because only a fraction become successful. Similarly, the psychological effects of competition may result in harm to those involved.

3) _____

There are three levels of economic competition. The most narrow form is direct competition (also called category competition or brand competition), where products that perform the same function compete against each other. For example, a brand of pick-up trucks competes with several different brands of pick-up trucks. Sometimes two companies are rivals and one adds new products to their line so that each company distributes the same thing and they compete. The next form is substitute competition, where products that are close substitutes for one another compete. For example, butter competes with margarine, mayonnaise, and other various sauces and spreads. The broadest form of competition is typically called budget competition. Included in this category is anything that the consumer might want to spend their available money on. For example, a family that has $20,000 available may choose to spend it on many different items, which can all be seen as competing with each other for the family's available money.

4) _____

Competition does not necessarily have to be between companies. For example, business writers sometimes refer to "internal competition". This is competition within companies. The idea was first introduced by Alfred Sloan[1] at General

---

1 Alfred Sloan was once chairman of GM, and is recognized as the inventor of the modern American corporation because of his revolutionary ideas about how to manage companies.

Motors in the 1920s. Sloan deliberately created areas of overlap between divisions of the company so that each division would be competing with the other divisions. For example, in 1931, Procter & Gamble initiated a deliberate system of internal brand versus brand rivalry. The company was organized around different brands, with each brand allocated resources, including a dedicated group of employees willing to champion the brand. Each brand manager was given responsibility for the success or failure of the brand and was compensated accordingly. This form of competition thus pitted a brand against another brand. Finally, most businesses also encourage competition between individual employees. An example of this is a contest between sales representatives. The sales representative with the highest sales (or the best improvement in sales) over a period of time would gain benefits from the employer.

2. **Read the passage concerning competition law and write questions that could produce the following answers.**

Competition law, known in the United States as antitrust law, has three main functions. Firstly, it prohibits agreements aimed to restrict free trading between business entities and their customers. For example, a cartel of sport shops who together fix football jersey prices higher than normal is illegal. Secondly, competition law can ban the existence or abusive behaviour of a firm dominating the market. One case in point could be a software company who through its monopoly on computer platforms makes consumers use its media player. Thirdly, to preserve competitive markets, the law supervises the mergers and acquisitions of very large corporations. Competition law aims to protect the welfare of consumers by ensuring business must compete for its share of the market economy.

In recent decades, competition law has also been sold as good medicine to provide better public services, traditionally funded by tax payers and administered by democratically accountable governments. Hence competition law is closely connected with law on deregulation of access to markets, providing state aids and subsidies, the privitisation of state owned assets and the use of independent sector regulators, such as the United Kingdom telecommunications watchdog Ofcom[1]. Behind the practice lies the theory, which over the last fifty years has been dominated by neo-classical economics. Markets are seen as the most efficient method of allocating resources, though sometimes they fail and regulation

---

1 Ofcom is the independent regulator and competition authority for the communication industries in the United Kingdom.

becomes necessary to protect the ideal market model. Behind the theory lies the history, reaching back further than the Roman Empire. The business practices of market traders, guilds and governments have always been subject to scrutiny, and sometimes severe sanctions. Since the twentieth century, competition law has become global. The two largest, most organised and influential systems of competition regulation are United States antitrust law and European Community competition law. The respective national authorities, the U.S. Department of Justice and the European Commission's Competition Directorate General have formed international support and enforcement networks. Competition law is growing in importance every day, which warrants for its careful study.

Questions for the answers below:

1) _____

— Competition law is known in the United States as antitrust law.

2) _____

— There are three: Encouraging free trade; banning monopoly; preserving competitive markets.

3) _____

— The welfare of consumers.

4) _____

— It is markets that are regarded as the most efficient method of allocating resources.

5) _____

— United States antitrust law and European Community competition law.

UNIT 2
Retailing

1. Discuss the following questions with your partners.

    1) List some of the retailers you know. Then answer the questions below.
        - Are they international or national retailers?
        - Are they big, midsized or small retailers?
        - When you want to shop, which ones would you prefer to visit? Why?

    2) As customers, we all have our own little pet peeves. Take a look at the following list. Does any of these situations affect your mood for shopping? What are the three situations that affect you most? What can retailers do to solve the three problems in your opinion?

        - Queues
        - No parking
        - Hard to find products
        - Inconvenient opening hours
        - Unpacking/poor packing
        - Lack of shopping carts/baskets
        - Messy dressing rooms
        - Disorganized checkout counters
        - Dirty bathrooms
        - Poor lighting
        - Offensive odors
        - Crowded aisles
        - Stained floor
        - Loud music
        - High price/cost

    3) Consider the interactions that you have witnessed or experienced as consumers and retailers have tried to work out disputes. How have these helped shape your ideas about what good retailers should and should not do?

2. In retailing, there are many misconceptions about what it takes to be successful. The following are some common retail myths. Work in groups to share your opinions about them in the perspective of retailers.

    - If you build it, they will come.
    - Small stores can't compete with chain stores.
    - Your best customer spends most.
    - Online shopping will replace retailing.

- Moving your store will hurt your business.
- The customer is always right.
- Good help is hard to find.
- You can't make a living in retailing.

Preview: Retailers, as resellers of products, offer many benefits to suppliers and customers. Consumers can purchase small quantities of a wide assortment of products at affordable prices. For suppliers the most important benefits relate to offering opportunities to reach their target market, build product demand through retail promotions, and provide consumer feedback to the product marketer.

The old model of retail sales is facing change as the Internet and big retailers work to redefine the sales model. Will small retailers still reach niche markets? Will big-box stores push mom-and-pop retailers out of the picture? Amy Tsao's article describes how the retailing industry has responded to the challenges of the Internet, the rise of big-box stores, and the use of technology. Understanding the unique challenges of these changes will enable retailers not only to survive, but also to thrive, Tsao says.

Retail's Little Guys Come Back

*Who's afraid of Wal-Mart? As holiday shopping revs up, specialty retailers and chains are **thriving** by offering what the big-box stores can't.*

By Amy Tsao

[1] The annual trip home to celebrate Thanksgiving for those with family in New Hampshire[1] has its **perks**. In the land of no state sales tax, the long weekend after the **turkey** offers opportunities to get a lot of holiday gift buying out of the way. I have relatives in Nashua[2], a retail **mecca** with several Wal-Marts, more than a few large chain stores, and dozens of regional retailers and independent outlets.

[2] Nashua is a **microcosm** of what's happening on the retail scene nationwide. Certainly, many midsize retail chains and mom-and-pop shops have been squeezed out of business by big-box stores over the past decade. Competition is intensifying all the

---

1 New Hampshire /-ˈhæmpʃɪə/ 美国新罕布什尔州
2 Nashua /ˈnɑːʃuə/ 纳殊尔，美国新罕布什尔州城市

time.

[3] Yet something very interesting is happening at the same time: Retailers — of every size and **persuasion** — are finding ways to get by or even thrive. And online retailing, with its own 800-pound gorilla in Amazon.com[1], is evolving and proving to be a marketplace with more **dynamism** and **diversity** than originally **anticipated**.

[4] Driving these changes in **cyberspace**, at shopping malls, and on Main Streets are consumers who want more than low prices and name brands. "We see Wal-Mart around for generations to come," says Candace Corlett, principal of consulting firm WSL Strategic Retail[2]. "But we're seeing on a day-to-day basis a shift in consciousness that there are other choices, which it's not always about the lowest price."

[5] Consumers want to be inspired and often desire products that can't be had at discount **behemoths**. Many retailers are using a strategy popularized by Target — signing big-name fashion designers to create a special line. Swedish clothing chain H&M's[3] fall **lineup** includes clothes by Karl Lagerfeld[4]. In a similar vein, Bath & Body Works[5] is selling $25 Henri Bendel[6] **scented** candles.

[6] Some things just aren't Wal-Mart's bag. Most sporting **gear** is better at stores that specialize in such products, says Irma Zandl, president of retail consultancy Zandl Group[7]. She notes that young adults she has **polled** are looking to buy from www.boardzone.com, a **snowboarding** Web site. Hot Topic[8] sells a comprehensive **array** of gifts featuring characters from the **foul-mouthed animated hit** *South Park*[9] — definitely not Wal-Mart's cup of tea.

[7] Specialty shops are focusing on "the environment, experience, and the art of **merchandising**," says Corlett. These are all components that have "**vanished** in big retail stores," she says. According to her firm's latest annual survey of shoppers, 45% of respondents (many of them baby boomers) said they would pay more for household

---

1 Amazon.com 美国亚马逊网站
2 WSL Strategic Retail WSL 战略零售公司，纽约的一家市场推广及零售咨询公司
3 H&M 瑞典时装零售连锁巨头
4 Karl Lagerfeld /kɑːl-ˈlɑːɡəfeld/ 卡尔·拉格斐，法国著名的时装设计大师，被人们称为"时装界的恺撒大帝"
5 Bath & Body Works 美国沐浴、护肤及保养产品品牌
6 Henri Bendel /henrɪ-ˈbendl/ 美国纽约的精品名店，专卖20年代的高雅迷人、价格昂贵的服饰，如手工鞋、珠宝等
7 Zandl Group 赞德尔公司，位于纽约苏荷区的一家潮流分析公司
8 Hot Topic 美国青年流行商品经销商
9 *South Park* 《南方公园》，美国动画剧

products if they could shop in a nicer environment. "That's a pretty strong minority," says Corlett.

[8] Wal-Mart's influence over shoppers "has peaked," says Zandl. Maybe consumers need to go to big-box retailers to buy toilet paper, cat food, and such everyday items. But shopping is about more than the necessities. And "more consumers today are looking for products and experiences that are more unique, more **stylish**, and more **sensory** than what Wal-Mart delivers." The retail giant did not return calls for comment.

[9] In a new report, "Challenges of the Future: The Rebirth of Small Independent Retail in America," the National Retail Federation[1] highlights several case studies of small retailers that aren't just surviving but growing. "I was sure we would find retail categories or locations where the independent retailer couldn't be successful," says Jim Baum, an author of the report and a shop owner in Morris, Ill.[2] "That simply is not true." In Baum's town, he says, the best retailers are small ones that focus on "different **niches** that Wal-Mart can't touch". A **fabric** store stresses crafts and **quilting**, while a stained-glass retailer and **kitschy** gift stores are also **flourishing**.

[10] Even within the most competitive merchandise categories — like toys — it's often the smaller-scale retailers that have found ways around the big-box approach. Some 30% of all dollars spent on toys go to Wal-Mart, but smaller toy stores continue to attract customers. At the Little House toy store in Baton Rouge, La.[3], young girls can dress up and throw tea parties like proper ladies. This kind of distinction sets it apart from Wal-Mart and helps Little House get its tiny slice of the $220 billion-a-year toy-retailing business.

[11] Others have made personalization and customization an **integral** part of their business models. Dollmaker[4] and retailer American Girl[5] and custom-teddy-bear **purveyor** Build-a-Bear Workshop[6] have emerged in recent years as two of the country's fastest-growing toy **outfits**. They're giving new meaning to classic toys by outfitting them to a child's particular tastes. Customization is a niche that even Target is trying out. It recently began a Web-based custom-clothing service for women's jeans and men's pants and dress shirts.

---

1 National Retail Federation　美国全国零售业联盟
2 Morris, Ill.　（Morris, Illinois）美国伊利诺伊州，莫里斯市
3 Baton Rouge, La.（Baton Rouge, Louisiana）　美国路易斯安那州，巴顿鲁治市
4 Dollmaker　美国玩具娃娃生产商
5 American Girl　美国女孩公司，生产深受美国小童欢迎的玩偶——美国女孩
6 Build-a-Bear Workshop　熊熊工作室，是一家可供客户个性化设计填充玩具的生产商和零售商

[12] In the online **arena**, Amazon and **auctioneer** eBay are the giants, but even there, smaller outfits are creating niches. This holiday season, sales via the Internet will grow in the **ballpark** of 19%, to about $21.6 billion, according to Jupiter Research[1]. Surprisingly, some of the best gains are expected from smaller pure plays like eBags[2] and Red Envelope[3]. "Online-only retailers have done a great job of cutting costs and offering a unique buying experience or alternative to traditional retailers," says Scott Silverman, executive director of Shop.org[4].

[13] Undoubtedly, technology will continue to drive how some of the smaller players can compete, experts say. The future holds more "multichannel" retailers — with store, catalog, and Web operations, says Wendy Farina, principal at New York-based consulting firm Kurt Salmon Associates[5]. Even a family-owned general store such as Vermont Country Store[6] in Manchester, Vt[7]., has adopted the three-channel strategy.

[14] As Americans digest their turkey dinners on Thanksgiving and prepare for the holiday shopping season ahead, they can rest assured that they have more choices than ever. Just a few years ago, experts were **gloomily** warning of the Wal-Martization of the retailing **landscape**. Today, although the behemoth discounter continues to grow, its dominance hasn't eliminated the diversity of holiday-shopping choices. Now that's something to be thankful for.

(1, 007 words)
From *Business Week*

New Words

thrive /θraɪv/
v. grow or develop well and vigorously, prosper 茁壮成长，蓬勃发展，繁荣

perk /pɜːk/
n. advantage or benefit of a particular job, one's position, etc.（工作、职位等带来的）好处，利益；便利，特权

turkey /ˈtɜːkɪ/
n. large bird reared to be eaten, esp. at Thanksgiving or Christmas 火鸡

mecca /ˈmekə/
n. a place that is regarded as the center of an

---

1 Jupiter Research   美国朱庇特市场研究公司
2 eBags   美国箱包零售网站
3 Red Envelope   销售满足客户个性化要求礼品的美国网站
4 Shop.org   美国零售商协会
5 Kurt Salmon Associates   科特·萨尔蒙协会，美国零售咨询公司
6 Vermont Country Store   佛蒙特乡村零售公司
7 Manchester, Vt.（Manchester, Vermont）   美国佛蒙特州，曼彻斯特市

activity or interest; place many people wish to visit, especially people with a shared interest 渴望去的地方；胜地

microcosm /ˈmaɪkrəkɒz(ə)m/
n. a thing, a place or a group that has all the features and qualities of something much larger 缩影；具体而微者

persuasion /pɜ(ː)ˈsweɪʒən/
n. something that one believes；conviction 信念；见解

dynamism /ˈdaɪnəmɪzəm/
n. quality of being energetic and forceful 精力，活力；干劲

diversity /daɪˈvɜːsɪtɪ/
n. state of being different; variety 多种多样；多样性

anticipate /ænˈtɪsɪpeɪt/
v. expect 期望；预料（某事物）

cyberspace /ˈsaɪbəspeɪs/
n. the imaginary place where electronic messages, pictures, etc. exist while they are being sent between computers 网络空间，计算机化世界

behemoth /bɪˈhiːmɒθ/
n. something that is very large 庞然大物

lineup /ˈlaɪnʌp/
n. a set of events, programs or things arranged to follow each other for a purpose 为某目的而安排的一批事情或项目；（用于同一用途的）一批东西

scented /ˈsentɪd/
a. with a particular smell, especially a pleasant 有香味的

gear /gɪə/
n. equipment, clothing, etc. needed for an expedition, a sport, etc.（远征、运动等需用的）设备、装备、衣物等

poll /pəʊl/
v. ask somebody's opinion as part of a public-opinion survey 对某人作民意调查

snowboarding /snəʊˈbɔːdɪŋ/
n. the sport of moving over snow on a long wide board called a snowboard, usually associated with young people 滑板滑雪运动

array /əˈreɪ/
n. a group or collection of things or people, often one that is large or impressive 大堆；大群；大量

foul-mouthed /faʊl-maʊðd/
a. using obscene and offensive language 口出恶言的，出言粗俗的

animated /ˈænɪmeɪtɪd/
a. given the appearance of movement 看起来活动的；动画的

hit /hɪt/
n. person or thing that is very popular; success 红极一时的人物或事物；成功

merchandising /ˈmɜːtʃəndaɪzɪŋ/
n. buying and selling (goods); promoting sales of (goods) 买卖（商品）；推销（商品）

vanish /ˈvænɪʃ/
v. disappear completely; stop to exist; fade away 完全消失；不复存在；消逝

stylish /ˈstaɪlɪʃ/
a. fashionable; elegant and attractive 时髦的，新潮的；高雅的

sensory /ˈsensərɪ/
a. connected with your physical senses 感觉的，感受的

niche /nɪtʃ/
n. a special area of demand for a product or service; a segment of the general market for a service or product line 产品或服务所需的特殊领域；利基（针对企业的优势细分出来的市场）；规模小但却有利可图的市场

fabric /ˈfæbrɪk/
n. type of cloth, esp. one that is woven 织物

quilting /ˈkwɪltɪŋ/
n. the work of making a quilt; a crafting hobby of many Americans, especially women （被子的）绗缝；一种手工艺爱好

kitschy /ˈkɪtʃɪ/
a. cheap, showy, vulgar or pretentious in art, design, etc.（艺术、设计等）俗气、矫饰的

flourish /ˈflʌrɪʃ/
v. develop quickly and be successful or common; thrive 昌盛，兴旺，繁荣

integral /ˈɪntɪgrəl/
a. necessary for completeness 构成整体所必需的

purveyor /pəˈveɪə(r)/
n. person or firm that supplies goods or services 供应货物或提供服务的人或公司

outfit /ˈaʊtfɪt/
n. an association of persons, especially a business organization 机构；商业组织
v. provide someone with a set of clothes or equipment for a special purpose 装备；配备；供给

arena /əˈriːnə/
n. place or scene of activity or conflict 活动或斗争的场所或场面

auctioneer /ˌɔːkʃəˈnɪə/
n. person whose job is conducting the activity of selling things in which each item is sold to the person who offers the most money for it 拍卖人

ballpark /ˈbɔːlpɑːk/
n. an area or a range within which an amount is likely to be correct or within which something can be measured （数额的）变动范围；变量范围

gloomily /ˈɡluːmɪlɪ/
ad. sadly and depressively 忧愁地，沮丧地

landscape /ˈlændskeɪp/
n. the general situation in which a particular activity takes place 全景

Phrases & Expressions

rev up
grow more intense; increase 增加，增长；更加活跃

specialty retailer
retailer concentrating on selling one merchandise line of goods for a particular and usually selective clientele 特种商品零售商；特色零售店

big-box store
a large, single story retail store which is usually free-standing, windowless, rectangular, and located in suburban or rural areas with expansive open air surface parking lots 占地面积很大的大零售商店；大规模商业中心

get by
manage to live, survive; manage 勉强维生；设法维持

shopping mall
a large, specially built covered area with many shops 大型零售购物中心

in a similar vein
in a similar manner, style or mood 同样地

cup of tea
something that one likes or excels in 喜爱的事物

baby boomer
someone born during a period when a lot of babies were born, especially between 1946 and 1964 生育高峰期出生的人

dress up
wear one's best clothes 穿上盛装

set apart from
make sb./sth. different from or superior to others 使某人/某事物与众不同或优于其他的

UNIT **2** Retailing

 Exercises

Comprehension

1. Answer the following questions with your partner.

    1) What is the meaning of "retail mecca"? Why is Nashua a retail mecca?
    2) What is the most prominent advantage of big-box-store to the consumers?
    3) Why can retailers of every size find ways to survive or even thrive?
    4) To buy necessities, which would consumers prefer to go to, a big-box retailer or a small stylish store? Why?
    5) To succeed in the future, what three channels ought to be adopted by retailers?
    6) According to the author, what is the survival and growth of Little House toy store in the competition with big-box-stores mainly attributed to?
    7) What are the strengths of online-only retailers?
    8) According to the passage, how are niches being created by smaller outfits as well as some bigger retailers?
    9) Which two companies have been quite successful in offering customized toys to consumers?
    10) Is the author for or against Wal-Martization? How do you know it?

2. The text can roughly be divided into four parts. Go through the text carefully to complete the outline below with the missing information from the text, and compare your answers with your partner's.

Part One (Para(s). 1 - 3)

Main idea: Though competition from big-box stores is intensifying all the time, retailers of every size, either traditional or online, can still find ways to survive or even thrive.

Part Two (Para(s). _____)

Main idea: _____

35

----------	Consumers can buy products of better quality in specialty shops.	----------	Consumers may go to big-box retailers to buy necessities, but more consumers now want unique products and experiences.

Part Three (Para(s). _____)

Main idea: _____
_____
_____

Part Four (Para(s).13-14)

Main idea: _____
_____
_____

Critical Thinking

Work in group to discuss the following questions.

1) Some business people choose to work directly with consumers, while others choose to work with other businesses, providing goods and services to them rather than consumers. What advantages might there be to work directly with consumers? What advantages might there be to work only with other businesses?

2) As you prepare for a career in business, what qualities will serve you well if you are going to work directly with consumers?

3) Retailing is all the activities involved in selling goods and services directly to final consumers for their personal, non-business use. Retail stores come in

a variety of shapes and sizes, and new retail types keep emerging. They can be classified by some characteristics. How do you classify the given retailers according to your understanding of the characteristics.

specialty stores	a shopping center	full service retailers
supermarkets	self-service retailers	the chain store
a department store	central business districts	convenience stores
a franchise	discount stores	factory outlets

Characteristics	Retailers
Amount of service (retailers classified by the amounts of service they provide):	
Product line (retailers classified by the depth and breadth of their product assortments):	
Relative prices (retailers classified by the prices they charge):	
Control of outlets (retailers classified by ownership):	
Type of store cluster (retailers clustering together to give consumers the convenience of one-stop shopping):	

Vocabulary

1. Use the words given below to write sentences with *retail*.

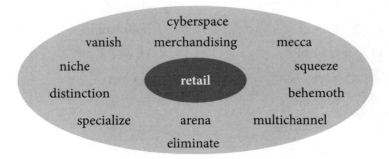

2. Replace a certain part in each of the following sentences with one of the words or expressions in the box. You may also use the phrase or the derivative of the word

or the expression you choose.

| set apart | highlight | poll | dress up | ballpark |
| perk | microcosm | integral | popularize | get by |

1) This book can serve as a good guide on how to wear formal clothes for cocktail parties or other formal occasions.

2) A rough estimate of the value of this property would be about $2,000,000.

3) We are all confused about how she manages to live on such a small salary.

4) The HR manager feels that it is a real challenge to distinguish Tom from the other candidates.

5) Train and bus services have been fully combined into an effective system.

6) These interview questions may make candidates' strengths and weaknesses easy to notice.

7) A majority of the managers we questioned said that they were overstressed.

8) This institute aims at making a lot of people know about the use of personal computers and enjoy it.

9) This car is given to him as one of the things provided by the company in addition to salary.

10) This small company contains the whole of society in miniature.

3. Link each word on the left with a noun on the right to make partnerships. Then complete the sentences below using the partnerships. You may have to make some changes to fit the grammar of the sentences.

A	B
specialty	director
big-name	strategy
baby	information
intensify	service
adopt	boomer
executive	retailer
customized	change
anticipate	store
digest	competition
big-box	designer

1) Those concentrating on selling one merchandise line of goods for a particular and usually selective clientele are _____.

2) Many experienced teachers say one of the symbols of smart students is that they can quickly _____ new _____.

3) We offer a _____ that can be tailored to the individual needs of our customers.

4) The introduction of foreign banks in China will _____ in the banking industry.

5) Some experts think the _____ are leading a consumer and workforce revolution that is changing the way we do business.

6) It is interesting that more _____ in fashion houses in the 20th century happen to be male.

7) In my opinion, being a(n) _____ can be lonely, frustrating and, in some circumstances, a miserable experience.

8) The executives are required to identify and _____ appropriate to their goals, such as expansion, diversification, specialization, integration, and internal organization.

9) Some manufacturers were lured from department stores and into _____, where their brands could be advertised directly to consumers.

10) Microsoft has always had to _____ in the software business and seize the opportunity to lead.

Translation

1. Translate the following paragraphs into Chinese.

   Even within the most competitive merchandise categories — like toys — it's often the smaller-scale retailers that have found ways around the big-box approach. Some 30% of all dollars spent on toys go to Wal-Mart, but smaller toy stores continue to attract customers. At the Little House toy store in Baton Rouge, La., young girls can dress up and throw tea parties like proper ladies. This kind of distinction sets it apart from Wal-Mart and helps Little House get its tiny slice of the $220 billion-a-year toy-retailing business.

   As Americans digest their turkey dinners on Thanksgiving and prepare for the holiday shopping season ahead, they can rest assured that they have more choices than ever. Just a few years ago, experts were gloomily warning of the Wal-Martization of the retailing landscape. Today, although the behemoth discounter continues to grow, its dominance hasn't eliminated the diversity of holiday-shopping choices. Now that's something to be thankful for.

2. **Put the following passage into English, using the words and phrases given in the box.**

intensify	multichannel	get by	personalization	customization
thrive	integration	niche	merchandising	behemoth

　　由于中小型零售商面临的来自"大型商业中心"的竞争加剧，对他们来说，如何寻找有效的市场利基、在竞争者中脱颖而出变得越来越重要。众多成功的中小型零售商采取的策略之一就是将个性化和顾客定制化纳入其商业理念中；策略之二便是充分利用科技力量构建多渠道的零售模式，如店铺零售和网上经营相结合。大型商业中心最具吸引力的口号是"天天低价"，但在购物环境、推销商品以及与顾客的关系方面却大大逊色于中小型零售商。正因为中小型零售商给顾客提供了大型商业巨鳄们所无法提供的特色服务和体验，在沃尔玛化全球盛行的今天，他们仍能生存，甚至繁荣兴旺。

Retailing Exchange Meeting

　　With the growing competition in the retailing world, it is becoming increasingly more difficult for retailers to survive. And for retailers to thrive today, they should often attend some retailing exchange activities where they can share some successful retailing experiences as well as the valuable lessons drawn from the mistakes some retailers made. Suppose you, as the retailers from different organizations, are invited to a retailing exchange meeting, at which you are given the information concerning the retail sales tips and common mistakes retail salespeople make. Discuss with your group members about how you understand the Tips and what lessons you can draw from the mistakes.

Retail Sales Tips

- In the world of retail sales, actions count, not words. Results count, not promises.
- Make big commitments, fulfill them all, and then give a little extra.
- Don't compete, create!
- Remember a picture is worth a thousand words!
- Selling is a combination of science and art.
- Sell benefits not products.
- Benefits help you tune-in to your customer's mental radio station.
- It is your obligation to close, and provide your customer with an opportunity to make a decision.
- Effective closing questions should be natural, sincere, yet assumptive (assume the sale).
- Objections do not mean "no".
- The READY formula suggests five ways to respond to an objection: reverse it, explain it, admit it, deny it, or ask "why".
- Develop a sense of belief / conviction about your service or product.
- Always maintain a positive attitude by visualizing the gainful end result of your work for your customer, company and yourself.
- Develop a follow-up schedule for customers who buy products from you.
- You don't have to work as hard to achieve your numbers if you leave such an impression with your customers that they always ask for you when they come back.

Common Mistakes Retail Salespeople Make

- Failing to build a rapport with the customer.
- Failing to find out customer's requirements.
- Focusing on their own agenda instead of customers'.
- Not giving customers the majority of the air time.
- Confusing "telling" with "selling".

- Not knowing the prevailing promotions, specials and regular pricing.
- Not differentiating the product/service/store/company enough to create additional value in the mind of the customer.
- Selling too fast, trying to close before the customer is ready to buy.
- Failing to address objections properly, and not realizing that satisfactory resolution is the shortest distance to purchase.
- Not taking advantage of add-on sales, as soon as the main purchase is done, which is when customer is most ready to entertain them.

Language Hints

Stating objectives
- What I want to introduce to you is...
- What I want to share with you is...
- ...

Clarifying
- I hope that make sense. In any case, ...
- ... by which I mean how we are going to distribute the product...
- ...

Referring to visual aids
- If you look at this mock-up drawing, you'll see that it consists of basically four elements...

Starting and closing
- To start with then, the product...

- I'd like to break this into two parts: firstly... secondly...
- However, there's an important aspect of... which I'd like to come onto to under my third heading of price.
- Is that all clear?
- ...

Concluding
- I'm also sure that you now share my enthusiasm for... which I've no doubt ...
- ...

Finishing
- Right, I'll stop there/here.
- That's all for today/this part.

An Invitation

Invitation is very common in the business circle. There are formal and informal invitations, depending on the importance of the occasion or the relationship between the inviter and the invitee. Invitations should be sent to all guests for their presence. Although there is no definite layout for business invitations, there are some indispensable structural parts.

Formal invitations:

- They usually apply the form of invitation cards.
- On them full names and official, business or professional titles of the host and the invitee, the nature of the event, the exact time and date, and the venue are made clear.
- They are written in the third person with formal and well-chosen words and expressions to convey the hospitality and courtesy of the host.
- If the invitation is issued by a firm or an organization, its full name should be given.
- The type of function should be specified and is generally capitalized, e.g. at a Reception, at Dinner, at a Banquet, etc.
- The sender can add some other items if necessary, such as the dress requirement for the occasion or the request for a reply.

In most cases, formal invitations require an immediate reply with R.S.V.P. (abbreviation for Répondez s'il vous plait, French) placed at the bottom right, which means "please reply". The receiver can use the reply card if enclosed or make a phone call if the phone number is provided, to express his or her gratitude for the invitation in the case of the acceptance or express his or her regrets and give a reason for the refusal. Sometimes "regrets only" instead of "R.S.V.P." is placed at the lower right-hand corner. In such cases, only those who are unable to be present are required to give a reply.

Informal invitations:

- They are usually presented in the form of a letter with detailed information about when, where and why of the invitation.
- Most are written in the first person in a sincere and courteous tone.
- They need to be short but persuasive.

It is polite for the receiver to reply the letter to show his/her gratitude for invitation and let the sender know whether he/she can be present or not.

Study the following samples and do the exercises according to the situation.

R.J. Roger
General director of the Canadian Trade Exhibition

Cordially invites the pleasure of
Victor Henry's company
at a buffet party
in Jin Jiang Hotel
378 Hong Qiao Road
Shanghai
at 6：30 p.m. on Friday
16 March 2008

Suggested dress code: formal

Mr. Richard Frazer
The President
Canadian Trade Exhibition

Regrets only
Tel. 021-68564476

To Welcome his Excellency Mr. Bo Xialai
Minister of the Ministry of Commerce of China
The Secretary of the State for Trade and Ms. Dell
Request the pleasure of the company of
Mr. Steven Chan
at Dinner
on August 8, 2008 at 18: 00 - 20: 30
at Hilton Hotel, #562 F Street, Washington
Dress formal, RSVP, Tel: 0718-2347788
Please present this invitation at the entrance

UNIT 2 Retailing

PJ Party

22 Yew Street, Cambridge, Ontario

Tel: 416-223-8900

April 7th, 2008

Dear Valued Customer:

Our records show that you have been a customer of PJ Party Inc. since our grand opening last year. We would like to thank you for your business by inviting you to our preferred customer Spring Extravaganza this Saturday.

Saturday's sales event is by invitation only. All of our stock, including pajamas and bedding will be marked down from 50%-80% off. Doors open at 9: 00 AM sharp. Complimentary coffee and donuts will be served. Public admission will commence at noon.

In addition, please accept the enclosed $10 gift certificate to use with your purchase of $75 or more.

We look forward to seeing you at PJ's on Saturday. Please bring this invitation with you and present it at the door.

Sincerely,

Linda Lane

Linda Lane

Store Manager

143 Elizabeth Avenue

Los Angeles, California

pjpartyinc@shoponline.com

*All sales are final. No exchanges.

Enclosure: Gift Certificate # 345 (not redeemable for cash)

Exercise:

Suppose you are one of the organizers of the Retailing Exchange Meeting in the oral task above. Write an invitation card and an invitation letter to a retailer to invite him to attend the meeting. Refer to the following Chinese hints and add anything necessary.

谨定于 2008 年 5 月 18 日（星期一）上午 9:30 在北京市朝阳区九仙桥路 10 号宇宙广场 3 号楼多功能展示厅举行零售经验交流会。

敬请乔治·李先生光临

请回复

查理斯·布朗

联系电话：010-68564476

尊敬的乔治·李先生：

　　如果您能光临这次零售经验交流会，我们将非常高兴。活动时间和地点是 2008 年 5 月 18 日（星期一）上午 9:30 在北京市朝阳区九仙桥路 10 号宇宙广场 3 号楼多功能展示厅。

　　我们还邀请了许多其他有影响的零售商。届时还有珍贵礼品送给大家。中午 12:30 还有招待午餐。这次活动仅凭邀请函参加。

　　感谢您长期以来一直积极参加我们组织的商务交流活动。我们期待着您的光临，希望能从与您的交流中受益。

查理斯·布朗

2008.5.8

Business Expressions

1. Look at the following words and expressions. Tick the odd one out.

   1) A. outlet　　　　　B. concessionaire　　C. franchise　　　　D. grocery

   2) A. hypermart　　　B. shopping mall　　　C. flagship store　　D. street vendor

   3) A. logistics　　　　B. packaging　　　　C. haulier　　　　　D. delivery

4) A. warehouse   B. stock   C. wholesale   D. inventory
5) A. cash refund   B. cash dispenser   C. cash register   D. POS systems
6) A. distressed goods   B. damaged merchandise
   C. shoddy goods   D. counterfeit goods
7) A. dump display   B. wall display
   C. window display   D. shop display
8) A. shelf tag   B. bin labels   C. price tag   D. shelf labels
9) A. brand leader   B. market leader   C. world leader   D. loss leader
10) A. odd price   B. budget price   C. exorbitant price   D. consumer price
11) A. credit voucher   B. sales voucher
    C. coupon   D. rebate
12) A. guarantee   B. warranty   C. commitment   D. maintenance
13) A. sales floor   B. showroom   C. selling floor   D. show house

2. **Complete the following sentences with the proper words or expressions in the box.**

cash-on-delivery	bins	stock turnover	goodwill	leader pricing
wholesale club	discount	staple goods	cashier	break-even point
brick and mortar	barcode	profit margin	mark-up	invoice dating

1) _____ is an encoded set of lines and spaces of different widths that can be scanned and interpreted into numbers to identify a product.

2) _____ are containers or fenced shelving for displaying merchandise.

3) _____ is when the customer pays for merchandise when it is delivered, instead of upfront.

4) _____ is a cash register operator.

5) _____ is the period allowed by vendors for the payment of bills.

6) _____ is reduction off of the price of an item or service.

7) _____ is an intangible asset of a business that is derived from its reputation, products, or services.

8) _____ is pricing products at lower than usual prices in order

to attract shoppers.

9) _____ is a measure for determining how quickly merchandise is being sold.

10) _____ is a retail store that sells a limited assortment of merchandise to customers who are "members" of the club.

11) _____ are products purchased regularly and out of necessity. Traditionally, these items have fewer markdowns and lower profit margins.

12) _____ is a ratio of profitability calculated as earnings divided by revenues. It measures how much out of every dollar of sales a retail business actually keeps in earnings.

13) _____ is a percentage added to the cost to get the retail selling price.

14) _____ refers to retail shops that are located in a building as opposed to an online shopping destination, door-to-door sales, kiosk or other similar site not housed within a structure.

15) _____ is the point in business where the sales equal to the expenses. There is no profit and no loss.

Specialized Reading

1. There are many types of non-traditional shops. Read the short passage below and put the underlined expressions into Chinese.

> Local shops can be known as 1) <u>brick and mortar stores</u> in the United States. Many shops are part of a chain: a number of similar shops with the same name selling the same products in different locations. The shops may be owned by one company, or there may be a 2) <u>franchising company</u> that has franchising agreements with the shop owners.
>
> Some shops sell 3) <u>second-hand goods</u>. Often the public can also sell goods to such shops, sometimes called 4) <u>"pawn" shops</u>. In other cases, especially in the case of 5) <u>a nonprofit shop</u>, the public donates goods to the shop, also called 6) <u>thrift store</u>, to be sold. In 7) <u>give-away shops</u> goods can be taken for free.

UNIT **2** Retailing

> There are also 8) "consignment" shops, which is where a person can place an item in a store, and if it is sold the person gives the shop owner a percentage of the sale price. The advantage of selling an item in this way is that the established shop gives the item exposure to more 9) potential buyers.
>
> The term *retailer* is also applied where 10) a service provider serves the needs of a large number of individuals, such as with telephone or electric power.

1) _____   2) _____
3) _____   4) _____
5) _____   6) _____
7) _____   8) _____
9) _____   10) _____

2. **Read more types of retailing and choose the best answer to each of the questions below.**

   There are three major types of retailing. The first is the market, a physical location where buyers and sellers converge. Usually this is done on town squares, sidewalks or designated streets and may involve the construction of temporary structures (market stalls). The second form is shop or store trading. Some shops use counter-service, where goods are out of reach of buyers, and must be obtained from the seller. This type of retail is common for small expensive items (e.g. jewelry) and controlled items like medicine and liquor. Self-service, where goods may be handled and examined prior to purchase, has become more common since the Twentieth Century. A third form of retail is virtual retail, where products are ordered via mail, telephone or online without having been examined physically but instead in a catalog, on television or on a website. Sometimes this kind of retailing replicates existing retail types such as online shops or virtual marketplaces such as eBay or Amazon.

   Buildings for retail have changed considerably over time. Market halls were constructed in the Middle Ages, which were essentially just covered marketplaces. The first shops in the modern sense used to deal with just one type of article, and usually adjoin the producer (baker, tailor, and cobbler). In the nineteenth century, in France, arcades (拱廊) were invented, which were a street of several different shops, roofed over. From this there soon developed, still in France, the notion of a large store of one ownership with many counters, each dealing with a different kind of article that was invented; it was called a department store. One of the novelties of the department store was the introduction of fixed prices, making haggling unnecessary, and browsing more enjoyable. This is commonly considered the birth of consumerism. In cities, these were multi-story buildings which pioneered the escalator.

In the 1920's the first supermarket opened in the United States, heralding in a new era of retail: self-service. Around the same time the first shopping mall was constructed which incorporated elements from both the arcade and the department store. A mall consists of several department stores linked by arcades (many of whose shops are owned by the same firm under different names). The design was perfected by the Austrian architect Victor Gruen. All the stores rent their space from the mall owner. By mid-century, most of these were being developed as single enclosed, climate-controlled, projects in suburban areas. The mall has had a considerable impact on the retail structure and urban development in the United States.

In addition to the enclosed malls, there are also strip malls which are 'outside' malls (in Britain they are called retail parks). These are often connected to supermarkets or big box stores. Also, in high traffic areas, other businesses may lease space from the supermarket or big-box store to sell their goods or services. A recent development is a very large shop called a superstore. These are sometimes located as stand-alone outlets, but more commonly are part of a strip mall or retail park.

1) Counter service is applied by some shops for _____.

   A. important and controlled items

   B. small and controlled articles

   C. expensive and controlled items

   D. small and expensive articles

2) If you want to examine the article you are buying personally, you may go to _____.

   A. counter service   B. online service

   C. self-service   D. door-to-door service

3) A department store originated from _____.

   A. covered marketplaces   B. market halls

           C. producers' shops   D. shopping arcades

4) Which of the following is true of the early department store according to the passage?

   A. It allowed customers to bargain over items.

   B. It made customers enjoy more articles.

   C. Articles there didn't come at bargain prices.

   D. The escalator was invented there.

5) What is the structural feature of the shopping mall in the United States?

   A. It is made up of department stores.

   B. It is constructed in shopping arcades.

   C. It incorporates a single enclosed project.

   D. It is linked by arcades.

6) What is the last paragraph about?

   A. Enclosed malls and "outside" malls.

   B. Structure of strip malls.

   C. Strip malls and a superstore.

   D. Big box stores and stand-alone outlets.

UNIT 3
E-Commerce

Lead-in

1. **Discuss the following questions with your partner.**

    1) What are your feelings about shopping on the Internet? What do you see as the advantages? What disadvantages are there?

    2) How do you feel about providing information to online services about yourself — for example, phone numbers, addresses, shopping preferences?

    3) Knowing that companies can track your online behavior, do you modify or alter your online profile or behavior to "hide" from them, or do you prefer that websites "recognize" you and your preferences? Do you think that online shoppers should be able to choose whether their behavior is tracked or not?

    4) Have you ever noticed that something on your computer screen has appeared automatically because of your online activity (advertisements for products you mention in an email to a friend, for example)? What was your reaction? Do you approve of such automation? Do you appreciate being informed of products or services in such a manner?

2. **Discuss with your group members what use you often make of the Internet. Tick the uses first and then talk about the strengths and weaknesses of doing them on the Internet.**

Uses	Your preferences	Strengths and weaknesses
Information searching		
E-mail		
Shopping		
Chatting		
Downloading video & music		

UNIT 3 E-Commerce

Preview: E-commerce can be defined as any business or commercial transaction carried out over the Internet. Nowadays, e-commerce is booming. Customers can buy air tickets, books, computers, flowers, music and a wide variety of other products over the Internet. E-commerce complements the traditional way of conducting business, with new technologies offering a wide range of ways in which a company can reach an appropriate consumer with their product message. These techniques border on the range of science fiction, and both consumers and sellers can benefit. The combination of e-commerce and high tech offers us a glamorous vista: enhanced interactivity, better visuals, more information, improved search results along with more personalized commercial service, and a lot more.

Taking E-Commerce to the Next Level

Coming soon: Improved recommendations and personalized pitches that actually work. But how much of this will shoppers stand for?

By Amey Stone

[1] This summer, Chester Yeum was watching Tom Cruise[1]'s **sci-fi thriller** *Minority Report*[2], set in the year 2054, when he realized he was helping make an element of it a reality today. The **epiphany** came as Cruise strode through a shopping **concourse** and **impromptu**, personalized advertising pitches **buffeted** him from all sides — just the kind of location-based marketing Yeum is trying to bring to market.

[2] Yeum's first step to a 2054-like world is SpotMeeting.com, a location-based online dating service. Romance seekers are linked to others near them through software that identifies their location. Today the site maps each member's Internet address, but an upcoming version will use global positioning technology to locate members on the go.

[3] Eventually, Yuem hopes to sign up retailers to send his customers pitches via their cell phones or handheld computers that will **entice** them into a store they're approaching, perhaps using a 10%-off coupon. Or maybe send them an e-mail reminding them that an **outfit** they abandoned in an online shopping cart is available in the store to try on.

[4] "I don't believe the mainstream market is ready for that right now," says

---

1 Tom Cruise / ˈtɒmˈkruːz / 汤姆·克鲁斯，美国影星
2 *Minority Report* 《少数派报告》，美国影片名

Yeum, who thinks that people first have to get comfortable disclosing their location and personal information — something they might be willing to do now for a chance at romance. Once his site establishes itself in dating, he says, "we will **stream** in **supplemental applications** that will plug right into e-commerce."

[5] It's back to the future for e-commerce, now that some of the technologies **envisioned** years ago are finally ready for prime time. With so many e-tailers profitable, they're finally ready to move ahead with adding new technologies that can take online shopping to the next level.

[6] For shoppers, the next level means more interactivity, better **visuals**, and improved search results with more product information. It also means being watched more closely by sites and receiving personalized pitches based on past browsing behavior — which can be a little **creepy**. For retailers, this next phase presents an opportunity to generate more sales volume, but it also requires treading carefully so as not to anger customers by invading their privacy.

[7] Web designers' widespread adoption of "meta data" and **XML** (extensible markup language), both standards for tagging data on Web pages, are making the **transition** easier. With such tagging in place, developers can create applications that **manipulate** information in new ways. Not only has this technology allowed for higher levels of interactivity but it has also **triggered** great advances in the ability to track customer behavior on e-commerce sites. That's rapidly leading to more personalization and smarter merchandising.

[8] Vastly improved search and site **navigation** probably represent the most important sales drivers for cutting-edge e-commerce sites today. One such company, Atomz[1], which hosts the Web applications it designs, has software that **trawls** a retailer's site gathering product information and creating advanced search functions. At Pacific Sunwear[2]'s site, customers can **drill** down from seeing all shirts, to just, say, girls' T-shirts in red. The retailer has some control over results, too, so higher-price items can be displayed first, says Atomz Chief Executive Officer Steve Kusmer.

[9] Atomz also can drive sales by allowing businesses to highlight special promotions tied to searches on their sites, like handheld maker PalmOne[3] does with a "noteworthy" box that appears along with search results. On PalmOne's site, type "Zire" into its search engine and up **pops** a box recommending the Zire 72, which comes with

---

1 Atomz / ˈætəmz / 美国亚腾公司
2 Pacific Sunwear / pəˈsɪfɪk ˈsʌnwɛə / 太平洋阳光服装公司
3 PalmOne / ˈpɑːm ˈwʌn / 奔迈有限公司，美国掌上电脑制造商

photo, video, and MP3 **capabilities**. The addition of a promotion box above the search results has increased the number of searchers **converted** to buyers by up to 60%, says Kusmer.

[10] Cutting-edge Web sites aren't just serving better information to customers; they're also tracking buyers' behavior much more closely. Web analytics companies Coremetrics[1] and Omniture[2] are thriving on new demand for their products, which analyze customer behavior. These are often sold as a hosted service for fees ranging from $30,000 to $100,000 a year, depending on the volume of traffic and the extent of the site analyzed, says Freeman Evans.

[11] Web analytics allows retailers to predict what customers might want to buy next by looking at their past purchasing history, as well as data generated from other shoppers. It also helps companies make important improvements in how easy their sites are to **navigate** and use. Sportsline.com announced in a May press release that it used Omniture's SiteCatalyst[3] to identify when customers dropped out of signing up for its **fantasy** football league, allowing Sportsline to improve its process and increase the number of paying customers.

[12] With so much data available at their fingertips, more retailers will be using Web analytics to personalize e-mail. For example, customers might get an e-mail letting them know that a sweater they **perused** but never bought is now available for 10% off. In retailing **lingo** this is called "remarketing".

[13] Retailers say higher-quality interactive images are driving sales, too. Lamps Plus[4], for one, is using **rich-media** software from Scene7 that allows customers to manipulate high-**resolution** photos, **zooming** in to see the **texture** of fabric, **spin** products around for a 360-degree view, or sample color swatches. Lamps Plus says the software has helped increase sales on its Web site and from in-store **kiosks** because customers can get a more realistic idea of a broad range of products.

[14] Creating a richer, more realistic online shopping experience is just one way retailers are getting customers to buy more. They're also employing so-called smart-pricing technology to **optimize** how much they charge for items on their sites. Plus, they're learning they can generate more sales by adding more information, such as customer **ratings** and reviews.

---

1 Coremetrics / kɔː'metrɪks /　美国核心网络分析公司
2 Omniture / 'ɒmnɪtʃə /　美国奥尼奇网络分析公司
3 SiteCatalyst / 'saɪt'kætəlɪst /　网站催化剂，奥尼奇网络分析公司的站点数据流量分析软件
4 Lamps Plus / 'læmps 'plʌs /　超级灯饰公司

80 [15] Too much computer-driven personalization can **backfire**, though, as Tom Cruise's character learned in the Big Brother-style world of *Minority Report*. "Retailers have to be careful to make sure shoppers don't feel they're being watched a little too closely," says Freeman Evans.

[16] That's why SpotMeeting's Yeum is happy to take a slow and steady pace in
85 bringing his brand of e-commerce to the next level. Your favorite clothing retailer won't be broadcasting a personalized message to you as you walk by for a while yet. But Yeum, for one, is confident that that'll happen sooner than you might think.

(1,056 words)
From *Business Week*

New Words

sci-fi /ˈsaɪˈfaɪ/
n. & a. science fiction; of, relating to science fiction 〈口〉科学幻想小说（的）

thriller /ˈθrɪlə/
n. a work of fiction or drama designed to hold the interest by the use of a high degree of intrigue, adventure, or suspense 惊险电影；恐怖电影

epiphany /ɪˈpɪfəni/
n. a sudden realization or revelation of the essential nature or meaning of something 对事物真谛的顿悟；事物本质的突然显露

concourse /ˈkɒŋkɔːs/
n. an open space or hall where crowds gather 群集场所；大厅；广场

impromptu /ɪmˈprɒmptjuː/
a. done without being planned, organized, or rehearsed 事先无准备的；即兴的

buffet /ˈbʌfɪt/
v. strike sharply or repeatedly 反复敲打，连续猛击

entice /ɪnˈtaɪs/
v. tempt 诱惑；吸引

outfit /ˈaʊtfɪt/
n. a set of clothes 全套服装

stream /striːm/
v. transmit (data) in real time, especially over the Internet 用计算机网络流媒体播放

supplemental /ˌsʌplɪˈmentəl/
a. additional, extra 补充的

application /ˌæplɪˈkeɪʃən/
n. a computer program or piece of software designed and written to fulfill a particular purpose of the user【计算机】应用程序；应用软件

envision /ɪnˈvɪʒən/
v. imagine 想象；展望

visual /ˈvɪzjuəl, -ʒuəl/
n. something that appeals to the sight and is variously used (as for illustration, demonstration, or promotion) 画面；图像

creepy /ˈkriːpi/
a. annoyingly unpleasant, repulsive; causing or having an unpleasant feeling of mild fear or horror 令人生厌的，令人反感的；令人毛骨悚然的，令人不寒而栗的

XML
abbr. (extensible markup language) a metalanguage which allows users to define their own customized markup languages, esp. in order to display documents on the World Wide Web 可扩展标记语言

transition /trænˈzɪʃən/

n. change; a development or evolution from one form, stage, or style to another 过渡，过渡时期；转变，变迁

manipulate /mə'nɪpjuleɪt/
v. manage or use skillfully（熟练地）操作；使用；巧妙地处理

trigger /'trɪgə/
v. cause sth. to begin to happen or exist 引起；促使

navigation /ˌnævɪ'geɪʃən/
n. the act of moving around a website, file, the Internet, etc.【计算机】浏览（网站、文件、因特网等）；导航

trawl /trɔːl/
v. search, search through a lot of documents, lists etc. in order to find out information 在……搜罗；查阅

drill (down) /drɪl/
v. access data which is in a lower level of a hierarchically structured database【计算机】提取多级数据库的低层数据

pop /pɒp/
v. go, come, or appear suddenly 冷不防地出现（或发生），（突然）冒出

capability /ˌkeɪpə'bɪlətɪ/
n. the ability or qualities necessary to do sth. 性能；功能

convert /kən'vɜːt/
v. bring over from one belief, view, or party to another 使转变

navigate /'nævɪgeɪt/
v. move around a website, file, the Internet, etc.【计算机】浏览（网站、文件、因特网等）；导航

fantasy /'fæntəsɪ/
n. a pleasant situation that you imagine but that is unlikely to happen 幻想

peruse /pə'ruːz/
v. examine or consider with attention and in detail; study 仔细观察；仔细考虑；仔细阅读

lingo /'lɪŋgəʊ/
n. the special vocabulary of a particular field of interest 行话，术语

rich-media /'rɪtʃ 'miːdjə/
a. consisting of any combination of graphics, audio, video and animation, which is more storage-and bandwidth-intensive than ordinary text 富媒体的（具有动画、声音、视频和/或交互性的信息传播方法）

resolution /ˌrezə'luːʃən/
n. 分辨率

zoom /zuːm/
v. focus more narrowly on an object so that the object's apparent distance from the observer changes（摄影机）迅速接近被摄对象；（用变焦距镜头）推近

texture /'tekstʃə/
n. the way a surface, substance or fabric looks or feels to the touch, i.e. its thickness, firmness, roughness, etc.（一物体表面、物质或织物的）质地；外观；手感（如厚薄、软硬、粗细等）

spin /spɪn/
v. turn around a central point 使旋转

kiosk /'kiːɒsk, kɪ'ɒsk/
n. a small building or structure from which people can buy things 售货亭

optimize /'ɒptɪmaɪz/
v. make as perfect, effective, or functional as possible 使尽可能完善

rating /'reɪtɪŋ/
n. a score or measurement of how good or popular sth. is 评定结果；评分

backfire /ˌbæk'faɪə/
v. have the opposite result to the one that was intended; have the reverse of the desired or expected effect 发生意外；产生事与愿违的结果

Phrases & Expressions

stand for
　　support 主张；支持

on the go
　　constantly or restlessly active〈口〉忙个不停

sign up
　　initiate a business deal with 与……达成交易

plug into
　　connect or become connected to 与……连接

prime time
　　the choicest or busiest time 黄金时间，全盛时期

sales volume
　　total amount of sales/revenue generated by a retail outlet or facility in a given period of time 销售额

meta data
　　a set of data that describes and gives information about other data 诠释数据

in place
　　working or being able to be used; working or ready to work 到位的；可用的

press release
　　a written statement about a matter of public interest which is given to the press by an organization concerned with the matter（通讯社或政府机构等发布的）新闻稿

drop out
　　withdraw from participation or membership; quit 退出

fantasy football
　　a competition in which participants select imaginary teams from among the players in a league and score points according to the actual performance of their players 空幻足球

at one's fingertips
　　instantly or readily available 近在手边；随时可供应用；立即可以得到

color swatch
　　a sample of a specified color 某种颜色的样本，色样

Exercises

Comprehension

1. Answer the following questions with your partner.

   1) What did *Minority Report* evoke in Chester Yeum's mind?

   2) How does Chester Yeum's SpotMeeting.com work?

   3) What technological advances has Chester Yeum been envisioning over the

UNIT **3** E-Commerce

recent years?

4) Does Chester Yeum think that the mainstream market will embrace his idea about e-commerce wholeheartedly right now? Why or why not?

5) What does it mean to take e-commerce to the next level, so far as customers are concerned?

6) From retailers' perspective, what does it mean to take e-commerce to the next level?

7) What implications does the adoption of "meta data" and XML have for e-commerce?

8) What are the major sales drivers for e-commerce sites today?

9) Does building a cutting-edge e-commerce web site solely mean feeding state-of-the-art information to customers? Why or why not?

10) According to Steve Kusmer, what purpose has the promotion box served?

11) How can retailers make business predictions on the basis of the customer data available?

2. The text can be roughly divided into four parts. Write the paragraph numbers of each part and then give its main idea. And compare your answers with your partner's.

Parts	Paragraphs	Main ideas
Part I	Paras. 1-4	Introduction: Chester Yeum's e-commerce venture
Part II	Paras. _____	_____
Part III	Paras. _____	_____
Part IV	Paras. _____	_____

Critical Thinking

Work in group to discuss the following questions.

1) As a business person, what advantages do you see in secretly identifying people who express an interest in products like yours in their online activity? What drawbacks do you see in taking advantage of that information?

61

2) How likely do you think it is, in the near future, that almost everyone will regularly use the Internet for e-commerce? Why? Will online shopping gradually take the place of other forms of shopping? Why or why not?

Vocabulary

1. Match the verbs with a similar meaning. Then think of a noun or a noun phrase to follow each pair of verbs.

    1) entice   imagine   _____
    2) disclose   change   _____
    3) envision   process   _____
    4) convert   improve   _____
    5) identify   reveal   _____
    6) optimize   examine   _____
    7) manipulate   cause   _____
    8) trigger   lure   _____
    9) peruse   discover   _____

2. Rewrite the following italicized parts by using the appropriate words or expressions from the text.

    1) The salesman works under great pressure and is *busy and active* all the time.

    2) They pushed hard to be part of the initiative from News Corp.'s Fox unit and NBC that will put *peak-time* TV shows on the Web as early as this summer.

    3) An errant supplier can delay a key product launch and *enrage* customers.

    4) Today, the potential from new technology is staggering. The Internet can increase grassroots democracy — or *infringe* on our privacy.

    5) Higher, higher, higher, then bam! Shanghai's pumped-up stock market fainted dead away on a black Tuesday. Many people wondered what on earth *set off* the slump.

    6) After years of taking abuse from counterfeiters, companies and even nations are turning to *state-of-the-art* technology to win back control of their brands and ward off accidents associated with fakes.

    7) Some companies are applying the latest *developments* in molecular science and nanotechnology to fight against counterfeits. Stores, customs officials,

or investigators will soon be able to see whether a product is real or fake by scanning it with a handheld reader and matching it against an electronic database.

8) The official said that government revenues might benefit in the short term, "but this could *have an opposite effect*, as they create significant disincentives to new investment in oil production, thus ultimately affecting the governments' long-run revenues."

9) Despite years of criticism from the West and some new anti-piracy technologies, the country's black market for counterfeit goods is *flourishing*.

10) Weather forecasts, directions, stock quotes, traffic reports, and more can be *instantly or readily available to us* with simple text messages on any mobile phone.

3. **Complete each sentence with the correct form of the words in capital letters.**

   1) THRILLER

   Sometimes getting promoted is a double-edged sword: _____, yes, but terrifying.

   2) PERSON

   The marketers can target the exact person who is most likely to buy a product at the precise moment they are most likely to buy it. It's the ad industry's dream come true: a perfect _____ pitch.

   3) IDENTIFY

   New Haven plans to offer a city _____ card that undocumented workers may use to access city services.

   4) DISCLOSE

   The company was strongly condemned for insufficient _____ of negative information.

   5) SUPPLEMENTAL

   President Bush's proposal for Personal Reemployment Accounts would _____ traditional unemployment insurance with an individually controlled account to fund training or provide income when an individual changes jobs.

   6) INTERACT

   TV on the Internet will, and should, closely resemble TV on television — save for some tinges of _____ like chat, and a thus-far unfulfilled promise of ultra-targeted ads.

7) OPTIMIZE

Now he is recalling the most important time of his business life, the years from 1972 to 1979, when he lived in Afghanistan and India, manufacturing and exporting women's clothing to luxury retailers in the West under less than _____ conditions.

8) REAL

Only 3% of senior management at FORTUNE 100 companies is black or Hispanic. Many nonwhite kids lack early exposure to the corporate world, and they often find a career at Goldman Sachs (高盛) a(n) _____ goal.

9) ANALYZE

A 15-year Walt Disney Co. veteran, he had risen to the chairmanship of the company's amusement parks and resorts unit. By nature a methodical thinker, he embraced market _____ and other researches to help him understand consumer spending patterns.

10) DEMAND

The processor of the computer is a 2.4 gigahertz Celeron (赛扬处理器), more than adequate for the relatively _____ use — mostly e-mail, Web browsing, and word processing.

Translation

1. Translate the following paragraphs into Chinese.

   It's back to the future for e-commerce, now that some of the technologies **envisioned** years ago are finally ready for prime time. With so many e-tailers profitable, they're finally ready to move ahead with adding new technologies that can take online shopping to the next level.

   For shoppers, the next level means more interactivity, better visuals, and improved search results with more product information. It also means being watched more closely by sites and receiving personalized pitches based on browsing preferences — which can be a little creepy. For retailers, this next phase presents an opportunity to generate more sales volume, but it also requires treading carefully so as not to anger customers by invading their privacy.

2. Put the following passage into English, using the words and phrases given in the box.

| cutting-edge | track | advance | at one's fingertips | pace |
| trigger | thrive | predict | personalize | demand |

最前沿的网络技术给商业带来了影响深远的进展。首先，它使得商家能够为顾客提供更多更好的商品信息。与此同时，它也使得网站有可能更密切地跟踪买家的行为。网络分析公司凭借市场对于其产品——对于顾客行为的分析——的需求而蓬勃发展。网络分析技术使得零售商能够通过观察顾客过往的购物历史来预测他们下一步可能买什么。零售商将会利用唾手可得的信息来为顾客定制电子邮件。不过，这里说一句警示性的话还是恰当的。虽然最新网络科技为零售商提供了一个拓展业务的机会，但也需要稳扎稳打、稳步推进，以免因侵犯顾客隐私而冒犯顾客。

Online Retailers

The Internet has opened a new world of opportunities for retailers. Retailers of any size can appear even more successful on the Internet with an effective service and sell site. The Web also offers a way for retailers to fill the gaps of their brick-and-mortar stores by offering more service online for their existing customers. Work in pairs first. Student A looks at the profile of Amazon.com Inc. on page 287; Student B looks at the profile of eBay Inc. on page 288 After reading the information, make a brief presentation about the retailer to your partner, and then work with another pair of students, discussing the following questions.

Visit our eBay Store

- They are the worldwide famous online retailer. What are they famous for respectively?
- How do they operate respectively?
- Do they offer any special services which the brick-and-mortar stores can't offer? If they do, what are the special services?
- What are their missions? How are they to accomplish their missions?
- What are the similarities and differences between these retailers?
- Do you have any shopping experiences with these retailers? If you do, tell your feelings about them.
- Can you think of any other similar online retailers? If you can, try to name a few.

Language Hints

Asking for views
- Peter, what are your views?
- Peter, what do you think?
- What do you make of it?
- What do you say?
- ...

Giving your views
- In my opinion, it ...
- Well, I must say...
- I'd just like to say...
- To my knowledge, they...
- ...

Hedging
- Do you think so?
- I'd rather not say anything about it.
- It's difficult to say.
- Can't say, really.
- It all depends.
- ...

Trying to change somebody's opinion
- But don't you think...?
- Hold on, it's too early to say that yet.
- Yes, but if we look at the whole picture, the situation...
- ...

An E-mail

E-mail, the short form for electronic mail, is a relatively new medium of communication. It is cheap, fast, and convenient. E-mail is briefer and less formal than regular letters although it can be written in the form of a letter. The layout of an e-mail message is made up of two parts — the head and the body.

The e-mail head is shown as below:

- To (name, title/department/company and e-mail address of the receiver)
- From (name, title/department/company and e-mail address of the sender)
- Subject (main idea of the e-mail message)
- Date (day/month/year)

The body text is usually written in short paragraphs and should be correct, clear, concise, complete, and courteous. The following e-mail etiquette may help you write effective professional e-mails.

- Distinguish between formal and informal situations and write accordingly.
- Never leave the subject line blank. Appropriate use of the subject line increases the chances your e-mail will be read and not deleted without so much as a glance.
- Write a brief and effective subject line, which inform the receiver of EXACTLY what the e-mail is about in a few well-chosen words.
- Keep the message focused and readable.
- Identify yourself clearly.
- Prior to sending it, proofread and double-check your e-mail message.
- If you are responding to an e-mail, include the original message in the reply, so the receiver can put your e-mail into the correct context. Also, respond within two business days.
- Keep your address simple, and avoid unprofessional sounding names like "studmuffin" or "partygirl".

Study the following sample, and then write a reply e-mail. Add anything necessary.

To:	Ms. Mary Brown, Sales Dept., Mayflower Company, marybrown@bigpond.com
From:	Mr. Mike Owen, Purchasing Dept., Kmart, mikeowen@kmart.com
Subject:	Asking for price reduction
Date:	08/11/2008

Dear Ms. Brown,

We have received both your quotation of October 31 and the samples of Men's suiting, and thank you for them. While appreciating the good quality of your suitings we find the prices of these materials rather high for the market we wish to supply. We have also to point out that very good suitings are now available in European countries from several other manufacturers and all of these are at prices from 10% to 15% below yours.

We would like to place our order with you, but must ask you to consider whether you can make us a more favorable offer. Is it possible to give us a 10% reduction? As your order would be worth around $100,000 you may think it worth while to make a concession.

A prompt reply would be appreciated.

Yours faithfully,

Mike Owen

Purchasing Dept., Kmart

Suggested key points of reply e-mail

- *Can not accept 10% reduction;*
- *Can only give 3% special discount;*
- *Considerable business has been done with many customers in European markets at these prices;*
- *The products are with high quality and better than similar articles from other sources;*
- *Minimum order quantity is 3,000 dozen.*

UNIT **3** E-Commerce

Business Expressions

1. Complete the words in the left column according to the definition in the right column.

Words	Definitions
1) _ _ _ _ _ space	a term coined to describe the sum total of computer accessible information in the world
2) d_ _ _ _ _ _ _	the transfer of information from the Internet to the browsing computer
3) b_ _ _ _ _ _	software that allows you to read information and navigate on the Internet
4) h_ _ _ _ _	a person who deliberately logs on to other computers by somehow bypassing the security system
5) f_ _ _ _ _ _ _	a combination of specialized hardware and software designed to keep unauthorized users from accessing information within a networked computer system
6) _ _ _ _ er	a component of a Web page containing an advertisement that is usually an inch or less tall and spans the width of the Web page
7) m_ _ _ _	the word come from the two words: Modulation and Demodulation, which refers to something used to convert information from analog to digital and vice versa
8) m_ _ _	a list of options presented to the user to enable them to perform a specific task
9) l_ _ _	a component of a hypertext document which, when selected with a mouse, takes the user to another document or a different section of the current document
10) _ _ _ _ _ net	an internal or company network that can be used by anyone who is directly connected to the company's computer network
11) in_ _ _ _ _ _	a world-wide computer network through which you can send a letter, chat with people electronically, or search for information on almost any subject

69

续表

Words	Definitions
12) s_ _ _ _ _	a host computer that stores information(e.g., Web sites) and responds to requests for information (e.g., links to another Web page)
13) s_ _ _	looking around the Internet, jumping from page to page, just going to wherever takes your fancy at that time
14) up_ _ _ _	to copy files from your own PC to another computer via a network or a modem
15) v_ _ _ _	a program that can damage your PC files, which is often created intentionally to do so
16) _ _ _ _ _ _ d	a word or phrase used in a search engine query, for example, to find Web documents related to a particular subject
17) _ _ _ _ _ _ _ th	the maximum speed at which data can be transmitted between computers in a network
18) multi_ _ _ _ _	the presentation of video, sound, graphics, text, or animation by software

2. Some abbreviations concerning e-commerce are scattered around a flower-shaped pattern. Write out the full name of the abbreviations with the proper words given inside the pattern.

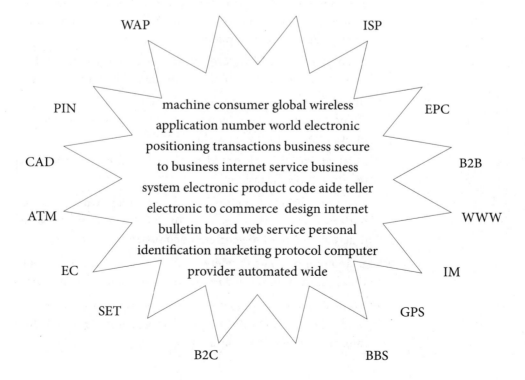

3. Complete the following sentences with the expressions in the box.

I-way	domain names	digital economy	e-logistics
cyber cash	welcome page	click(s)-and-mortar	web hosts
shopping cart	virtual	marketplace	

1) The _____ is ideal for companies with an established market position and a clearly-defined customer base who want to offer a more complete service and a better on-line experience to their customers, simply and profitably.

2) It is useful to think of the _____ as having three primary components — supporting infrastructure, electronic business processes(how business is conducted), and electronic commerce transactions (selling of goods and services online).

3) Our integrated _____ solutions can help you manage resources allocation, supply chain, inventory, logistics flow and warehouse operations.

4) You're reading the _____, but the daily "front page" is here.

5) _____ are companies that provide space on a server they own for use by their clients as well as providing Internet connectivity, typically in a data center.

6) _____ are sometimes colloquially (and incorrectly) referred to by marketers as "web addresses".

7) In British English, _____ is generally known as a shopping basket, almost exclusively shortened on websites to "basket".

8) _____ refers to a shop that exists both online and in the physical world.

9) There may be many popular meanings for _____ with the most popular definition being that of Information high way.

10) For those concerned primarily with payment protection, however, SET technologies and e-cash or _____ are the best bets.

Specialized Reading

1. E-commerce should take customers into consideration and avoid its problems. Read the following passage and choose the topic sentence marked A-H to complete the gap.

> A. Providing service and performance
> B. Providing value to customers

> C. Providing personal attention
> D. Providing an incentive for customers to buy and to return
> E. Providing a sense of community
> F. Helping customers do their job of consuming
> G. Owning the customer's total experience
> H. Letting customers help themselves

A successful e-commerce organization must provide an enjoyable and rewarding experience to its customers. Many factors go into making this possible. Such factors include:

1) _____. Vendors can achieve this by offering a product or product-line that attracts potential customers at a competitive price, as in non-electronic commerce.

2) _____. Offering a responsive, user-friendly purchasing experience, just like a flesh-and-blood retailer, may go some way to achieving these goals.

3) _____. Sales promotions to this end can involve coupons, special offers, and discounts. Cross-linked websites and advertising affiliate programs can also help.

4) _____. Personalized web sites, purchase suggestions, and personalized special offers may go some of the way to substituting for the face-to-face human interaction found at a traditional point of sale.

5) _____. Chat rooms, discussion boards, soliciting customer input and loyalty programs (sometimes called affinity programs) can help in this respect.

6) _____. E-tailers foster this by treating any contacts with a customer as part of a total experience, an experience that becomes synonymous with the brand.

7) _____. Provision of a self-serve site, easy to use without assistance, can help in this respect. This implies that all product information is available, cross-sell information, advice for product alternatives, and supplies & accessory selectors.

8) _____. E-tailing and online shopping directories can provide such help through ample comparative information and good search facilities. Provision of component information and safety-and-health comments may assist e-tailers to define the customers' jobs.

2. **Another side of the picture is the problems of e-commerce. Read the passage and complete the headings that summarize the specific paragraphs.**

Even if a provider of E-commerce goods and services rigorously follows the "key factors" to devise an exemplary e-commerce strategy, problems can still arise. Sources of such problems include:

Failure to understand customers, why they buy and how they buy. Even a product with a sound value proposition can fail if producers and retailers do not understand customer habits, expectations, and motivations. E-commerce can potentially mitigate this potential problem with proactive and focused marketing research, just as traditional retailers may do.

Failure to consider the competitive situation. One may have the will to construct a viable book e-tailing business model, but lack the capability to compete with Amazon.com.

1) Inability to predict _____. What will competitors do? Will they introduce competitive brands or competitive web sites? Will they supplement their service offerings? Will they try to sabotage a competitor's site? Will price war break out? What will the government do? Research into competitors, industries and markets may mitigate some consequences here, just as in non-electronic commerce.

2) Over-estimation of _____. Can staff, hardware, software, and processes handle the proposed strategy? Have e-tailers failed to develop employee and management skills? These issues may call for thorough resource planning and employee training.

Failure to coordinate. If existing reporting and control relationships do not suffice, one can move towards a flat, accountable, and flexible organizational structure, which may or may not aid coordination.

Failure to obtain senior management commitment. This often results in a failure to gain sufficient corporate resources to accomplish a task. It may help to get top management involved right from the start.

3) Failure to obtain _____. If planners do not explain their strategy well to employees, or fail to give employees the whole picture, then training and setting up incentives for workers to embrace the strategy may assist.

4) Under-estimation of _____. Setting up an e-commerce venture can take considerable time and money, and failure to understand the timing and sequencing of tasks can lead to significant cost overruns. Basic project

planning, critical path, critical chain, or PERT analysis may mitigate such failings. Profitability may have to wait for the achievement of market share.

5) Failure to follow _____. Poor follow-through after the initial planning, and insufficient tracking of progress against a plan can result in problems. One may mitigate such problems with standard tools: benchmarking, milestones, variance tracking, and penalties and rewards for variances.

6) Becoming the _____. Many syndicates have caught on to the potential of the Internet as a new revenue stream. Two main methods are as follows: (1) Using identity theft techniques to order expensive goods and bill them to some innocent person, then liquidating the goods for quick cash; (2) Extortion by using a network of compromised "zombie" computers to engage in distributed denial of service attacks against the target Web site until it starts paying protection money.

7) Failure to _____. Too often new businesses do not take into account the amount of time, money or resources needed to complete a project and often find themselves without the necessary components to become successful.

UNIT 4
Communication

1. **Discuss the following questions with your partner.**

    1) In recent surveys conducted across industries, and especially the IT industry, money is a distant second reason why employees choose to be part of an organization. What do you think is the primary reason for employees' loyalty?

    2) Internal communications include all forms of contact within an organization. What forms of communication can you think of? Complete the following table.

Oral Forms	Written Forms

    3) To allow effective communication to take place, an organization should have a number of internal communication channels available depending on its needs. How many channels can you list? Which of them do you think is the most reliable today?

    4) Some experts assert that while formal channels are important, it is critical to make informal communication a continuous effort. What informal channels can you think of?

2. **Work with your group members on the following questions.**

    1) List at least five reasons why internal communication is so important for an organization:

    a. _____

    b. _____

c. _____

d. _____

e. _____

2) List at least four features of effective internal communications:

a. _____

b. _____

c. _____

d. _____

3) List respectively at least three long-term and short-term results of ineffective internal communication:

Short-term Fallout	Long-term Fallout

Preview: Internal communication is an important tool for binding an organization, enhancing employee morale, promoting openness and improving employee loyalty. Ironically, while everybody understands and talks about the significance of internal communication, very few are able to manage it efficiently. The communication in many companies leaves their employees wondering what is going on. The following passage presents some findings based on a survey about internal communication. It defines four types of communicators and their strengths and weaknesses. The author also emphasizes the importance of openness, honesty, authenticity and two-way communication.

Employees Want to Hear It "Straight" from the Boss's Mouth

*Workers prefer their corporate leader to speak directly to them and **disdain*** *the "performance" style.*

By Alison Maitland

[1] In a much-visited video **clip** on Google, Steve Ballmer, Microsoft's chief executive, can be seen bouncing around the stage to dance music, screaming, **whooping** and **exhorting** his **hyped-up** audience to "COME AARN, GED UP." He then pauses, **panting**, before shouting at the top of his voice: "I HAVE FOUR WORDS FOR YOU:
5 I-LOVE-THIS-COMPANY...**YEAHHHS**!"

[2] Mr. Ballmer evidently took to heart — and to the extreme — that **cliché** of leadership that you can never communicate enough with your employees. Chief executives routinely pay homage to Communication and boast about the ways they "reach out" to their people — through "town hall" meetings, site visits, **newsletters**,
10 open doors and, now, blogs. Those on the receiving end, however, are often left feeling **bemused** or, worse, cheated. What employees really want, according to a new survey, are **straight-talkers** who keep them up to date with bad, as well as good, news. They also want leaders who stay true to themselves instead of putting on a performance or **preaching** through PowerPoint[1].

15 [3] The 1,000 employees surveyed regard communicating with staff as a more important leadership quality than having a clear vision for the company. Only 40 per cent say their boss communicates effectively.

[4] The report, "Straight Talking," by CHA[2], a workplace communications consultancy, says the findings suggest four categories of communicators. The
20 "considerate" ones talk directly to staff rather than through managers or the media, **invite** feedback and value people's views. About a third of employees have bosses like this — considerate, sincere and **motivating**.

[5] On the other hand, a third say their bosses fail to provide enough information about plans, communicate too late or not at all and talk at them rather than having a
25 conversation.

[6] These "controlling" communicators also tend to **underestimate** the intelligence of their workers and how far they can trust them. They are keener to talk to industry **peers** than to their staff, according to the survey by Explorandum[3], a market research company.

---

1 PowerPoint   微软公司生产的制作幻灯片及简报的软件
2 CHA   英国一家公共关系咨询公司
3 Explorandum / ɪksplə'rændəm /   英国一家市场调查公司

[7] Many respondents complain of the lack of face-to-face contact with their leaders. "Nobody at floor level ever gets asked their opinion, even though they are the ones dealing directly with the customers and the ones with the real experience of what people need," says one employee.

[8] Another says that, if she was in charge, she would "try to remember who works for me, and why, and their names; show some interest in what they have to say and actually try to act on it; be less **aloof** and proud and feel free to admit when I am wrong or need help."

[9] Two other communication styles emerge from the survey: the "**charismatic**," **exemplified** by Sir Richard Branson, and the "**understated**," where the leader is often admired but so **reserved** that he or she leaves people guessing and wanting more. Phil Knight, chairman of Nike, and Sven-Goran Eriksson, the former England manager, are **cited** as cases in point. Some leaders fit more than one category — Jack Welch, for example, could be **categorized** both as controlling and charismatic.

[10] Can bad communicators change fundamentally, or is it all rooted in personality? Bob Ayling, the unpopular British Airways[1] chief executive **ousted** several years ago, came across as a distant and **abrasive** leader unable to connect with his employees.

[11] "Leaders can learn to tell the truth, to admit what they don't know and to admit mistakes," says Jeffrey Pfeffer, professor of organizational learning at Stanford's Graduate School of Business[2]. "They can also learn to be less controlling. People want to make decisions at work and have some control and responsibility, just as they do in other **spheres** of their lives."

[12] Prof. Pfeffer gives an example in a **forthcoming** book, *What Were They Thinking? Unconventional Wisdom about Management*, to be published by Harvard Business School Press[3].

[13] "When Anne Mulcahy became CEO of Xerox[4], after just five months on the job she told Wall Street[5] the company's business model was **flawed**," he writes. "Then she explained to employees, directly and honestly, the challenges they faced, the first step in creating a remarkable **turnaround** at Xerox. That honesty, although possibly

---

1 British Airways　英国航空公司
2 Stanford's Graduate School of Business　斯坦福大学商学院
3 Harvard Business School Press　哈佛商学院出版社
4 Xerox / ˈzɪərɒks /　美国施乐公司，主要生产计算机办公设备
5 Wall Street　华尔街，位于纽约市曼哈顿区南部，是美国的金融中心

60　unexpected, told employees the person in charge actually knew and was willing to talk about the truth and had a plan for making things better."

[14] What matters most is **authenticity**. Steve Ballmer's stage performance was **jaw-dropping**. But it represented the way he is, says Darren Briggs, a partner at The Company Agency, which advises corporate leaders on communications.

65　[15] Mr. Briggs, who worked at Microsoft 12 years ago, says Mr. Ballmer had a reputation for being loud, direct and not particularly good at listening — the opposite of Bill Gates[1]. "But people accept that behaviour because that's what he's like. It's not a show he's putting on. If he'd been calmer on the stage and discussed things, people would have said: 'What happened to Steve Ballmer?'"

(831 words)
From *Financial Times*

New Words

disdain /dɪsˈdeɪn/
v. treat with feeling that sb./sth. is not good enough to deserve one's respect 鄙视, 不屑

clip /klɪp/
n. a short extract, especially a video clip 节选, 片段

whoop /huːp/
v. utter a loud cry, usually of happiness 大叫, 高声喊叫

exhort /ɪgˈzɔːt/
v. encourage especially by cheers and shouts; advise strongly or earnestly 恳切地、通常令人激动地劝告、建议或请求

hyped-up /haɪptʌp/
a. stimulated by sth. exciting 被刺激兴奋起来的

pant /pænt/
v. breathe with short quick breaths 喘气

yeahhhs /jeəs/
int. an exclamation to show excitement 耶

cliché /ˈkliːʃeɪ/
n. a phrase or idea which is used so often that it has become stale or meaningless 陈词滥调, 老套

newsletter /ˈnjuːzˌletə/
n. an informal printed report giving information and regularly sent to members of a club, society, etc. 时事通讯, 新闻快报

bemused /bɪˈmjuːzd/
a. bewildered or confused 困惑的, 茫然的, 不知所措的

straight-talkers /streɪtˈtɔːkəs/
n. persons who talk honestly and frankly 言语坦率者, 直言不讳者

preach /priːtʃ/
v. give unwanted advice esp. in a persistent, annoying manner 说教; 鼓吹

invite /ɪnˈvaɪt/
v. be open to; ask for (comments, suggestions, etc.) 征求; 请求

motivating /ˈməʊtɪveɪtɪŋ/

1　Bill Gates / bɪlgeɪts /　比尔·盖茨, 是全球个人计算机软件的领先供应商——微软公司的创始人、前任董事长和首席执行官

UNIT 4 Communication

a. inspiring 激励的，鼓舞人的

underestimate /ˌʌndərˈestɪmeɪt/
v. think or guess that something is smaller, cheaper, easier etc. than it really is 低估，看轻

peer /pɪə(r)/
n. a person who is equal to another in rank, status or merit 同等之人，同辈

aloof /əˈluːf/
a. cool and remote in character 冷淡的，疏远的

charismatic /ˌkærɪzˈmætɪk/
a. having charisma 有号召力的；有神授能力的

exemplify /ɪɡˈzemplɪfaɪ/
v. illustrate by examples 例证

understated /ˌʌndəˈsteɪtɪd/
a. expressing in a very controlled way 表达简略的；不充分的

reserved /rɪˈzɜːvd/
a. slow to show feelings or express opinions 有所保留的；含蓄的

cite /saɪt/
v. quote or refer to 引用，引证

categorize /ˈkætəɡəraɪz/
v. place sth. in class or group 分类

oust /aʊst/
v. remove sb. (from a position, job, etc.) in order to take his place 驱逐；撵走从而取代

abrasive /əˈbreɪsɪv/
a. harsh and offensive 粗鲁的

sphere /sfɪə(r)/
n. range or extent 方面；领域

forthcoming /ˌfɔːˈθkʌmɪŋ/
a. about to happen or appear in the near future 即将来临的

unconventional /ˌʌnkənˈvenʃənl/
a. not following what is traditional or customary 非传统的

flawed /flɔːd/
a. imperfect 有缺陷的

turnaround /ˌtɜːnəˈraʊnd/
n. a complete change, e.g. from a very bad situation to a good one (经济、经营等的)彻底转变

authenticity /ˌɔːθenˈtɪsəti/
n. quality of being true or genuine 真实性

jaw-dropping /ˈdʒɔːˈdrɒpɪŋ/
a. showing sudden surprise or disappointment 令人瞠目的；让人大跌眼镜的

Phrases & Expressions

at top of one's voice
as loudly as one can 提高嗓门，声嘶力竭

take... to heart
take... seriously; be particular about; believe in 很在乎某事，对某事看得很重

to the extreme
of the highest degree 极度地，非常地

pay homage to
show respect for 对……表示尊敬或尊重

reach out to sb.
show people that you are interested in them and want to talk to them 向人们表示你对他们感兴趣，愿意和他们交流

town hall
building containing local government offices and usually a hall for public meetings, concerts,

etc. 市政厅

keep... up to date
keep sb. informed of what is going on 使……及时了解

put on
pretend; deceive 装作有某事物，假装采纳某事物

rather than
and not; instead of 而不是……，而非……；替代……

talk at
speak to sb. without listening to his replies 对……唠叨不休

in charge
in a position of control or command 主管

act on
take action in accordance with or as a result of sth. 按照……行事

cases in point
examples connected with the subject being discussed 适当的例子

root in
establish sth. deeply and firmly 植根于

come across
make an impression of the specified type 使人产生某种印象

Exercises

Comprehension

1. Mark the following statements T (true) or F (false) or NM (not mentioned) according to the passage. Discuss with your partner about the supporting points for each statement.

    1) _____ Steve Ballmer, the chief executive of Microsoft is fond of bouncing around the stage to dance music.

    2) _____ What employees really want are leaders who can talk to them directly.

    3) _____ In a survey, effective communication with staff and having a clear vision for the company are considered as equally important leadership qualities.

    4) _____ "Considerate" communicators always talk to staff through managers or the media.

    5) _____ Those who are keener to talk to industry peers tend to underestimate the intelligence of their staff.

6) _____ Many employees dealing directly with the customers are more likely to have face-to-face contact with their leaders.

7) _____ Jack Welch is also a typical example of the leaders with the "understated" communication style.

8) _____ Leaders can learn to tell the truth, to admit what they don't know and to admit mistakes.

9) _____ Prof. Pfeffer took Bob Ayling as one of the examples in his book to illustrate unconventional wisdom about management.

10) _____ Just opposite of Steve Ballmer, Bill Gates is not particularly good at listening.

2. This passage can be roughly divided into three parts. Put down the paragraph numbers and main idea of each part. Then compare your answers with your partner's.

Parts	Paragraphs	Main ideas
Part I	Paras. _____	_____
Part II	Paras. _____	_____
Part III	Paras. _____	_____

Critical Thinking

Work in group to discuss the following questions.

1) Some leaders mistake communications, thinking they're the same as paperwork and so they're averse to a high degree of communications. The followings are taken as the common causes of problems in internal communications. Explain the problem with each statement.

- *If I know it, then everyone must know it.*
- *I told everyone, or some people, or...?*
- *Did you hear what I meant for you to hear?*
- *Our problems are too big to have to listen to each other!*
- *So what's to talk about?*
- *If I need your opinion, I'll tell it to you.*

2) Internal communication should take place as a series of steps and not as an isolated event. The details of how one plans for internal communication to create a coherent culture will vary depending on a number of factors, especially the size of the organization. The following are steps for a general process of internal communication in a random order. Discuss with your group members to put them in the best order.

   a. *Plan for remediation.*

   b. *Determine what tools are suited to which goals.*

   c. *Plan for implementation.*

   d. *Develop a description of how each tool will be used.*

   e. *Identify the common culture needed/wanted.*

   f. *Implement.*

   g. *Continuously monitor and revise.*

   h. *Identify the available communication tools (Paper-based, general meetings, E-mail, web sites and intranets, surveys...).*

3) While formulating internal communication strategies, what factors should be taken care of?

Vocabulary

1. **Rewrite the following italicized parts by using the appropriate words or expressions from the text. Make some changes if necessary.**

   1) Make sure that your subsidiaries and foreign offices take up the responsibility to *keep you informed*.

   2) The moment you are *in the position* as the chief executive, you're the prisoner of your organization.

   3) The workers were told to *follow* the instructions very carefully when operating the new machine.

   4) To create a sense of community, management need to provide a trusting and safe environment, in which workers are free to express their ideas *instead of* trying to please the managers.

   5) When management are blinded by greed and ambition, they are likely to make some *imperfect* decisions.

   6) All great companies endure because they serve a higher purpose. Anita

Roddick, founder of the Body Shop, is *one example*.

7) Though business people like to think of themselves as realists, the fact is that wishful thinking, denial, and other forms of avoiding reality are *deeply established in* most corporate cultures.

8) People-centered organizations embrace the core ideology of *showing great respect to* individual employees, regardless of their positions in the company.

9) Peter Drucker has *made a deep impression on us* as a management guru.

10) Effective managers concentrate not only on conducting the task, but also on *keeping close* to their subsidiaries.

2. **Choose the correct word to complete each sentence with the proper form.**

1) communication, conversation

   a. English is the language of business _____ the world over.

   b. Employees of some joint-ventures are not allowed to hold a private _____ during working hours.

2) vision, view

   a. This report gives the people of business circles an inside _____ of the conglomerate.

   b. He had a clear _____ of how he hoped the company would develop.

3) category, classification

   a. In essence, a basic _____ system for business reports may be based on a report's function, subject matter, direction, and format.

   b. Seats of that grand theater are available in eight of the 10 price _____.

4) considerate, considerable

   a. In order to maintain a stable and motivated workforce, companies must be _____ towards their employees and sensitive to their personal needs.

   b. Its billion-customer market and _____ supply of cheap labor beckon seductively, yet the market seems always out of reach.

5) illustrate, exemplify

   a. The fact that different companies have different ways of expressing its core values can be _____ by Southwest Airlines as well.

   b. The case also _____ a fundamental weakness in their marketing strategy.

6) boast, preach

   a. He is always _____ of his performance in the company.

   b. You are in no position to _____ to me about efficiency.

7) truth, authenticity

   a. We know the _____ that the widest variety of content possible is the best way to build the largest consumer base possible.

   b. The _____ of community lies in a safe environment in which every worker is treated as a valuable member.

8) effectively, efficiently

   a. The second step is _____ managing those search terms and listings to receive maximum Return on Investment and high sales conversions from a search advertising campaign.

   b. To be a good manager today, you need the versatility to communicate with people _____ and to require that they produce results.

3. Choose the correct prefix for each word in the oval. Then complete the sentences below with the appropriate new words.

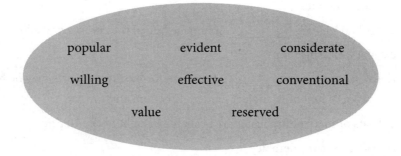

popular   evident   considerate
willing   effective conventional
     value   reserved

in-	un-	de-

UNIT 4 Communication

1) Prospective employees are _____ to join a company that has a history of treating its people badly.

2) When there is an _____ leadership, each department, in fact, each individual does whatever they want.

3) They spread tales about her in an attempt to _____ her work.

4) Jones' lawyers are seeking an _____ apology from the newspaper.

5) There is a pervasive, restless creative energy, constantly seeking and creating _____ ideas and new markets.

6) She has not made a sale for several days because of falling demand, so she's rather _____ with her boss at the moment.

7) Because of the maximum sensitivity of this view, future development would need to be _____.

8) Unclear, inaccurate, or _____ business communication can waste valuable time, alienate employees or customers, and destroy goodwill toward management or the overall business.

Translation

1. Translate the following paragraph into Chinese.

    Mr. Ballmer evidently took to heart — and to the extreme — that cliché of leadership that you can never communicate enough with your employees. Chief executives routinely pay homage to Communication and boast about the ways they "reach out" to their people — through "town hall" meetings, site visits, newsletters, open doors and, now, blogs. Those on the receiving end, however, are often left feeling bemused or, worse, cheated. What employees really want, according to a new survey, are straight-talkers who keep them up to date with bad, as well as good, news. They also want leaders who stay true to themselves instead of putting on a performance or preaching through PowerPoint.

2. Put the following paragraph into English, using the words and phrases given in the box. Change the form if necessary.

    | pay homage to | invite | charismatic | peer | preach |
    | considerate | come across | aloof | underestimate | vision |

    如今公司领导越来越重视内部沟通，因为他们懂得来自基层的信息反馈

87

有助于提高公司的管理水平；有效的内部沟通还有助于员工了解公司的发展前景，提高员工的士气和工作积极性。然而，不少公司的员工对目前的沟通状况仍旧不满意。他们抱怨领导与员工之间缺少面对面的交流，不少领导常常低估员工的智商和可信度，宁愿与业内其他同行沟通，也不愿与自己的员工交流。许多员工讨厌那种冷淡自负、使人无法接近的领导。他们认为，一个真正称职且有魅力的领导应该是善解人意、坦率真诚，而不是只善于演戏或说教。只有懂得沟通并善于沟通的领导才能使企业不断发展，取得成功。

Meetings

As a standard form of business communication, a face-to-face meeting is one of the wonderful tools for generating ideas, expanding on thoughts and managing group activities. Just like many other forms of communication, a business meeting is expected to and should follow certain rules of etiquette to help make the experience pleasant and productive for all those involved.

The following is an example of a typical business meeting. There are usually five parts in such kind of meeting: *Introductions, Reviewing Past Business, Beginning the Meeting, Discussing Items, and Finishing the Meeting*. **Read the dialogue with your partner and divide it into such five parts.**

Chairman:	If we are all here, let's get started. First of all, I'd like you to join me in welcoming Jack Peterson, our Southwest Area Sales Vice President.
Jack:	Thank you for having me. I'm looking forward to today's meeting.
Chairman:	I'd also like to introduce Margaret Simmons who recently joined our team.
Margaret:	May I also introduce my assistant, Bob Hamp.
Chairman:	Welcome, Bob. I'm afraid our national sales director, Anne Trusting, can't be with us today. She is in Kobe at the moment, developing our Far East sales force.

Chairman:	Let's get started. We're here today to discuss ways of improving sales in rural market areas. First, let's go over the report from the last meeting which was held on June 24th. Right, Tom, over to you.
Tom:	Thank you, Mark. Let me just summarize the main points of the last meeting. We began the meeting by approving the changes in our sales reporting system discussed on May 30th. After briefly revising the changes that will take place, we moved on to a brainstorming session concerning after sales customer support improvements. You'll find a copy of the main ideas developed and discussed in these sessions in the photocopies in front of you. The meeting was declared closed at 11:30.
Chairman:	Thank you, Tom. So, if there is nothing else we need to discuss, let's move on to today's agenda. Have you all received a copy of today's agenda? If you don't mind, I'd like to skip item 1 and move on to item 2: Sales improvement in rural market areas. Jack has kindly agreed to give us a report on this matter. Jack?
Jack:	Before I begin the report, I'd like to get some ideas from you all. How do you feel about rural sales in your sales districts? I suggest we go round the table first to get all of your input.
John:	In my opinion, we have been focusing too much on urban customers and their needs. The way I see things, we need to return to our rural base by developing an advertising campaign to focus on their particular needs.
Alice:	I'm afraid I can't agree with you. I think rural customers want to feel as important as our customers living in cities. I suggest we give our rural sales teams more help with advanced customer information reporting.
Donald:	Excuse me, I didn't catch that. Could you repeat that, please?
Alice:	I just stated that we need to give our rural sales teams better customer information reporting.
John:	I don't quite follow you. What exactly do you mean?
Alice:	Well, we provide our city sales staff with database information on all of our larger clients. We should be providing the same sort of knowledge on our rural customers to our sales staff there.
Jack:	Would you like to add anything, Jennifer?
Jennifer:	I must admit I never thought about rural sales that way before. I have to agree with Alice.
Jack:	Well, let me begin with this Power Point presentation (Jack presents his report).

Jack:	As you can see, we are developing new methods to reach out to our rural customers.
John:	I suggest we break up into groups and discuss the ideas we've seen presented.
Chairman:	Unfortunately, we're running short of time. We'll have to leave that to another time.
Jack:	Before we close, let me just summarize the main points: • Rural customers need special help to feel more valued. • Our sales teams need more accurate information on our customers. • A survey will be completed to collect data on spending habits in these areas. • The results of this survey will be delivered to our sales teams. We are considering specific data mining procedures to help deepen our understanding.
Chairman:	Thank you very much, Jack. Right, it looks as though we've covered the main items. Is there any other business?
Donald:	Can we fix the next meeting, please?
Chairman:	Good idea, Donald. How does Friday in two weeks time sound to everyone? Let's meet at the same time, 9 o'clock. Is that OK for everyone? Excellent. I'd like to thank Jack for coming to our meeting today. The meeting is closed.

Practice running your own meeting now.

Suppose you work in one of the sections at Nortel Networks. Now a flexible work schedule has been proposed, and you need to run a further meeting to discuss necessity and feasibility of the schedule. Work in groups. Set the meeting chairman and then hold the meeting. Refer to the related information given below and work on the following questions.

- Why do you think it necessary to implement flexible work arrangements and practices?
- What are the benefits of flexible work time for employers and employees respectively?
- What is the proper way to implement the flexible work schedule? How can employers and workers agree on work patterns that suit everyone?
- What do you think are the practical difficulties managers or employers may face when trying to implement quality flexible work arrangements?

UNIT 4 Communication

- *What do you think can make it hard for employees to ask for flexible work arrangements?*
- *Do you think different types of employers, types of work or workplaces, or occupations face particular challenges in providing for flexible work? What are these challenges? What is needed to meet these challenges?*

Implementing time flexibility in the workplace means a variation from the traditional 9-5 system. Beyond that, there is a wide variety of practices, offering different amounts of structure, regularity and flexibility. Common types of flexible working are:

- part-time: working less than the normal hours, perhaps by working fewer days per week;
- flexi-time: choosing when to work (there's usually a core period during which you have to work);
- annualized hours: your hours are worked out over a year (often set shifts with you deciding when to work the other hours);
- compressed hours: working your agreed hours over fewer days;
- staggered hours: different starting, break and finishing times for employees in the same workplace;
- job sharing: sharing a job designed for one person with someone else;
- home working: working from home.

You can combine any of these working patterns to come up with something to suit your circumstances.

Language Hints

Opening
- Good morning/afternoon, everyone.
- If we are all here, let's get started / start the meeting / start.
- ...

Stating the principal objectives
- We're here today to...
- Our main aim today is to...
- I've called this meeting in order to...
- ...

Introducing the agenda
- Have you all received a copy of the agenda?
- There are X items on the agenda. First, ...second,...third,...lastly,...
- Shall we take the points in this order?
- ...

Introducing the first item on the agenda
- So, let's start with...
- I'd suggest we start with...
- So, the first item on the agenda is...
- Shall we start with...
- ...

Closing an item
- I think that takes care of the first item.
- If nobody has anything else to add, let's...
- ...

Moving to the next item
- Let's move onto the next item.
- Now that we've discussed X, let's now...
- Now we come to the question of...
- ...

Summarizing
- Before we close today's meeting, let me just summarize the main points.
- Let me quickly go over today's main points.
- To sum up,...
- In brief,...
- ...

Finishing up
- Right, it looks as though we've covered the main items.
- If there are no other comments, I'd like to wrap this meeting up.
- Let's bring this to a close for today.
- ...

Thanking participants for attending
- Thank you all for attending.
- Thanks for your participation.
- ...

Minutes

Minutes are a formal brief summary of proceedings at meetings. The main reasons for keeping minutes are to:

- provide an authoritative source and permanent record of proceedings for future reference;
- provide formal evidence of decisions, e.g. appointments, financial allocations, authorized actions;
- provide a record of policy decisions made and the basis for them;
- provide a starting point for action to be taken in future;
- create an official record which can be used in legal proceedings;
- inform members not present at the meeting and any others of the actions of the body concerned;
- assist in the conduct of subsequent meetings;
- set out precedents for future occasions, in the case of rulings from the chair;

UNIT 4 Communication

- provide documentary evidence for audit purposes.

At some meetings, especially of bodies with less formal accountabilities, the term 'minutes' is sometimes replaced by the term 'notes'. Notes differ from minutes in that, typically, they are less formal, depending on the status of the committee/working party concerned. They typically:

- are less detailed, involving a shorter précis of discussion;
- emphasize action to be taken after the meeting;
- do not need to be approved at the next meeting.

Usually, formal minutes include the following items: title, time, venue, participants, the body of the minutes, minutes taker and chairperson. When keeping the record, the recorder must be exact and objective. Passive voice, past tense and indirect speech can be employed to show its objectivity.

Study the following sample and then do the exercises according to the directions.

Sample

Minutes of the Managers' Meeting

Time: 3 p.m., Friday, December 12, 2008
Venue: Conference Room 217, Shanghai Branch
Presiding: Mr. Robin Hill
Present: Miss Sue Chen, Mr. David Wang, Mr. Tony Smith, Mr. Edward Lee, and Daisy Liu

After the meeting was declared open, Mr. Robin Hill's report on the state of the company's business was read by the secretary.

The attendants discussed how to expand business in China.

- Mr. Tony Smith suggested technical experts go around branch offices to stimulate the interflow of technique and experience.
- Miss Sue Chen proposed that two new branch offices be established in Shenyang and Zhuhai. The motion was seconded by Mr. David Wang

and carried unanimously.
- Mr. Edward Lee presented his idea on the cutting-down on lunch allowance, which was opposed by Miss Sue Chen and Mr. David Wang. The Chairman decided to discuss the problem later.

The Chairman made a brief explanation of the 2009's plan of the company. Each branch office was assigned a turnover about US$ 6,000,000 for this year.

The meeting closed at 4:30 p.m.

Daisy Liu
(Secretary)
Robin Hill
(Chairman)

1. Look at the situation in the section of Meeting. Please compose the minutes with the notes you made for the meeting concerning Flexible Work Schedule.

2. You are Doris Franklin, a secretary to the Welfare Committee of A & D Company. You are asked to sort out the minutes of the monthly meeting presided over by Mr. Ian Falk at 9:30 a.m., Friday, November 21, 2008 in Meeting Room 502. Members present included Mr. Lee Baum, Ms. Sarah Jones, Mr. Jack Fenster, Ms. Liu Dan, and Ms. Sun Li. The following are the notes you took at the meeting.

> 1) Apology for absence was received from Ms. Vicki Zhang
> 2) Minutes of the last meeting approved
> 3) Mr. Jack Fenster; complaints from sanitary workers; pouring of unfinished coffee in dustbin; a plastic dustbin be placed near; discharge of liquid
> 4) Ms. Sun Li; complaints by the staff on the stuffy air; contact the janitorial department; adjustment of air-conditioning temperatures; cleaning of the air-conditioner nets
> 5) Ms. Liu Dan; Christmas Party; sample menus obtained from hotels; Regent Hotel Tuesday, December 23 chosen; responsible for making all arrangements
> 6) Next meeting at 14:00 p.m., Wednesday, December 10.

UNIT 4 Communication

Relevant Extension

Business Expressions

1. Make 13 two-word expressions connected with business communication by combining words from the two lists: A and B. Then match each of the expressions with the corresponding explanation below. Use each word once.

A	B
persuasive	groups
focus	ground
eye	sample
guided	audience
hot	presentation
news	question
watchdog	slang
active	messages
random	contact
interpersonal	discussion
business	buttons
common	listening
branching	release

   1) a presentation that motivates the audience to act or to believe

   _____

   2) small groups who come in to talk with a skilled leader about a potential product

   _____

   3) issues to which the audience has a strong emotional response

   _____

   4) messages that package information about a company and that the writer would like to announce in local and national media

   _____

5) a presentation in which the speaker presents the questions or issues that both the speaker and the audience have agreed on in advance, and the speaker serves as a facilitator to help the audience tap its own knowledge
   _____

6) a sample for which each person of the population theoretically has an equal chance of being chosen
   _____

7) looking another person directly in the eye
   _____

8) messages promoting friendliness, cooperation, and group loyalty
   _____

9) an audience that has political, social, or economic power and that may base future actions on its evaluation of your message
   _____

10) feeding back the literal meaning or the emotional content or both so that the speaker knows that the listener has heard and understood
    _____

11) terms that have technical meaning but are used in more general senses
    _____

12) a question that sends respondents who answer differently to different parts of the questionnaire
    _____

13) values and goals that the writer and the reader share
    _____

2. **Write in the central box one of the given words which goes together with each of the four words to make four collocations concerning communication. The first one has been done for you.**

| communication | presentation | letter | telephone | negotiation |
| report | interview | language | chart | conference |

1)

```
       press              |           |    panel
   ----------             | interview |   ---------
      referral            |           |    stress
```

UNIT **4** Communication

2)
pie		flip
flow		progress

3)
breakdown		channels
network		mass

4)
media		committee
justification		status

5)
sales		slide
monologue		goodwill

6)
claim		resignation
rejection		bomb

7)
session		season
complex		programme

8)
sign		body
computer		everyday

9)
message		helpline
query		contact

10)
process		pay
collapse		trade

3. **Spell the following words according to their definitions and first letters. Then complete the sentences using the appropriate words you have spelt.**

j_____	technical or specialized words used by a particular group of people and difficult for others to understand

97

m_____	an official written record of what is said and decided at a meeting
b_____	a method of shared problem solving in which all members of a group spontaneously contribute ideas
e_____	the ability to understand other people's feelings and problems
e_____	put it into a code or express it in a different form or system of language
f_____	information about a product, etc. that a user gives back to its supplier, maker, etc.
e_____	make (sth.) seem larger, better, worse, etc. than it really is; stretch (a description) beyond the truth
d_____	find the meaning of something that is difficult to read or understand

1) It is important to develop the _____ between service contact persons and their customers.

2) The secretary studied the envelope, trying to _____ the handwriting.

3) The manual is full of _____ and slang of self-improvement courses.

4) The _____ of certain entities, such as a corporate board of directors, must be kept and they are important legal documents.

5) Let's have a _____ session to come up with slogans for new products.

6) We need more _____ from the consumers in order to improve our goods.

7) The two parties _____ confidential data in a form that is not directly readable by the other party.

8) Sheila admitted that she did sometimes _____ the demands of her job.

Specialized Reading

1. Read the passage through carefully and select one word for each blank from a list of choices given in the word bank following the passage.

　　Internal communication departments have broken away from HR since the 80's and 90's and now __1)__ directly to senior management in most organizations. In some organizations where internal communication has not been established as a separate communication function, it may be __2)__ by Human Resources, Marketing and PR departments.

　　Internal communication helps employees to understand the organization's

3)___, values, and culture. It may involve staff members in issues that affect working life and keeps staff   4)___ on important decisions taken by management. Furthermore, internal communication, when implemented effectively, can be   5)___ in a time of crisis, providing employees with not only a strategy to   6)___ a crisis, but the facts surrounding such an event. As arguably some of the most invested individuals in an organization, trusted and valued employees can prove to be excellent partners when addressing a crisis. By   7)___ open lines of communication between management and employees, effective internal communication can enhance stronger   8)___ throughout all levels of the organization and forge a sense of community.

Excellent internal communication cannot simply be   9)___ and left alone; the process must be ever-changing and   10)___ for success. While more and more organizations begin to spend more time identifying special interest groups within their own walls, internal communication methods are becoming increasingly   11)___ to match the varying needs of each organizations' internal staff and   12)___.

The way messages are presented can have a negative or positive   13)___ upon the reader, regardless of the core content of the message. While this could be condemned as spin, organizations who strive to practice excellent public relations will avoid manipulative and ambiguous messages as they   14)___ trust in the organisation. The most effective way is to find a   15)___ between being "his Master's voice" and representing employees' interests.

A. diverse	G. stakeholders	M. impact
B. balance	H. maintaining	N. handle
C. informed	I. crucial	O. report
D. destroy	J. coordinated	P. implemented
E. increase	K. relationships	Q. vision
F. adaptable	L. organised	R. critical

2. **Identifying communication styles properly is very important for business success. Read the following passage and correct each sentence below so that it reflects the meaning of the passage.**

Faxes, teleconferences, the World Wide Web, and other technological advancements guarantee that we can communicate with virtually anyone, anywhere. However, it's up to us to ensure that the messages we send are clearly understood by the recipient.

Whether it's a face-to-face meeting or an overseas transmission, communication is a complex process that requires constant attention so that intended messages are sent and received. Inadequate communication is the source of conflict and misunderstanding. It interferes with productivity and profitability. Virtually everyone in business has experienced times when they were frustrated because they just couldn't "get through" to someone. They felt as if they were speaking an unknown language or were on a different "wave length". Communicating effectively is much more than just saying or writing the correct words. How we communicate is affected by frame of reference, emotional states, the situation, and preferred styles of communication.

Our perceptions are directly related to the senses — visual, auditory, or kinesthetic/tactile (movement, touch, taste, and smell). Although everyone uses all three styles or modes to interact with the world, most people have a primary one. Research indicates that most people are visually-oriented, whereas the fewest number of people are auditorially-oriented. To ensure that messages are conveyed, it's important to learn how to communicate in another's particular style. To discover someone's primary mode: (1) Listen to the verbs they use; (2) Watch their eye movements during a discussion; (3) Observe their behavior; (4) Ask how they prefer to receive new information; and (5) Be aware of your own preferences. Let's consider each mode.

The Visual Mode. Visually-oriented people interact with the world by creating mental pictures. They'll often make statements such as "I don't *see* it that way" or "It *looks* good to me." When responding to questions or making comments, their eyes will go up to create a picture. They also may blink to "clear the screen" in their mind's eye or they may look directly at you in response to your questions. They will use verbs such as *look, see, picture*, and *imagine*. When presenting new information to them, use colorful pictures, charts, or displays.

The Auditory Mode. "I *hear* what you're *saying*" or "It doesn't *sound* that way to me" are typical statements made by those whose primary way of interacting with the world is auditory. They like to discuss and listen to recorded information and music. When responding to questions or making comments, their eyes will go over to the side, often repeating out loud or in their mind's ear the question or statement made. They will use verbs such as *hear, listen, debate*, and *talk*. When presenting new information to them, take the time to discuss it and answer all of their questions.

The Kinesthetic/Tactile Mode. Many people are doers and are quite demonstrative, preferring movement in their interactions. They often make statements such as "I *feel* this is the best solution" or "I just can't *grasp* the idea." When responding to questions or making comments, their eyes will go down to get in touch with emotions and the motion involved in the statement or question. They will use action-oriented verbs such as *feel, touch, run, hold*, and *move*. When presenting new information, use hands-on activities, such as actually going through the motions of a new procedure.

In these times of doing more with less and increased use of technology, it's imperative to remember to do whatever we can to foster effective communication. By looking at the world from another's point of view, your employees, co-workers, customers, and vendors will feel that you're really listening to them. Listening and responding in a way that makes sense to them will improve relationships, enhance performance, increase productivity, and positively impact the bottom line.

1) When it is a face-to-face meeting, the communication process is becoming simple and clear.
2) The visually-oriented people like to discuss and listen to recorded information and music.
3) According to the research, most people are auditorially-oriented.
4) A typical visually-oriented person will say "It doesn't sound that way to me".
5) Many people of the kinesthetic/tactile mode prefer discussing in their interactions.
6) When presenting new information, people of the auditory mode use hands-on activities.
7) With the increasing use of technology, an effective communication is generally considered necessary.
8) In addition to a primary mode, three other modes — mentioned-visual mode, auditory mode, and Kinesthetic/tactile mode — are used by most people.

3. **Discuss the following questions with your group members.**

   1) Given the range of different communications that businesses have to make, it is not surprising that mistakes are made and that sometimes communication breaks down. What are the possible sources of barriers to successful communication?
   2) In each of the following cases, what sort of response do you think the source will be looking for as evidence that the communication has been successful?

What other reactions might the source get as a result of the message being sent?

a. A manager posts a notice to all staff in her section telling them that there will be a staff meeting at 3:30 that afternoon.

b. A small business places an advert in the local press telling prospective customers that next Saturday they will be offered a two-for-one promotion between 10:00 a.m. and 1:00 p.m.

c. A receptionist leaves a message on the answer phone of a member of staff asking the individual to phone back Mike Burks in Sales before 5:00 p.m.

d. A large business announces to suppliers that it is going to increase the length of the credit terms it has from 28 days to 60 days.

e. A new office worker on his first day in a new job sends a joke he has heard over the weekend to his new boss via e-mail.

f. An employer sends a text message to 40 of his staff telling them they are out of work because the company is insolvent.

g. A company encloses a slip of paper in every employee's salary information sheet at the end of a month informing them of the new mission statement that the company has decided upon.

UNIT 5

Customer Service

Lead-in

1. **Discuss the following questions with your partner.**

   1) What is "Customer Service" in your opinion? Which of the following two definitions provides a better model? Why?

      - *"Customer Service is a function of how well an organization meets the needs of its customers."*
      - *"Customer Service is a function of how well an organization is able to constantly and consistently exceed the customer's expectations."*

   2) Have you ever experienced any of the following situations? Recall what you did when you encountered the situation and how your attitude toward the company was affected.

      - *Long lines and uninformed sales staff in shopping;*
      - *No actual person to talk to on 24-hour service line;*
      - *A disinterested person to speak to on the phone;*
      - *Several numbers to dial before getting the right person;*
      - *Delays in shipping;*
      - *Delays in repairs;*
      - *Delays in getting the money back for refunds.*

   3) After some unpleasant experiences with customer service, do you usually stay quiet about them or share them with others? Why?

2. **All of us are consumers in one way or another. We associate some characteristics with good customer service. Discuss with your group members, adding at least five characteristics to the following list and giving explanations to each point.**

A qualified customer service representative should:
● *be friendly;*
● *not impose some solution on the customer;*
●
●

A qualified customer service representative should:
•
•
•
•
•

Preview: How do companies provide good customer service? You can find the answer in this article —helping employees become more empathetic toward customers. The creative but practical approach adopted by *Southwest Airlines* when trouble arises and by *Four Seasons* as a standard procedure reveals one of the most powerful secrets of world-class service: providing great customer service takes coordination from the top, bringing together people, management, technology, and processes to put customers' needs first. So, "empathy engine" is stressed here in customer service, i.e., helping employees to understand what it feels like to be a customer.

Customer Service Champs

By Jena McGregor

[1] Bob Emig was flying home from St. Louis[1] on Southwest Airlines[2] this past December when an all-too-familiar travel nightmare began to **unfold**. After his airplane backed away from the gate, he and his fellow passengers were told the plane would need to be **de-iced**. When the aircraft was ready to fly two and a half hours later, the pilot had reached the hour limit set by the Federal Aviation Administration[3], and a new pilot was required. By that time, the plane had to be de-iced again. Five hours after the scheduled departure time, Emig's flight was finally ready for takeoff.

[2] A customer service disaster, right? Not to hear Emig tell it. The pilot walked the aisles, answering questions and offering constant updates. Flight attendants, who Emig

---

1 St. Louis 圣·路易斯（美国密苏里州东部港市）
2 Southwest Airlines 西南航空公司（美国）
3 Federal Aviation Administration 联邦航空局（美国）

10 says "really seemed like they cared," kept up with the news on connecting flights. And within a couple of days of arriving home, Emig, who travels frequently, received a letter from Southwest that included two free round-trip ticket **vouchers**. "I could not believe they acknowledged the situation and apologized," says Emig. "Then they gave me a gift, for all intents and purposes, to make up for the time spent sitting on the runway."

15 [3] Emig's "gift" from the airline was not the result of an unusually kind customer service agent who took pity on his **plight**. Nor was it a **scramble** to make amends after a disastrous operational **fiasco**, as JetBlue Airways Corp[1]. experienced recently. Rather, it was standard procedure for Southwest Airlines, which almost six years ago created a new high-level job that oversees all **proactive** customer communications with
20 customers. Fred Taylor, who was plucked from the field by President Colleen C. Barrett to fill the role, **coordinates** information that's sent to all frontline reps in the event of major flight **disruptions**. But he's also charged with sending out letters, and in many cases flight vouchers, to customers caught in major storms, air traffic **snarls**, or other travel messes — even those beyond Southwest's control — that would fry the nerves of
25 a seasoned traveler. "It's not something we had to do," says Taylor. "It's just something we feel our customers deserve."

[4] As Southwest recognizes, providing great customer service is much more than just a job for the front lines or the call centers. It takes coordination from the top, bringing together people, management, technology, and processes to put customers'
30 needs first. That's true today more than ever. Technology is leveling the barriers between **alpha** companies and **also-rans**, making great customer service one of the few ways companies can distinguish themselves. Retail, online, and phone shopping channels are expanding, increasingly **prompting** customers to demand a **seamless** — and painless — experience. Refining time-tested concepts and coming up with **cutting-edge** ideas is
35 critical for managing **rank-and-file** workers and measuring what customers think.

[5] For most of us customer service is an **aggravating maze** of automated phone trees and **scripted** voices **resonating** from halfway around the world. But while offshoring call-center work is still growing steadily, companies are getting smarter about what they send overseas. "I think we're seeing some **backlash**," says Bruce Temkin,
40 Forrester Research Inc.'s[2] principal analyst for customer experience. "Companies are pulling some (more complex types of calls) back from offshore, and in other cases are recognizing they need to invest more in those facilities to give reps more tools and

---

1 JetBlue Airways Corp.　捷蓝航空公司（美国）
2 Forrester Research Inc.　佛瑞斯特研究公司（美国）

training."

[6] One encouraging alternative trend is "homeshoring," in which service agents armed with a broadband line, a computer, and a quiet corner in their spare bedroom respond to calls at their homes. Service can be better for customers because homeshoring attracts more experienced workers with more education than do regular call centers. Stay-at-home moms are a big part of the labor pool and like the flexibility and nonexistent **commuting** costs of the home-based model. That makes them more loyal, keeping **turnover** lower and experience levels higher. Companies that outsource calls to home-based agents report turnover rates in the 10% to 30% range, compared with anywhere from 60% to 100% in the average call center. The home-based outsourcing model, with its more experienced agents working at home in jeans and slippers, fits well with the idea that happier frontline folks will make for happier customers.

[7] The connection between satisfied employees and contented customers is hardly a new concept: Any business-school student can recite by heart the concept of the "service-profit chain," which draws the **inextricable** link between the front line and satisfied customers. But new research from Katzenbach Partners[1] offers an updated metaphor. The firm stresses the importance of an "**empathy** engine," which looks at the role of the entire organization, including middle and senior management, in providing great service. If that engine is thought of as a heart, "the whole company has to pump the customer through it," says Traci Entel, a principal at Katzenbach Partners who recently studied 13 leading service companies' best practices. "It starts much further back, with how they organize themselves, and how they place value on thinking about the customer."

[8] Helping employees become more empathetic with customers was a common focus. For instance, all frontline workers at Cabela's[2], the **outfitter** famous for its massive retail **shrines** to hunting, fishing, and camping, partake in a free product-loaner program. Staffers are encouraged to borrow any of the company's more than 200,000 products for up to two months, so long as they write a review that's shared via a companywide software system when the goods are returned. That's not only a perk for employees; it also helps them better **empathize** with product issues customers might have.

---

1 Katzenbach Partners / ˈkætzənbætʃ ˈpɑːtnəz /　卡岑巴赫咨询公司（美国）
2 Cabela's / ˈkæbeləz /　坎贝拉，美国最大的户外用品零售商，同时还是美国名列前茅的户外用品生产商

[9] But few places make empathizing with customers quite as **luxurious** an experience as Four Seasons Hotels[1]. At most of its properties, the final piece of the seven-step employee **orientation** is something the chain's executives call a "familiarization stay" or "fam trip." Each worker in these hotels, from housekeepers to front-desk clerks, is given a free night's stay for themselves and a guest, along with free dining.

[10] While there, employees are asked to grade the hotels on such measures as the number of times the phone rings when calling room service to how long it takes to get items to a room. "We **bill** it as a training **session**," says Ellen Dubois du Bellay, vice-president of learning and development. "They're learning what it looks like to receive service from the other side."

[11] That's key when your product is out of range for many employees — a $400 room rate isn't exactly easy to swing on a housekeeper's budget. But the perk doesn't stop at orientation: After six months of service, employees may stay up to three nights a year for free. By 10 years, they get 20 free stays. As you'd imagine, "there's a very healthy **uptake**," says du Bellay. Four Seasons' creative but practical approach reveals one of the most powerful secrets of world-class service: helping employees to understand what it feels like to be a customer. Thinking like that distinguishes our customer service champs from the rest of the field.

(1175 words)
From *Business Week*

New Words

unfold /ʌnˈfəʊld/
v. (cause sth. to) be revealed or made known （使某事物）显露，展现

de-ice
v. remove the ice from sth. 除去……上的冰

voucher /ˈvaʊtʃə(r)/
n. a document, showing that money has been paid or promised, which can be exchanged for certain goods or services （代替现金的）凭单，凭证，代金券

plight /plaɪt/
n. a difficult or distressing situation that is full of problems 困境

scramble /ˈskræmbl/
n. rough struggle (to get sth.) 争夺，抢夺

fiasco /fiˈæskəʊ/
n. complete and ridiculous failure 彻底的失败，惨败

proactive /prəʊˈæktɪv/
a. (of a person or policy) controlling a situation by making things happen rather than waiting for things to happen and then

---

1 Four Seasons Hotels　四季酒店，总部在加拿大，五星级豪华世界连锁酒店

UNIT 5 Customer Service

reacting to them 积极主动的；先发制人的

coordinate /kəʊˈɔːdɪneɪt/
v. bring together; integrate; organize 协调；综合；管理

disruption /dɪsˈrʌpʃən/
n. an action that prevents something from continuing in its usual way 中断；扰乱

snarl /snɑːl/
n. tangled or jammed state, esp. of traffic 拥挤、阻塞的状态（尤指交通）

alpha /ˈælfə/
n. (fig.) the first or the best, someone or something that is successful; the first letter of the Greek alphabet 〈喻〉成功者；希腊字母表的第一个字母

also-ran
n. (fig.) person who fails to gain success or distinction 〈喻〉没有成功或无成就的人

prompt /prɒmpt/
v. cause or incite (sb.) to do sth. 促使或激励（某人）做某事

seamless /ˈsiːmlɪs/
a. done or made so smoothly that you cannot tell where one thing stops and another begins; without a gap 平滑的；浑然一体的；无裂缝的；无伤痕的

cutting-edge
a. newest, most advanced 最领先的，最前沿的

rank-and-file
a. ordinary, not special 普通的，一般的

aggravating /ˈæɡrəveɪtɪŋ/
a. irritating; annoying 令人恼怒的，使人烦恼的

maze /meɪz/
n. a confused collection or complicated mass (of facts, etc.)（事情等的）错综，复杂

scripted /ˈskrɪptɪd/
a. carefully planned, read from a script 照稿读的

resonate /ˈrezəneɪt/
v. make a deep, clear sound that continues for a long time, have a long-term effect 产生共鸣；发出回响，回荡

backlash /ˈbæklæʃ/
n. a strong but usually delayed reaction against recent events（对重大事件等）强烈反应；反冲

commute /kəˈmjuːt/
v. travel every day between your home and the place of work 每天往返于家和工作单位之间

turnover
n. the rate at which people leave an organization and are replaced by others 人事变更率，人员调整率

inextricable /ɪnˈekstrɪkəbl/
a. (two things) cannot be separated; closely connected 分不开的，紧密联系的

empathy /ˈempəθɪ/
n. the ability to imagine and share another person's feelings, experience, etc. 感情移入，同感；（对他人的感情、经历等的）想象力和感受

outfitter
n. a shop that sells clothes and equipment for a specific purpose （专营）商店

shrine /ʃraɪn/
n. a place that people visit because it is connected with sb./sth. that is important to them 具有重要意义的地方

empathize /ˈempəθaɪz/
v. understand another person's situation, problems or feelings because you have been in the similar situation 理解；移情

luxurious /lʌɡˈʒʊərɪəs/
a. supplied with luxuries; very comfortable 奢侈的；极舒适的

orientation /ˌɒ(ː)rɪenˈteɪʃən/
n. basic information or training that is given to people starting a new job, school or course 培训，训练

bill
v. announce or advertise; put in a programme 宣布；贴广告；列入节目单

session /ˈseʃən/
n. a single continuous period spent in one activity （进行某活动连续的）一段时间

uptake
n. understanding, comprehension 理解，领会

Phrases & Expressions

for all intents and purposes
in all important respects; almost competetly; virtually 在一切重要方面；实际上；几乎完全

take pity on...
act out of sympathy for; feel sorry for sb. because of their situation 同情

make amends
do sth. for sb. in order to show that you are sorry for sth. wrong or unfair that has been done 补偿；赔偿；将功补过

pluck sb. from the field
give an important job or role to someone unknown working in obscurity 成功提拔；成功地重用（不知名的人）

frontline reps
frontline representatives — those who work most directly with customers 第一线的工作人员

in the event of
if sth. happens 如果……发生

come up with
think of an idea, answer etc. 提出（建议），拿出（主意）

pull back
decide not to do sth. that you were intending to do because of possible problems; withdraw 退出

Exercises

Comprehension

1. Mark the following statements with T(true) or F(false) or NM(not mentioned) in the passage. Discuss with your partner about the supporting points for each statement.

    1) _____ Bob Emig, who travelled little, encountered a rare flight disaster when he was to take a Southwest Airlines flight home.

    2) _____ During the waiting period, the customers never heard the news connecting flights with air company from an officer.

    3) _____ Dealing well with customers in Southwest Airlines is not only an emergency action in the event of travel disruptions, but also a standard procedure coordinated by higher management.

    4) _____ In the past, dominant companies and smaller ones differentiated from each other in the services they provided, but technology is

UNIT **5** Customer Service

changing that tendency.

5) _____ For many people, customer service means providing a series of toll-free service phone numbers and scripted voices on the phone.

6) _____ Today, companies are reluctant to rely on "homeshoring" customer service calls for complex calls because it is too costly.

7) _____ The homeshoring model allows more stay-at-home moms to work at home, which not only keeps turnover lower but also provides better service to customers.

8) _____ "Empathy engine" stresses the importance of high-level management sharing the feelings and emotions of employees and customers.

9) _____ Cabela's helps its employees become more empathetic with customers by allowing them to borrow products for up to two months. Employees are only required to return it on schedule.

10) _____ Four Seasons Hotels provide the "fam trip" as the final piece of the seven-step employee orientation to successfully provide world-class service to customers.

2. The author uses some successful and unsuccessful cases of customer service to illustrate the importance of good service, and especially gives us some good examples of several companies as customer service champs. Please write down the specific experience of each company listed below and compare your answers with your partner's.

Companies	Experiences
Southwest Airlines	
JetBlue Airways Corp.	
Four Seasons Hotels	
Cabela's	

Critical Thinking

Work in group to discuss the following questions.

1) What is the main reason customer service is so important to a successful business?

2) A company's most vital asset is its customers. Without them, a company would not and could not exist in business. The practice of customer service should be as present on the show floor as it is in any other sales environment. Look at some commandments of customer service below and tell how you understand them.

- *Know who is boss.*
- *Identify and anticipate needs.*
- *Appreciate the power of "Yes."*
- *Give more than expected.*
- *Take the extra step.*

3) Look at the following case of customer service. What do you think the rental car agency could have done differently?

> A trainer was staying in a hotel in Denver. When she went to her rental car the first morning of her workshop, she discovered a dead-battery. She made a desperate call to the rental car agency and was told that it would be two hours before they could come out. They offered no other option for her to get to the seminar. In effect, they've said, "You've got a problem. Here's our policy. Like it or rent elsewhere next time."

Vocabulary

1. Write out the synonyms or the near-synonyms of the following words. The first letter of each word has been given to you.

planned	s_____	recognize	a_____
expose	u_____	failure	f_____
involvement	p_____	organize	c_____
congestion	s_____	obstacle	b_____
satisfied	c_____	possessions	p_____

UNIT 5 Customer Service

2. The underlined words are wrongly used in the following sentences. Choose a proper word from the box to replace them.

| commute | nightmare | backlash | voucher | empathize | disruption |
| pluck | proactive | prompt | cutting-edge | resonate | offshoring |

1) Gas prices are sky-high; parking rates are increasing; so <u>working</u> by car is getting more expensive every day.

2) E-commerce, a <u>lagged</u> business, has unleashed a new revolution, totally transforming traditional commerce and trade.

3) There's a bit of <u>reply</u> going on against Southwest Airlines' for changing their family first boarding policy.

4) Collaborative workflows and advanced technologies will <u>demand</u> customers to engage bank personnel in advisory discussions on personal finance, thus leading to incremental business.

5) In sum, this company has to be very <u>positive</u> and seize on any available opportunity to win.

6) Companies have been outsourcing work for many years. This trend has been carried to an extreme in the case of <u>globalizing</u> — sending work and jobs to other countries where labor is cheaper.

7) We <u>agree</u> with our clients. We understand their problems and pressures; we respect their budgets and deadlines, and we deliver solutions they can use and grow as their businesses evolve.

8) Sometimes you can get a <u>ticket</u> for the next breakfast there when you consume in a KFC, which is exciting for many children who love western food.

9) Today, we often read reports and comments on terrible tourist experience — it is advertised and imagined as a fabulous journey at first but often turns out a <u>terror</u>.

10) His voice as a local business leader will <u>echo</u> loudly in Washington and Springfield, helping the company secure the support it needs from their legislators.

3. Complete the following dialogues with the given phrases.

   1) out of range

      a. What do you think of the price of this new digital camera?

   ___

113

b. Do you know how a company can provide a satisfied service to customers now?
___

2) recite by heart

   a. How do you deal with so many rules of customer service?
   ___

   b. Do you want to be a lawyer in the future?
   ___

3) send out

   a. What do you usually do if you are interested in a position advertised on newspaper?
   ___

   b. How do businesses promote their sales during the Christmas Season?
   ___

4) keep up with

   a. How do you keep developing a business in the information age?
   ___

   b. How do you effectively improve customer service?
   ___

5) in the event of

   a. What are the basic requirements for your staff in customer service?
   ___

   b. Are you satisfied with the traffic management in your city?
   ___

6) be charged with

   a. Do you know what happened to the manager of this hotel?
   ___

   b. What if some company managers buy off the local government officials for an unfair business?
   ___

7) take pity on

   a. I've heard a toy shop sent out some food and toys to the homeless children on Christmas Day. What do you think of it?

b. How do you feel about donations made by some businessmen? If you were a millionaire, would you make donations to an orphanage?

8) think...as...

a. Do you know why some companies stress the importance of "empathy engine?"

b. What do you think of the role of business in our society?

Translation

1. **Translate the following paragraphs into Chinese.**

   But few places make empathizing with customers quite as luxurious an experience as Four Seasons Hotels. At most of its properties, the final piece of the seven-step employee orientation is something the chain's executives call a "familiarization stay" or "fam trip." Each worker in these hotels, from housekeepers to front-desk clerks, is given a free night's stay for themselves and a guest, along with free dining.

   While there, employees are asked to grade the hotels on such measures as the number of times the phone rings when calling room service to how long it takes to get items to a room. "We bill it as a training session," says Ellen Dubois du Bellay, vice-president of learning and development. "They're learning what it looks like to receive service from the other side."

2. **Put the following passage into English, using the proper forms of the words and phrases given in the box.**

for all intents and purposes	turnover	coordination	homeshore	offshore
customer service		outsource	cutting-edge	unfold	plight

   如今，客户服务"离岸外包"越来越和它的胞兄"境内外包"联系紧密。有专家认为，"离岸外包"是一种先进的贸易形式，对公司走出贸易困境有所帮助。他们还认为，实际上，通过外包业务，公司可以避免各部门之间协

调的麻烦，保持较低的人事变更率，同时为社会提供更多的就业机会。

一家名为佛瑞斯特的研究组织曾经断言，明年将有 330 万美国白领的工作流向如印度这样的海外国家。麦肯锡全球机构（McKinsey Global institute）最近的一个报告显示，"离岸外包"的过程对所涉及的两个国家都有利，是一个双赢方案。

Complaint Handling

A pleasant consumer experience often results in a repeat venture to the same business establishment. Providing good customer service is important to a company because it keeps their loyal customers coming back and helps to build new customer-business relationships every day. On a larger scale, the customer can receive a quality product and great customer service while the establishment can continually improve their business. The following are the typical scenarios often happening in customers' experiences. Work in pairs/groups to do the following tasks:

1) Read the scenarios to ensure you understand them completely.

2) Discuss with your partner about the ways to handle them.

3) Role-play the scenarios with ANOTHER pair, calling the repres entatives of the service providers or the sellers to make complaints and discuss the way to solve the problems. You should include the following points into your practice:

- *Listen to their complaints patiently;*
- *Convey your apology sincerely;*
- *Tell the way to solve the problem;*
- *Ask whether they are satisfied with the solution.*
- *Others...*

4) Reverse your roles to go on with another scenario.

5) Work in groups to discuss what lessons you can learn from the cases and how you can avoid the similar problems in the future.

Scenario 1

On-demand Sollutions.com has just moved into their new offices. They have contracted AdvancedTelecom.org to provide the necessary telecommunications infrastructure for these offices. Parties are now disputing the delay in establishing the connection for telephone and Internet. The contractually agreed upon term of 8 weeks for AdvancedTelecom.org to provide the connection is long overdue and the client is furious. Moreover they are completely at a loss as they have no means of contacting their clients. A little more than 60% of their turnover is generated through the Internet and On-demand Sollutions.com is predicting considerable losses in revenues if the problem is not resolved with further delay.

Multiple phone calls with various representatives of AdvancedTelecom.org have taken place without any success. On-demand Sollutions.com insists on compliance with the terms of the agreement. Advanced Telecom.org's representatives, however, refer to external factors that are beyond their control, due to which a firm commitment to effectuate the connection can only be given two weeks from now.

Scenario 2

A consumer in Orlando purchases a brand-name watch for several hundred US dollars on the Internet from an online merchant in Boston. The purchaser and online merchant both meet the agreed conditions of the transaction. The watch is paid for by the purchaser and is dispatched and received by post. When, a few days following its receipt, the watch no longer functions, the purchaser telephones the online merchant, who advises the buyer to place a new battery in the watch. However, this fails to rectify the problem. The buyer takes the watch to an authorized dealer, who questions the authenticity of the watch. The buyer is angry and feels deceived. The online merchant is a small company of good standing and the fact that the watch is not what it appears to be comes as an unpleasant surprise. He is keen to solve the problem and it is in his best interests to maintain his good name in the online market.

Scenario 3

Ms A saw an advertisement in the paper for a service offering loans to bankrupts and those with a poor credit history, with no application fees. Applications were via a 190 number, charged at $5 per minute. She called the service twice, and tried to speak to a manager to find out if it would be worth her applying for a loan. On her third call she answered the application questions asked by an operator on the service, and was asked to call back with further information. She did this, often repeating information at the request of the operator. She was told to call back on the 190 number to check on the progress of her application, and received a fax from the company explaining that when her loan was approved, an administration fee of $98 would be payable. Her loan application was initially unsuccessful, however she was told that the company made three attempts to arrange a loan, and asked if she wished to continue. She agreed, but her application was ultimately not approved. She was charged approximately $350 for her calls to the service.

Language Hints

Breaking bad news
- Hello, I'm sorry to trouble you but...
- Hello, my name is...The reason I'm calling you is that...
- I'm afraid I have some rather bad news.
- I'm very sorry about this but...
- ...

Apologizing
- I'm really very sorry about this. Is there anything I can do to help?
- I'd like to apologize for this.
- I'll certainly make sure it doesn't happen again.
- May I offer you my sincere apologies for...?
- ...

Reacting to bad news
- Yes, what seems to be the problem?
- Oh, Mr./Ms...., what happened?
- Yes, I understand.
- ...

Reacting to an apology
- Don't worry, it doesn't really matter.
- It's OK really. I hope it won't happen again.
- It's not your fault.
- Please don't blame yourself.
- Don't think any more about it.
- Don't let it worry you.
- ...

Delaying
- Could you hold the line a moment, please? I'll need to ask my colleague.
- I'm not quite sure about that. Could I call you back in a few minutes, please?
- I don't really want to give a quick answer, I need to check that.
- Can I get back to you with an answer? I'll have to check.
- ...

Don't know
- I'm afraid I can't answer that question.
- I really don't know. I'm afraid.
- I'm not really sure of the answer.
- ...

UNIT 5 Customer Service

A Letter of Apology

After receiving a letter of complaint, one is expected to respond with a prompt investigation and then give a reply. The structure of a letter of apology usually goes as follows:

- Thank the buyer for the letter;
- Express your regrets and apologize;
- State your reasons;
- Offer settlement.

If the complaint is unjustified, it is advisable to explain the matter clearly to the other party so that you can continue doing business successfully in the future.

The letter needs to be well organized and written with a sensible tone that should be apologetic and informative.

The key to language use in a letter is to be clear and polite. If you are in doubt about word choice and structure, try to think what you would say if the person was in front of you. In that way, you will usually make the right choice. Always bear in mind to be courteous, sincere, and cooperative.

Remember that a letter must be paragraphed, and you may use graphic devices.

Write letters according to the following situations. The letter for Situation 1 is given as a model.

1. You work at Supple Shoes, 64 South Mall, Cork, Ireland (telephone +353 25 33507). Mr. Sean Supple, the owner of the firm, hands you a letter (the letter below) and asks you to draft a reply to it ready for his signature. Mr. Supple says:

> I have looked in our customer file. Mr Ryan is a regular client of ours who has introduced several of his friends to our service…
>
> We really ought to have sent him some sort of message by now! Apologize to him. Explain to him that the shoes he ordered are from a new manufacturer and the sizes are slightly different from our normal stock. Tell him that we will send him a pair of the next larger size in about 7 days as soon as the supplies are available.

Letter from the customer, Brendan Ryan

39 Kerrymount Rise
Dublin 18

June 15, 2008

Supple Shoes
64 South Mall
Cork

Dear Sirs

Re: Shoes (Cavalier Style) Size 10 Brown

I have been ordering my shoes from you for more than 6 years and I have always been very satisfied with the quality of the footwear and the speed of your postal service.

Unhappily the last shoes which I received, brown Cavalier Style size 10, were not satisfactory. They were far too small despite the label on them claiming they were size 10.

I returned them with a written explanation and asked either for a pair which did fit or for my check to be returned.

After 3 weeks, I still have received neither my money nor my shoes.

What do you intend to do?

Yours faithfully

Brendan Ryan
Brendan Ryan

Model Answer to Situation 1

Supple Shoes
64 South Mall, Cork
Telephone: + 353 25 33507

June 25, 2008

Mr. Brendan Ryan
39 Kerrymount Rise
Dublin 18

Dear Mr. Ryan

I am sorry that you had a problem with the fit of your shoes: brown-Cavalier style-size 10 and we are particularly keen to continue to satisfy a valued customer like you.

We apologize for not realizing that the footwear, from a new supplier, was sized slightly differently from our usual stock. I am sure, however, that if you accept our sending you the next larger size, it will fit you well and that the shoes will prove to be of the quality we like to provide.

Please also accept our apologies for the delay in replying to your original letter. Normally we rectify problems immediately and there is no need to send a separate response. However, because of the huge demand for this product we were temporarily out of stock.

New supplies have been promised within 7 days and we shall send your shoes as soon as we receive them.

We thank you for your custom and hope you will allow us to continue to supply you in future.

Yours sincerely

Sean Supple

Sean Supple
Proprietor

2. Mr. Andrew Perry, head of the Sales Department at Electrostatic Plant Systems, West Bromwich (telephone 0121 553 7760), asks you to reply to a letter of complaint as follows.

BENNETT AND SMITH

"Hire all your decorating equipment from the specialists."

43-45 Gauze Street Paisley Scotland G52 3KF

Telephone and fax 0141 889 2461

Electrostatic Plant Systems   May 8, 2008
Bromford Park Industrial Estate
West Bromwich
West Midlands
B70 6BG

Dear Sirs,

Re: Order Number 91198

We ordered 12 'Quick Start' Paint Sprayers from you on April 30 and were told that they would be delivered to us within 5 working days. However, we still have not received them.

There have been similar delays on several occasions recently and we have to say that we must consider trying a different supplier if you cannot improve your delivery.

We thank you for the excellent service you formerly offered and regret having to think about taking our business elsewhere. Unfortunately, because of the inefficient supply we now receive from you, we find ourselves unable to offer our customers guarantees that the equipment they need will be available at a specific time.

We look for a satisfactory response including, of course, improved delivery.

Yours faithfully

Harold Bennett

Harold Bennett
(Partner)

UNIT **5** Customer Service

Mr Andrew Perry asks you to be tactful, especially since Mr Bennett is an established customer and has been buying from Electrostatic Plant Systems for more than 10 years. He adds:

> This is the first I have heard of any delays with deliveries to Bennett and Smith. I think it must be a problem with the new firm of carriers that we are using for sending goods to Scotland. I've checked here at EPS and the paint sprayers were forwarded the same day that we had the order....It would be a nice idea to thank Mr Bennett for letting us know that there could be a similar difficulty with other clients in Scotland. In fact I shall phone some of them now to check that everything has been received by them.

The warehouse staff tells you:

> ...there are enough supplies of the paint sprayers to send a new consignment immediately and a different firm of carriers has promised delivery within 48 hours.

3. Mrs Pearce, head of Tracer Ltd. (134-138 Sidmouth Road Exeter Devon EXI 9BG, Telephone 01392 286334 and 286335, Fax 01392 286336) asks you to answer the following letter that she has received.

> ★★★★★★★★★★★ **FAX TRANSMISSION** ★★★★★★★★★★★
>
> To: Customer Service Dept.
> From: John Rees
> Date: 6 November, 2008
>
> Dear Sirs,
>
> On April 5 I had a burglar alarm fitted by Tracer Ltd. As a special offer, you installed a fire alarm free of charge. I have had problems with both.

123

> Every time we cook anything, it sets off the smoke alarm. This is hardly satisfactory as it means that we cannot prepare a meal without worrying if the alarm is going to sound.
>
> The burglar alarm is almost as bad. Twice recently my wife and I have returned home after an evening out to be met by the police since our alarm had been disturbing the neighbors. On neither occasion had there been any attempted burglary.
>
> I worry particularly that, if a burglar did attempt to break in, everyone would think there was another false alarm.
>
> Please do something soon!
>
> Yours faithfully
>
> John Rees

Mrs Pearce suggests that you should discuss the problem with Paul Turner, who had fitted the burglar alarm system at Mr Ree's home (17 York Road Exeter Devon EX6 3DA). She adds:

> …Whatever the cause, arrange to fix it immediately. Dissatisfied customers are bad publicity for us.

After talking with Paul Turner you have sorted out the notes as follows:

> Smoke alarm — is it positioned too close to doorway of kitchen?
> 'I did warn the customer that it could be a problem' — Paul Turner.
> (Advise customer only solution — to reposition?)
>
> Burglar alarm problem COULD BE:
> - family pet (a dog?) left in house
> - external doors not closed properly
> - faulty sensor
> - many other possible causes
>
> Suggest customer phones for appointment — Paul Turner to check and rectify (matter of urgency).
>
> Stress no charge.

UNIT 5 Customer Service

Relevant Extension

Business Expressions

1. Choose ten adjectives and ten nouns from the boxes to make respective collocations with CUSTOMER, e.g. loyal customer, customer care.

Adjectives			Nouns
favored			care
common			support
major			attraction
long-standing			regulations
loyal			account
regular			requirements
inside			back
prospective	CUSTOMER	CUSTOMER	reaction
long-run			items
external			complaints
favorite			profiles
domestic			specifications
personal			budget
home			expectation
industrial			preference

2. Complete the following sentences with the expressions in the box.

end-user	a great many of customers	customer-oriented market
customized products	target customers	personalized service
refund policy	potential customers	consumer sovereignty
customer base	after-sale service	consumer welfare

1) The _____ or consumer may differ from the customer, who might buy the product, but doesn't necessarily use it.

2) Knowing this vital information not only helps the inventor know who _____

125

are, but also leads the way for all strategic marketing endeavors.

3) Now Google is the first among them to provide a real _____ for users to play with for web page search refinement.

4) This website contains information on _____, which is targeted to a wide range of audiences and could contain product details.

5) If the refund is for a recurring billing product, then the _____ allows for the most recent payment to be returned.

6) _____ refers to the individual benefits derived from the consumption of goods and services.

7) The Music Workshop will attract _____ from advance musicians to the novice (beginners).

8) Marketing managers are shifting to a _____ plan to improve the market-share.

9) Smaller shops lose _____ when supermarkets open nearby.

10) _____ is the idea that in economic transactions the "Customer is King," which means the producer is forced to mould everything around the customer and satisfy his needs as closely as possible in order to survive.

11) By sufficient spares supply and timely _____, we may guarantee the max profit during the operation of our products.

12) They are hoping that TV advertising will increase their _____.

3. Match the verbs in the left column with the nouns or noun phrases in the right column, and then use them to complete the text below, changing the form where necessary.

deal with	various CRM projects
pursue	customers
implement	data
gather	a company's specific situation
win	their data
want	numerous awards
provide	the assurance
consider	a benefit
access	a CRM strategy

appreciate   some relevant offers

CRM (Customer Relationship Management) is a holistic approach to an organization in 1) _____. The objectives of a CRM strategy must 2) _____ and its customers' needs and expectations.

While there are numerous reports that "failed" to 3) _____, these are often the result of unrealistic high expectations and exaggerated claims by CRM vendors.

In contrast there are a growing number of successes. One example is the National Australia Bank (NAB) which has 4) _____ for over ten years and has 5) _____ for its efforts.

To 6) _____, CRM must consider customer privacy and data security. Customers 7) _____ that third parties should not share their data without their consent and they should not 8) _____ illegally.

Customers also want their data used by companies to 9) _____ for them. For instance, an increase in unsolicited telemarketing calls is generally resented by customers while customers generally 10) _____.

Specialized Reading

1. Marketing has exerted a great influence over people's daily life. Here is the passage about criticism of marketing from the perspective of customers. Read the passage, choose the author's viewpoints out of some statements and translate the underlined sentences into Chinese.

    1) Critics acknowledge that marketing has legitimate uses in connecting goods and services to the consumers who want them. Critics also point out that marketing techniques have been used to achieve morally dubious ends by businesses, governments and criminals. Critics see a systemic social evil inherent in marketing. Marketing is accused of creating ruthless exploitation of both consumers and workers by treating people as commodities whose purpose is to consume.

    2) Most marketers believe that marketing techniques themselves are amoral. While it is ethically neutral, it can be used for negative purposes, such as selling unhealthy food to obese people or selling SUVs in a time of global warming, but it can also have a positive influence on consumer welfare.

    3) The Observer's survey among 1,206 UK adult consumers highlighted some of the stark changes our society has gone through in the last two decades. This

raises a question on the effective definition of marketing (anticipating, identifying and satisfying customer needs profitably), mainly in consumer marketing. There are similar concerns in industrial markets, also known as business-to-business or B2B. Industrial market segmentation attempts to provide some answers.

Marketing has made and can make to customers' satisfaction and economic value.

4) <u>It has contributed to both customers' and suppliers' quality of life by selecting profitable customer satisfaction as its sole objective</u>. The marketing concept, together with other business disciplines, helped the UK to make the transition from a 19th-century manufacturing economy to a modern model of success in the service industry, creating an economic growth period never seen before in the United Kingdom.

5) <u>Marketing has helped create value through customized products, no-questions-asked refund policies, comfortable cars, environmental attention, shopkeepers' smile, and guaranteed delivery dates</u>. Even some government departments address the public not as 'the Queen's subjects' or 'the applicants' any more but as 'customers.' Of course all of the above is done for economic or political gain, for better or worse.

Which of the following statements does the author of the article believe?

A. Marketing has made great contribution to customer satisfaction.

B. Marketing techniques are used to achieve morally dubious purposes.

C. Marketing techniques themselves are ethically neutral.

D. Marketing techniques can be used for negative purposes.

E. Marketing has helped to create value through various approaches.

F. Customer satisfaction should be the sole objective of the society.

Translation:

1) _____

2) _____

3) _____

4) _____

5) _____

2. Read the following information about customer relationship management. Look at the 15 statements below it, and then classify the statements under three headings marked A, B and C.

Customer relationship management (CRM) is a broad term that covers concepts used by companies to manage their relationships with customers, including the capture, storage and analysis of customer information. There are three aspects of CRM which can each be implemented in isolation from each other: Operational CRM, Analytical CRM and Collaborative CRM.

Operational CRM

Operational CRM provides support to "front office" business processes, including sales, marketing and service. Each interaction with a customer is generally added to a customer's contact history, and staff can retrieve information on customers from the database as necessary.

One of the main benefits of this contact history is that customers can interact with different people or different contact "channels" in a company over time without having to repeat the history of their interaction each time.

Consequently, many call centers use some kind of CRM software to support their call centre agents.

Analytical CRM

Analytical CRM analyses customer data for a variety of purposes including:
- design and execution of targeted marketing campaigns to optimize marketing effectiveness;
- design and execution of specific customer campaigns, including customer acquisition, cross-selling, up-selling, retention;
- analysis of customer behavior to aid product and service decision making (e.g. pricing, new product development etc.);
- management decisions, e.g. financial forecasting and customer profitability analysis;
- prediction of the probability of customer defection.

Analytical CRM generally makes heavy use of predictive analytics.

Collaborative CRM

Collaborative CRM covers the direct interaction with customers. This can include a variety of channels, such as internet, email, automated phone (Automated Voice Response AVR). It can generally be equated with "self service". The objectives of Collaborative CRM can be broad, including cost reduction and service improvements.

> A. Operational CRM
> B. Analytical CRM
> C. Collaborative CRM

1) Staff members can obtain information on customer's contact history.
2) Direct interaction with customers will be covered.
3) Customers' data can be analyzed for multi-purposes.
4) It means self service in another sense.
5) Front office business processes including sales, marketing and service will be supported.
6) It can predict whether the customer is likely to be loyal to the product.
7) It can help make decisions such as pricing by analyzing customer behavior.
8) It can be implemented to support customer processes.
9) It can design some campaigns to optimize marketing effectiveness.
10) One of the objectives is to cut down on cost.
11) It can forecast financial profit.
12) Customers can keep in touch with different people in a company.
13) It usually makes full use of predictive analytics.
14) Service improvement is one of its broad objectives.
15) It has got many accesses to customers such as internet and email.

3. Discuss the following questions with your group members.

1) If you, as a manager, have just taken over an operation with a reputation for less than ideal customer service, what can you do about it? What should you do first?
2) How do you quantify good customer service and measure it?

UNIT 6
Human Resources

1. Discuss the following questions with your partner.

   1) What do you think is the prime source of competitive advantage for most companies today?

   2) Someone says that today recruiting the right people has become not just difficult, but a full-blown battle. Do you agree with it? How do you define the expression "a full-blown battle" here?

   3) Suppose you were the boss of a company. What would you offer to attract talents?

2. Work in groups.

   1) Some experts believe that in order to win the talent wars, managers must welcome some new changes to the Old Way to fight the war. Look at the following guidelines for the New Way, and match them to the proper points of the Old Way. Discuss the nature of the differences in their approaches.

      Guidelines for the new way:

      - Recruiting is like marketing.
      - We fuel development primarily through stretch jobs, coaching and mentoring.
      - We affirm all our people, but invest differentially in A, B and C players.
      - All managers, starting with the CEO, are accountable for strengthening their talent pools.
      - We shape our company, our jobs, even our strategy, to appeal to talented people.

Guidelines for the old way	Guidelines for the new way
HR is responsible for people management.	
We provide good pay and benefits.	
Recruiting is like purchasing.	
We think development happens in training programs.	
We treat everyone the same and like to think that everyone is equally capable.	

2) If you were the HR manager of a company, what qualifications or credentials would you value most in job applicants?

3) Suppose you, a talented person, had received a job offer from a multinational company. Evaluate it from the following perspectives. Rank the factors in descending order of importance. Remember to justify your ranking.

Factors	Ranking	Justification
distance to home		
remuneration		
corporate culture		
job security		
opportunity of advancement		
opportunity of global business travel		
training program		
...		

Preview: The global economy is going through a huge shift from capital investment to intellectual capital, especially talent, which has become the world's most sought-after commodity because it is so rare in our society. More and more people, especially business executives, have realized its value and rarity. Brainpower is in ever-greater demand as economies get more sophisticated. Talent shortages are a problem in rich countries as well as in many developing ones. Attracting, cultivating, and retaining talent is a major concern for executives in an era when people matter more than ever. In the foreseeable future, the global war for talent is likely to intensify.

The Search for Talent

The world's most valuable commodity is getting harder to find.

By Bill Frymire

[1] These are **heady** days for most companies. Profits are up. Capital is **footloose** and **fancyfree**. Trade unions are getting weaker. India and some other countries are adding billions of new cheap workers and consumers to the world economy. This week

the Dow Jones Industrial Average[1] hit a new high.

[2] But talk to bosses and you discover a **gnawing** worry about the supply of talent. "Talent" is one of those **irritating** words that has been **hijacked** by management **gurus**. It used to mean **innate** ability, but in modern business it has become a **synonym** for brain power (both natural and trained) and especially the ability to think creatively. That may sound **waffly**; but look around the business world and two things stand out: the modern economy places an enormous premium on brainpower; and there is not enough to go round.

[3] The best evidence of a "talent shortage" can be seen in high-tech firms. The likes of Yahoo! and Microsoft are battling for the world's best computer scientists. Google, founded by two **brainboxes**, uses billboards bearing a mathematical problem: solve it for the telephone number to call. And once you have been **lured** in, they fight like hell to keep you: hence the growing number of Silicon Valley[2] **lawsuits**.

[4] Such worries are common in just about every business nowadays. Companies of all sorts are taking longer to fill jobs and say they are having to make do with **substandard** employees. Ever more money is being thrown at the problem — last year 2,300 firms adopted some form of talent-management technology — and the status and size of human-resource departments have risen **accordingly**. These days Goldman Sachs[3] has a "university", McKinsey[4] has a "people com-mittee" and Singapore's Ministry of Manpower[5] has an international talent division.

[5] Some of this **panic** is **overdone** and linked to the business cycle: there was much **ado** about "a war for talent" in America in the 1990s, until the dotcom bubble burst. People often talk about shortages when they should really be discussing price. Eventually, supply will rise to meet demand and the market will adjust. But, while you wait, your firm might go bust. For the evidence is that the talent shortage is likely to get worse.

[6] Nobody really disputes the idea that the demand for talent-intensive skills is rising. The value of "**intangible**" assets — everything from skilled workers to **patents** to **know-how** — has **ballooned** from 20% of the value of companies in the S&P 500 to

---

1 Dow Jones Industrial Average 道琼斯工业平均指数，是 30 种在纽约股票交易所及纳斯达克交易所买卖的重要股票的股价加权平均。
2 Silicon Valley 硅谷，旧金山东南圣克拉拉谷的别称，美国主要微电子公司集中于此
3 Goldman Sachs 高盛，美国著名投资银行
4 McKinsey 麦肯锡，美国著名咨询公司
5 Singapore's Ministry of Manpower 新加坡人力资源部

70% today. The proportion of American workers doing jobs that call for complex skills has grown three times as fast as employment in general. As other economies move in the same direction, the global demand is rising quickly.

[7] As for supply, the picture in much of the developed world is **haunted** by **demography**. By 2025 the number of people aged 15 - 64 is **projected** to fall by 7% in Germany, 9% in Italy and 14% in Japan. Even in still growing America, the **imminent** retirement of the **baby-boomers** means that companies will lose large numbers of experienced workers, in a short space of time (by one count half the top people at America's 500 leading companies will go in the next five years). Meanwhile, two things are making it much harder for companies to adjust.

[8] The first is the collapse of loyalty. Companies happily **chopped** out layers of managers during the 1990s; now people are likely to repay them by moving to the highest **bidder**. The second is the mismatch between what schools are producing and what companies need. In most Western countries schools are churning out too few scientists and engineers and far too many people who lack the skills to work in a modern economy (that's why there are talent shortages at the top **alongside** structural unemployment for the low-skilled).

[9] What about all those billions of people in the developing world? **Alas**, adding willing hands to the global economy is not the same as adding trained brains. Some developing countries are suffering from acute skills shortages at the more sophisticated end of their economies. Wage inflation in Bangalore[1] is close to 20%, and job turnover is double that ("**Trespassers** will be recruited" reads a sign in one office). The few **elite institutions**, such as India's Institutes of Technology, cannot meet demand. And there are also cultural **legacies** to deal with: India's Licence Raj[2] destroyed management skills.

[10] This poses different challenges for companies, governments and individuals. For companies the main task is simply to end up with more talented people than their competitors. Firms will surely have to cast their net wider, employing more part-time workers and more older workers, and spending yet more on training, even in places where workers seem cheap: the training budget at Infosys[3], an Indian tech giant, is now well above $100m. Human-resource managers, once **second-tier** figures, now often rank among the highest-paid people at American firms; they will have to **justify** that status.

[11] But governments too need to act. Removing barriers is a priority: even

---

1 Bangalore / ˈbæŋgəˈlɔː/ 班加罗尔，印度南部一个城市
2 India's Licence Raj 印度的许可证制度
3 Infosys 印度印孚瑟斯技术有限公司，一信息技术有限公司

65 America still **rations** the number of highly skilled immigrants it lets in, and Japan and many European countries, do far worse. But education inevitably matters most. How can India talk about its IT economy lifting the country out of poverty when 40% of its population cannot read? As for the richer world, it is hard to say which throw more talent away — America's **dire** public schools or Europe's dire universities. Both suffer
70 from too little competition and what George Bush has called "the soft **bigotry** of low expectations".

[12] And the talented would do well to **intervene** in this debate on the side of the disadvantaged. For one last thing is sure to flow from the hunt for talent: even greater inequality. Most societies will tolerate the idea of well-rewarded winners, as long as
75 there is equality of opportunity and the losers also clearly gain something from the system. If those conditions are not met, **populist** politicians from Toledo[1] to Tokyo[2] will clamp down and everyone will be poorer for it. A global **meritocracy** is in all our interests. Be prepared to fight for it.

(1049 words)
From *The Economist*

New Words

heady /ˈhedɪ/
a. having a strong or exhilarating effect; exciting 易使人醉的；使人兴奋的

footloose /ˈfʊtluːs/
a. having no ties; free to move about 自由自在的，行动无拘束的

fancy-free /ˈfænsɪˈfriː/
a. having no commitments or restrictions; carefree 随心所欲的，无义务或约束的；无忧无虑的

gnawing /ˈnɔːɪŋ/
a. worrying; causing pain 折磨人的，令人痛苦的

irritating /ˈɪrɪˌteɪtɪŋ/
a. causing anger or displeasure 使人不愉快的，恼人的，使人烦恼的

hijack /ˈhaɪdʒæk/
v.(infml.) steal idea, take somebody else's idea and use it, especially to the exclusion or detriment of the person from whom it was taken; misuse 〈非正式〉盗用；滥用

guru /ˈgʊruː/
n. a person with knowledge or expertise; expert 专家；权威

innate /ˌɪˈneɪt/
a. possessed at birth; inborn 先天的，天生的

synonym /ˈsɪnənɪm/
n. one of two or more words or expressions of the same language that have the same or nearly the same meaning in some or all senses 同义词

waffly /ˈwɒflɪ/
a. in an evasive manner, with vague or nonsensical words (in speech or writing) 含

---

1 Toledo /təˈliːdəʊ/ 托莱多，美国俄亥俄州西北部港口城市
2 Tokyo /ˈtəʊkjəʊ/ 东京，日本首都

糊其辞的，模棱两可的

brainbox /ˈbreɪnbɒks/
n. (infml.) a very intelligent person〈非正式〉非常聪明的人

lure /ljuə/
v. attract 吸引，引诱

lawsuit /ˈlɔːsjuːt/
n. a suit in law; a case before a court 诉讼（尤指非刑事案件）

sub-standard /ˌsʌbˈstændəd/
a. below the usual or required standard 不够标准的，在标准以下的

accordingly /əˈkɔːdɪŋlɪ/
ad. in accordance; correspondingly 相应地

panic /ˈpænɪk/
n. a very strong feeling of anxiety or fear, which makes one act without thinking carefully 恐慌，惊慌

overdo /ˌəʊvəˈduː/
v. exaggerate 把……做得过分；过于夸张

ado /əˈduː/
n. bustle; fuss; trouble; bother 纷扰；忙乱；小题大做；麻烦；困扰

intangible /ɪnˈtændʒəbl/
a. unable to be touched or grasped; not having physical presence 触摸不到的；无形的

patent /ˈpeɪtnt/
n. an official document conferring a right or privilege, especially for the legal right to an invention 专利

know-how /ˈnəʊhaʊ/
n. knowledge of how to do something smoothly and efficiently; expertise〈口〉技术；实际知识，技能

balloon /bəˈluːn/
v. swell; expand; increase rapidly 大大增加；激增

haunt /hɔːnt/
v. make someone worry or make them sad 缠扰，烦扰

demography /dɪˈmɒɡrəfɪ/
n. the composition of a particular human population 人口组成（或构成）

project /prɒˈdʒekt/
v. plan, figure, or estimate for the future 预计；推断

imminent /ˈɪmɪnənt/
a. ready to take place; about to happen 邻近的；即将发生的；逼近的

baby-boomer /ˈbeɪbɪˈbuːmə/
n. someone who was born during the years after the end of World War II, especially from 1946—1965, when there was a marked rise in birthrate （第二次世界大战后的）生育高峰期出生的人

chop /tʃɒp/
v. dismiss from employment, cut 解雇；削减

bidder /ˈbɪdə/
n. a person who offers to pay a certain amount of money for sth. that is being sold 出价人；竞标人

alongside /əˈlɒŋˈsaɪd/
ad. in company with; together with; at the same time as or in coexistence with 与……同时；与……共存

alas /əˈlæs/
int. (表示遗憾等的惊叹声) 哎呀；唉

trespasser /ˈtrespəsə/
n. a person who enters sb.'s land or property without his permission or other authority 非法侵入某人地界者

elite /eɪˈliːt/
n. social group considered to be the best or most important because of their power, talent, wealth, etc. （由于有权力、才能、财富等）被视为最好的或最重要的社会集团；精英；尖子

institution /ˌɪnstɪˈtjuːʃən/
n. a (usually) large important organization 社会公共机构

legacy /ˈleɡəsɪ/
n. sth. transmitted by or received from an ancestor or predecessor or from the past 遗赠，遗赠的财物；遗产

second-tier /ˈsekənd-ˈtɪə/
a. second-class, second-level 二线的，二流的

justify /ˈdʒʌstɪfaɪ/
v. prove or show to be just, right, or reasonable 证明……正当（或有理、正确）

ration /ˈræʃən/
v. allow to have only a fixed amount of a certain commodity 配给供应，定量供应

dire /daɪə/
a. awful; tragic; of very low quality 极糟的；可怕的

bigotry /ˈbɪgətrɪ/
n. the possession or expression of strong, unreasonable prejudices or opinions 偏见；偏执的行为

intervene (in) /ˌɪntəˈviːn/
v. become involved in an argument, fight, or other difficult situation in order to change what happens 介入；干预；调停，调解，斡旋

populist /ˈpɒpjʊlɪst/
n. a supporter of the rights and power of the people 平民主义者

meritocracy /ˌmerɪˈtɒkrəsɪ/
n. a system in which the talented are chosen and moved ahead on the basis of their achievement 精英领导

Phrases & Expressions

trade union
an organization of workers formed for the purpose of advancing its members' interests in respect to wages, benefits, and working conditions 工会

place/put a premium on
attach special value or importance to sb./sth. 高度评价；高度重视

stand out
be easily noticeable; be prominent or conspicuous 引人注目

go round
(of a number or quantity of sth.) be enough for everyone to have a share （指某物的数或量）足够每人一份

like hell
(infml.) very much, hard, etc. (used for emphasis) 〈非正式〉拼命地

make do (with)
manage with the limited or inadequate means available 凑合着对付过去；将就使用，勉强应付

business cycle
a sequence of economic activity typically characterized by recession, fiscal recovery, growth, and fiscal decline 经济周期（以衰退、财政复苏、增长、财政下跌为典型特征）

go bust
go bankrupt; go broke 〈俚〉破产

call for
require; demand 要求；需要

as for
with regard to; concerning 至于

UNIT **6** Human Resources

churn out
produce large quantities of sth. very quickly 大量地生产出

structural unemployment
unemployment resulting from industrial reorganization, typically due to technological change, rather than fluctuations in supply or demand（指因工业改组，尤指因技术进步而非供需变化造成的）结构性失业

end up (with)
be in a particular situation, state, or place after a series of events, especially when you did not plan it 以……告终

cast/spread one's net wide
consider or try as many things as possible in order to find what one wants 想尽办法寻找，千方百计搜罗

throw sth. away
waste something good that you have, for example a skill or an opportunity 浪费掉（本领）；错过（机会）

do well
be wise; be successful 明智；做得好，进展好

flow from sth.
happen as a result of something 来自，产生于，源于

clamp down (on)
impose restrictions; crack down（对……）进行压制；（对……）强行限制；（对……）进行取缔

in sb.'s interest(s)
for or to sb.'s advantage 为某人的利益，对某人有好处，有利于某人

Exercises

Comprehension

1. Mark the following statements with T (true) or F (false) or NM (not mentioned) according to the passage. Discuss with your partner about the supporting points for each statement.

    1) _____ On the global market, there is a lack of capital, which gives most companies a big headache.

    2) _____ Management experts often kidnap talented people, those with spectacular innate ability or rich hands-on experience.

    3) _____ The word talent once meant natural ability, but it has come to include trained ability and creativity as well.

    4) _____ In the 1990s, companies happily fired managers, and those who were lucky to stay now repay their employers for their kindness by moving upward along the corporate ladder.

    5) _____ Cultural heritage has implications for corporate management.

    6) _____ High-tech firms offer the paradigmatic example of a talent

shortage.

7) _____ The demand for labor force exceeds its supply at every level on the job market.

8) _____ Talent shortage is a problem that plagues the developing world only.

9) _____ Those people who were smart enough to solve the mathematical problem placed on the billboards could make a phone call for an interview from Google.

10) _____ Currently the concern about talent shortage that is palpable throughout the business world is completely unwarranted.

2. With subheadings the organization of the text can be made very clear. The text can be granted four subheadings, and the first one is given. Now write down the rest by completing the following table.

Parts	Paragraphs	Subheadings
I	Paras. 1-2	Introduction: a global talent shortage
II	Paras. _____	_____
III	Paras. _____	_____
IV	Paras. _____	_____

Critical Thinking

Work in group to discuss the following questions.

1) Why are talents the most important factor in a company's success?

2) What kinds of recruitment campaigns attract the most talented people?

3) During a job interview, the employer must discover whether the candidate is able to work effectively with a variety of people and whether he possesses the aptitudes that fit the needs of the position. Usually, tough questions during job interviews are to be expected. The answers to these questions are so crucial that they can determine a candidate's prospects. Learning how to answer them takes planning and preparation. Work with your group members and discuss how you would answer the following interview questions.

   a. What is the thing that you have experienced that best prepares you for the job here?

UNIT **6** Human Resources

   b. *Where do you see yourself in five years?*
   c. *Why should we hire you?*
   d. *If you were a tree, what kind of tree would you be?*
   e. *Describe one of the greatest challenges you have faced and how you overcame it.*
   f. *Describe a difficult person you have had to work with and what you did to deal with that person.*
   g. *You are preparing to make a presentation to your supervisors about a project you have been working on as a team. When you discover that one member of your team has used information stolen from a competitor, what do you do?*

Vocabulary

1. **Find from the text the equivalent expressions of the following definitions.**

   1) persons who work for only part of each day or week

   _____

   2) economy covering or affecting the whole world

   _____

   3) the division of an organization dealing with the management of people to achieve individual behavior and performance that will enhance the organization's effectiveness

   _____

   4) the process by which investment, output, and employment in an economy tend to fluctuate up and down in a regular pattern causing booms and depressions, with recession and recovery as intermediate stages

   _____

   5) change in employment during a given period of time

   _____

   6) unemployment resulting from changes in the basic composition of the economy

   _____

   7) something of value that cannot be physically touched, such as a brand, franchise, trademark, etc.

   _____

8) a speculative bubble covering roughly 1995-2001 during which countless Internet companies were riding an enormous wave of enthusiasm that pushed their stock valua-tions into the stratosphere even though they never made a penny

9) intellectual capacity; people of well-developed mental abilities

10) an organization whose principal purposes include the regulation of relations between employees and employers or employers associations

2. **The underlined words are wrongly used in the following sentences. Choose a proper word or phrase from the text to replace them.**

1) The housing shortage is more urgent than first thought.

2) The chief economist of this renowned investment bank predicted that the bubble in the property market of Shanghai would break in the coming two years.

3) As the Dow Jones industrial average hit new heights on Oct. 1, some investors were putting money in another bull market: fine art.

4) Much more commonly, you find smart, capable people stalled because they lack the instinctive ability to win hearts and minds.

5) With new governance rules placing a value on independent directors, many boards are on the prowl for new members, and they are not limiting themselves to the executive suite.

6) We anticipate continued market volatility and periodic stock specific investment opportunities. In accordance, we remain alert to summer season buying opportunities.

7) These years London is attracting money — and talent — at an accelerating pace. Estimates vary, but by one account, Britain has about 700 hedge-fund managers today.

8) This marketing problem may lie in a discontinuity between a regulatory objective and the technique chosen to achieve it .

9) Even business educators acknowledged that their discipline was ill-defined and lack of standards.

UNIT **6** Human Resources

10) The financial newsletter audience is dwindling fast, and unless the industry alters its focus, more losses seem <u>indispensable</u>.

3. **Complete the following dialogues with the given phrases.**

   1) intervene in

      What is the independent arbiter supposed to do in the event of a contract dispute?

      _____

   2) in sb.'s interest

      Does a stock option （优先认股权） do good to both the company and the employee that receives it?

      _____

   3) clamp down

      Piracy is so rampant that record sales suffer a lot. What should the government do?

      _____

   4) call for

      What are the prerequisites for a job in high technology?

      _____

   5) chop out

      How did layers of middle management fare during the depression years?

      _____

   6) churn out

      Why is the loyalty to this brand of washing machine declining so fast?

      _____

   7) like hell

      Wow! You've finished this project within such a short period of time! How did you manage to meet the deadline?

      _____

   8) make do with

      The doctor said Peter was overweight and had better drink fat-free milk. What if there is no fat-free milk in the supermarket?

      _____

9) end up

What happened to those American families stricken by the property bust?

_____

10) go round

What is the secretary supposed to do before the conference?

_____

Translation

1. Translate the following paragraphs into Chinese.

These are heady days for most companies. Profits are up. Capital is footloose and fancy-free. Trade unions are getting weaker. India and China are adding billions of new cheap workers and consumers to the world economy. This week the Dow Jones Industrial Average hit a new high.

But talk to bosses and you discover a gnawing worry — about the supply of talent. "Talent" is one of those irritating words that has been hijacked by management gurus. It used to mean innate ability, but in modern business it has become a synonym for brainpower (both natural and trained) and especially the ability to think creatively. That may sound waffly; but look around the business world and two things stand out: the modern economy places an enormous premium on brainpower; and there is not enough to go round.

2. Put the following passage into English, using the words and phrases given in the box.

supply	priority	asset	capital	balloon
resource	brainpower	premium	end up	lure

对处于互联网时代风口浪尖的公司来说，最稀缺的资源既不是原材料，也不是资金，既不是科技，也不是市场。让这些公司的经理们彻夜难眠的是人才的匮乏。难怪计算机行业的巨头迈克尔·戴尔将员工列为经理人必须优先考虑的十大因素之首。随着各公司对智能密集型技术需求的不断增长，人才被视为公司极其宝贵的资源。大公司往往极为重视培养和留住人才，而小企业经常通过提供有竞争力的薪酬将顶尖的人才从大公司挖过来。那些不重视人才的企业将以失败告终。只有人才才能给梦想插上翅膀，使未来以光速变成现在。

UNIT 6 Human Resources

Business Practice

Job Interview

Interviewing effectively is the single most important aspect of the job search. It is your best and oftentimes only chance to demonstrate to an employer that you have the skills and experience necessary to do the job. Becoming comfortable with the interview process is crucial, as employers, regardless of their fields, constantly seek to hire poised, well  spoken, directed individuals. Nowadays it is not uncommon that companies conduct group interviews, at which several applicants are interviewed at the same time by a panel of interviewers. In this activity, you work in group of six or eight with half being the applicants and the other a panel of interviewers. You should first look at the related information given below, and then do the activity, following the listed steps.

Beijing Huiyuan

Join us!

We are a leading Food & Beverage company and we offer you a challenging and fulfilling post-Director of Customer Service

You'll

- develop and maintain an effective department through proper selection, training, and assignment of personnel;
- evaluate, promote, terminate employees, and recommend promotions and increases;
- assist subordinates in day-to-day problems and personal counseling;
- regularly review the progress of work in the department;
- handle customer correspondence, complaints, and inquiries, especially on major accounts, and with the executive level of all accounts.

> **A great opportunity for the right kind of person!**
>
> Job requirement:
>
> - University graduate: major in engineering, sales & marketing will be preferred;
> - At least 4 years related sales experiences in industrial and food & beverage area;
> - Account service or sales & marketing work experience will be highly preferred;
> - Strong interpersonal skills;
> - Good command of English language skills.
>
>
>
> **Interview today in Hotel Sheraton**
>
> **from 9:00 to 5:00 in Suite 101**
>
>

Beijing Huiyuan Beverage & Food Group Co., Ltd. was founded in 1992. It is a large modern enterprise group engaged in the production of 100% Fruit and Vegetable Juice, Nectars, Juice Drinks, Milky Juice Drinks, Tea Drinks, etc.

The Group has built more than 20 modern plants throughout the country. More than 100 advanced Aseptic Filling Lines are introduced from abroad. Huiyuan has built and promoted to build more than 60 raw materials bases of fruits, vegetables, tea and milk. Over 10 categories of more than 400 kinds of products are available in the Group.

Huiyuan has gained the certification of ISO9000 and HACCP, and has accredited as "Safety Drinks" by Chinese authorities. The company has been awarded many prizes such as "Reliable Products for the Chinese Consumers", "The First Brand of Quality Satisfaction in China's Beverage Market". The products have been exported to more than 20 countries and regions. Huiyuan Juice has been ranking No. 1 in the domestic market in terms of sales revenue and sales quantity in the industry.

For applicants:

- *Discuss to predict what questions the interviewers will ask.*
- *Discuss to prepare some questions to ask the interviewers.*
- *The interview begins. Each interviewer asks at least two different questions to each*

applicant.

- *Each applicant asks at least two questions to the interview panel.*
- *Discuss your performance and decide which interviewer asked the most effective questions.*
- *Find out who is to get the jobs.*

For interview panels:

- *Discuss to prepare some suitable questions to ask each applicant.*
- *The interview begins. Each interviewer asks at least two different questions to each applicant.*
- *Discuss and choose one or two applicants for the job.*
- *Announce who is to get the job.*

Tips for Interview Success

An interview is your opportunity to shine. Take the time to prepare yourself for this important moment. How will you prove you are the ideal candidate? Start by reviewing your background carefully to look for clues. Draw from every part of your life—academic, work, community, athletic, leadership, volunteer, travel—to display this. Since employers are hiring a colleague as well, your personal characteristics count. Be sure to convey these through your thoughtful and well-prepared answers to traditional interview questions as well as behavioral-based interview questions. Keep the following tips in your mind when you are having an interview:

- *Clarify the details of the interview in advance — date, location, schedule, attire.*
- *Arrive 10 minutes earlier.*
- *Bring several copies of your resume — you never know who in addition to the interviewer you may meet.*
- *Bring your portfolio or samples of your work, if appropriate for your field.*
- *Bring a list of references, if you are graduating this year.*
- *Bring an unofficial copy of your transcript.*
- *Be a good listener. Let the interviewer guide you.*
- *Ask for clarification if you are unsure of the question.*

- *Be honest if you are asked a question you are unable to answer. Offer a thoughtful way in which you would attempt to find the answer.*
- *Be positive about yourself and your experiences.*
- *Display energy and enthusiasm for your field and the organization.*
- *Adjust your answers as the situation demands. You may use more technical terminology while speaking with someone in your field.*
- *If you are asked the question, "tell me about yourself" — get right to the point by saying what makes you ideal for the job.*
- *Be prepared to give specific examples to back up statements you make about yourself. These can be from academic, professional, and personal experiences.*
- *Watch your body language — smile, practice a firm handshake, maintain good eye contact, sit and stand in an attentive manner, stay focused on the conversation at hand while in a group setting.*
- *Look for opportunities to match your background to their needs.*
- *Conclude with a sincere statement of interest in the position.*
- *Thank the interviewer for their time and ask about next steps in the process.*
- *Follow up with a thank you note — emailed, typed, or handwritten.*

Language Hints

For interviewers
- What attracts you to this job?
- Have you any relevant experience?
- Are you sure you could cope with...?
- ...

For candidates
- Could you tell me something about...?
- I'd like to know...
- There's one other thing...
- ...

Resume and Cover Letter

Resume Tips

The purpose of a resume is to disclose your accomplishments and qualifications to a potential employer. If the employer likes what she sees, she will contact you for a face-to-face meeting. Your resume is also an example of your communication and organizational skills. A well done resume is itself another reminder of what kind of valuable employee you would be. So follow the tips below when you are writing a resume:

- *Think of your resume as a promotional brochure about you. Your strategy should be to emphasize the experience and skills that a particular employer is looking for.*
- *Keep it concise. Resumes should be one page, if possible, and two if absolutely necessary to describe relevant work experience.*
- *Make your words count. Your use of language is extremely important; address your potential employer's needs with a clearly written, compelling resume.*
- *Avoid large paragraphs(over six or seven lines). Use action verbs such as"developed,""managed," and"designed" to emphasize your accomplish-ments.*
- *Don't use declarative sentences like"I developed the..."or"I assisted in..."; leave out the "I."*
- *Don't be vague. Describe things that can be measured objectively. Tell them that you"cut requisition costs by 20%, saving the company $3,800 for the fiscal year". And be honest.*
- *Remember to only include the experience that is relevant to the job.*
- *Don't mention personal characteristics such as age, height, and marital status.*
- *List your hobbies and interests only if you can relate them to the position you're applying for. If you need room to describe your work experience, avoid this altogether.*
- *The phrase "References available upon request" should be left off if you need room to describe your work experience.*
- *Avoid the "Objective" statement — your objective should be clearly articulated in your cover letter. If you do include an objective, be specific.*
- *Check your resume for proper grammar and correct spelling — evidence of good communication skills and attention to detail.*
- *Make your resume easy on the eyes. Use normal margins and allow for some breathing room between the different sections. Avoid unusual or exotic font styles; use simple fonts with a professional look.*

Cover Letter Writing Tips

Whether you e-mail, fax or snail-mail your resume, you'll want to include a cover letter. This document can direct the reader to the meat of your resume and establish rapport between you and the potential employer. More than just window dressing for your resume, a cover letter is like a partner to that all-important document. Many employers today won't even look at your resume if you don't submit it with a cover letter. Your cover letter gives employers the opportunity to evaluate your ability to communicate — Do you know the proper form for a business letter? Can you string together coherent sentences? Are you able to express yourself well on paper? Your cover letter will give employers insight into all of these things. Here are some things to consider when putting your cover letter together:

- *Your cover letter should draw employers to your resume. Don't clutter it with needless facts.*
- *Keep it brief. No employer wants to read your life's history.*
- *Tailor it to the position and company for which you are applying. A cover letter shouldn't be "canned."*
- *Open by explaining why you are writing and where you heard about the opportunity.*
- *Be sure to say why you think you would be a good match for the position. If the advertisement lists several traits or skills the employer wants to see in job applicants, refer to those skills in your letter and say how you exemplify them. Mention traits that will set you apart from other candidates.*
- *Refer the employer to your resume — "you can see from my resume that I have the experience you are looking for" may be a good way to do so.*
- *Maintain the initiative by suggesting a meeting and that you will call for an appointment.*
- *Remember to sign your cover letter.*
- *Note "enclosure" or "enc." several lines after your signature if your resume is enclosed.*
- *Proof your letters carefully. Have someone else review them. Don't rely on a computer spell-checker. A word may be correctly spelled but inappropriate for the context.*

Study the following samples and do the exercises according to the directions.

Sample resume

Sarah E. Madison
2000 Nord Avenue Chico, CA 95929 (530) 892-5555
e-mail: goodgolly@hotrocks.com

EDUCATION CALIFORNIA STATE UNIVERSITY, CHICO

Bachelor of Science in Business Administration, Graduation: May 2008

Option: **Management Information Systems**

Option: **Production Operations Management** Overall GPA: **3.30**

Earn 100% of education and living expenses through work and loans.

Special Projects:

System Development: As project manager, coordinated the efforts of six teams of students working on highly interdependent phases.

SAP R/3 Implementation Team Member — Learn the basic architecture and operations of the SAP R/3 system. Work with other team members and faculty members to implement SAP R/3 modules into the business curriculum.

COMPUTER SKILLS **Operating Systems:** Windows, UNIX

Languages: IBM-AIX, COBOL, HTML

Applications: JDE, Siebel, SAP R/3, SQL, Microsoft Office, Lotus Notes/Domino, Word Perfect, RBASE.

EXPERIENCE Intern

DATA RESOURCE GROUP, Scottsdale, AZ (July 2007-August 2007)

Assisted with development of home page. Programmed "hot keys" from DRG to IBM and other vendor's sites. Developed the graphical presentation of upcoming sales specials and new products. Created custom reports from DRG's database.

Data Entry Specialist

A.S. BUSINESS OFFICE, CSU, Chico, CA (September 2005-June 2006)

Entered all transactions for two businesses. This included journal entries, cash receipts, accounts receivable, accounts payable, and canceled checks.

Office Manager

NATIONAL PIZZA COMPANY, Westlake Village, CA (January 2005-July 2005)

Interfaced with all levels of personnel. Responsible for biweekly payroll. Maintained personnel files and office supplies. Pre-interviewed job applicants. Trained new office employees. Approved and sent bills to the corporate office for payment.

Information Specialist

JB TECHNOLOGIES, INC., Moorpark, CA (February 2002-January 2004)

Revamped order processing system. Generated flow charts of company procedure. Implemented new order system which involved training of employees. Helped with innovation and installation of new software package and trained employees to use it.

Quality Control Assistant

Warranty evaluation. Manipulated customer and bar code information on a network system. Assisted in testing and formatting of computer disk drives.

ACTIVITIES & HONORS	MIS Society, CSU, Chico: **V.P. Administration** (Spring 2008, Fall 2007) **Member**, Golden Key National Honor Society (Spring 2007, Fall 2007) Dean's List (Spring 2007, Fall 2007)

UNIT 6 Human Resources

Sample cover letter

Sarah E. Madison
2000 Nord Avenue
Chico, CA 95929
(530) 892-5555
e-mail: goodgolly@hotrocks.com

April 9, 2008

Nicholas Slick
Ace Communications
100 Fifth Ave.
New York, New York 10011

Dear Mr. Slick:

If your organization is seeking a skilled and experienced Project Manager, I would appreciate the opportunity to discuss your needs and objectives with you. The accomplishments noted within the accompanying resume will illustrate the value and vision that I can bring to your team.

For the last five years, I have led various project implementations, providing Business Data Management, Personal Management, Revampment of Order Processing System and Quality Evaluation. I have demonstrated success in managing these full project lifecycles, which have resulted in numerous savings for this company. I possess a deep understanding of how to utilize technology in order to deliver enterprise

> Make every effort to get a specific name. If you absolutely cannot, address your letter to the right department, making sure you know the current name of the department, for example, Human Resources vs. Personnel.

> Indicate the reason for writing, the specific position for which you are applying, and, if there is a position opening, the source from which you learned of the job and the date it was posted. If you are inquiring about jobs in general and no opening was advertised, indicate your interest in career opportunities in your field.

solutions that meet requirements of business.

My expertise includes strong hands-on technical skills with CRM software applications including JDE and Siebel. I am highly skilled in database development, object-oriented analysis/design, data modeling, client/server applications development and data warehousing/knowledge management. Furthermore, I have proven the ability to manage large scale projects, consistently delivering these engagements within time and budget constraints. I possess a solid track record for leading and motivating technical professionals in order to achieve high levels of performance. These trends I intend to continue long into the future.

> Mention why you are interested in the position or organization and its products or services. Relate your academic or work background to the position for which you are applying. Point out your practical work experience, specific achievements, and unique qualifications. Mention information other than what is on your resume.

In review of your company's objectives and possible openings, I believe that my experience is in perfect line with your current needs. If your firm is looking for a dependable, results-oriented professional with a solid performance track, I would be interested in speaking with you to discuss the value that my strengths and experience can bring to your search.

I would appreciate an interview with you at your convenience. I can be reached in confidence at one of the above telephone numbers and look forward to hearing from you.

Thank you for your consideration.

> Include a final sentence which summarizes the strength of your candidacy. Provide the reader with additional information and again emphasize your career objective. Restate your interest and indicate your eagerness to meet personally to learn more about the position. Thank the reader for taking the time to read your letter and resume.

Sincerely yours

Sarah E. Madison

Sarah E. Madison

Enclosure

> Refers to enclosed resume, reference list, etc.

UNIT **6** Human Resources

1. Read the job advertisement in the section of Job Interview. Then design a resume and write a related cover letter to apply for the post. You may do it based on the information about yourself, or invent any name, experiences and qualifications you think relevant to the requirements.

2. Carl Furman, a graduate student, got to know some job information, through the Career Development Center of Northwest University, for a position of customer service manager by Frito-Lay Co., a famous multinational company. Design a resume based on the following details and write a cover letter for him. The letter should be written to Ms. Stephanie P. Tatoe, HR Manager of Frito-Lay Company at P.O. Box 789 Dallas, TX 75235.

> Carl Furman, 123, Ellis Street, Boston, MA, 01234, (123) 456 789...part-time student for Master Of Public Health in NORTHWESTERN UNIVERSITY SCHOOL OF PUBLIC HEALTH, Evanston, IL:...to get degree in May, 2008. ... studied in NORTHWESTERN UNIVERSITY, Evanston, IL in 2005 for B.S., Business Administration/Marketing...a then member of Alpha Beta Gamma, National Business Honor Society, Varsity Soccer...once got a Certificate of Award for Outstanding Business Administration Graduates...studied for A.A., Merchandising in Professional Modeling in LARSON COLLEGE, Malibu, CA 1998...studied with an emphasis on Communication and Public Presentation...
>
> Started from 2003...have been working as an information consultant in Present RED SAVIOR INSURANCE, Elsah, IL...trained on all contracts and systems...assist Department Supervisor as required with responsibility for work assignments, quality control, and troubleshooting...including educating public on applicable BC/BS policies, guidelines and procedures, resolve complaints and disputes in billing or contract specifications, research and write customer requests for appeal and present findings...selected to assist the Consumer Relations Department with inquiries from the media and third party inquiries from the Division of Insurance...got P.A.C.E. 5 Awards (Public Acknowledgment for Conscientious Effort)...worked as a senior information representative from 2001 to 2003...experienced assisting in training and orientation of new information representatives, interacting directly with Research on legal cases for Law Department, responding to inquiries, identified and researched subscriber problems and drafting series of form letters to accompany payments to participating medical providers...from 1998 to 2000 worked as a sales associate with responsibility for customer sales and service...assisted with new employee training...ranked among top 15 salespeople in the country in THE CLOTHES CRITERION, Chicago, IL...

Relevant Extension

Business Expressions

1. Make 18 collocations connected with human resources by choosing one word from Column A and another one from Column B. Translate the expressions into Chinese.

A	B
core	leave
unemployment	appraisal
bonus	setting
emotional	competency
job	mobility
human	intelligence
incentive	planning
employee	vitae
goal	compensation
curriculum	structure
comp	wages
labor	description
peer	pay
lump sum	training
minimum	capital
succession	time
occupational	retention
diversity	payment

1) _____ 2) _____
3) _____ 4) _____
5) _____ 6) _____

UNIT 6 Human Resources

7) _____   8) _____
9) _____   10) _____
11) _____   12) _____
13) _____   14) _____
15) _____   16) _____
17) _____   18) _____

2. Complete the following sentences with the appropriate words in the box.

turnover	nepotism	retirement	recruitment	attrition
induction	empowerment	resignation	suspension	mentoring
union	motivation	probation	layoff	outplacement
outsourcing	redundancy	orientation		

1) A reduction of employment to the university workforce, or _____, sometimes becomes necessary due to lack of funds, lack of work, or material changes in duties or organization.

2) When an employee chooses to leave a position it is considered a _____, as opposed to termination, which occurs when the employee involuntarily loses a job.

3) Nowadays most developed nations have systems to provide pensions on _____ in old age, which may be sponsored by employers or the state.

4) _____ is the process of increasing the capacity of individuals or groups to make choices and to transform those choices into desired actions and outcomes.

5) There's a three-month period of _____ for new recruits in many companies.

6) If companies take proper steps and adopt methods to serve their employees' needs, the challenge of managing _____ will remain low.

7) There is no such thing as a standard programme because _____ is unique to each new employee. But you can expect to work with and observe other employees in action.

8) In work environments, money may provide a more powerful extrinsic factor than the intrinsic _____ provided by an enjoyable workplace.

9) Offering employment to a relative, despite the fact that there are others who are

better qualified and willing to perform the job, would be considered _____.

10) _____ is to support and encourage people to manage their own learning in order that they may maximize their potential, develop their skills, improve their performance and become the person they want to be.

11) This half day _____ event will help make new employees' transition to their new company life a success.

12) Individuals seek out _____ or career management assistance when they need help to structure their job search, have been out of the job seekers market for some time or want to consider a new career direction.

13) _____ involves the transfer of the management and/or day-to-day execution of an entire business function to an external service provider.

14) The online software provided by those who specialize in online _____ helps organizations attract, test, recruit, employ and retain quality staff with a minimal amount of administration.

15) A _____ situation may arise where a business continues to operate but there is no longer a need for the skills for which the employee was taken on.

16) Work _____ occur when a business manager/supervisor deems an action of an employee, whether intentional or unintentional, to be a violation of policy that should result in a course of punishment.

17) If an employer is said to have a high _____, it most often means that employees of that company have a shorter tenure than those of other companies in that same industry.

18) The organization of workers, through its leadership, bargains with the employer on behalf of _____ members and negotiates labor contracts with employers.

Specialized Reading

1. Read the passage through carefully and fill in the missing words based on the first letters given.

The Human Resources Management (HRM) function includes a variety of activities, and key among them is deciding what staffing n __1)__ you have and whether to use independent contractors or hire e __2)__ to fill these needs, recruiting and training the best employees, ensuring they are high p __3)__, dealing with performance issues, and ensuring your personnel and management practices conform to various r ___4)___ . Activities also include managing your approach to employee benefits and compensation, employee records and personnel policies. Usually small businesses (for-profit or nonprofit) have to carry out these activities themselves because they can't yet afford part-or f ___5)___ -time help. However, they should always e ___6)___ that employees have — and are aware of — personnel policies which conform to current regulations. These policies are often in the form of employee manuals, which all employees have. Note that some people d ___7)___ a difference between HRM (a major management activity) and HRD (Human Resource Development, a profession). Those people might include HRM in HRD, explaining that HRD includes the broader range of activities to develop p ___8)___ inside of organizations, including, eg, career development, training, organization development.

2. **Read about the lessons from the AT&T layoffs and answer the following questions.**

The Wall Street Journal yesterday announced the layoff of 4,600 AT&T employees. (You must be a subscriber to access the story.) These layoffs have significant implications for employees in workplaces everywhere. The reason? AT&T plans to create about the same number of jobs going forward, so in many ways, the layoffs are a wash. Not good news for the people, mostly white collar, management employees in the landline phone division, who are affected, but for the company as a whole, the news represents movement into the future.

The future is proving painful for many employees who work in positions that are not needed for the future. These white collar employees will be replaced by "guys in trucks getting U-Verse into people's homes, he (UBS analyst John Hodulik) added, referring to AT&T's television and high-speed Internet offering." This is significant because there are lessons to learn from this downsizing.

No job is safe when the world is changing as fast as ours is. People who fail to keep up with or embrace new knowledge and skills are in trouble. One of my top ten reasons to quit your job has to do with this scenario. Employees need to constantly remain in touch with the direction of their industry, their company, and their job skills.

And, it's not easy being over forty and out of work. But people can make job searching easier on themselves. A client company interviewed an older individual recently. The applicant had not read the company Website, had not reviewed the company' products, and his main qualification, as stated by the candidate in the interview, was that he could do the job. Obviously, this didn't fly well with the interviewers.

1) What was the news in yesterday's Wall Street Journal?
2) Why is AT&T's downsizing significant?
3) Is the AT&T layoff a piece of good news or bad news?
4) Who will be the new employees in AT&T?
5) What lessons can we learn from the layoff?

3. Read the following passage about human resource management and choose the most suitable heading from the box for each paragraph. There is one extra heading which you do not need.

> A. HRM techniques in the eyes of practitioners
> B. Definition of personnel management
> C. Assumption of employees in the theoretical discipline
> D. Definition of HRM with comparison to personnel management
> E. Traditional characters of HRM
> F. Comparison between HRM theories and practice

1) _____

Human resource management(HRM) is the strategic and coherent approach to the management of an organization's most valued assets — the people working there who individually and collectively contribute to the achievement of the objectives of the business. The terms "human resource management" and "human resources"(HR) have largely replaced the term "personnel management" as a description of the processes involved in managing people in organizations. Human resource management is evolving rapidly. Human resource management is both an academic theory and a business practice that addresses the theoretical and practical techniques of managing a workforce.

2) _____

Its features include: personnel administration; personnel management; manpower management; industrial management. But these traditional expressions are becoming less common for the theoretical discipline. Sometimes even industrial relations and employee relations are confusingly listed as synonyms, although these normally refer to the relationship between management and workers and the behavior of workers in companies.

3) _____

The theoretical discipline is based primarily on the assumption that employees are individuals with varying goals and needs, and as such should not be thought of as basic business resources, such as trucks and filing cabinets. The field takes a positive view of workers, assuming that virtually all wish to contribute to the enterprise productively, and that the main obstacles to their endeavors are lack of knowledge, insufficient training, and failures of process.

4) _____

HRM is seen by practitioners in the field as a more innovative view of workplace management than the traditional approach. Its techniques force the managers of an enterprise to express their goals with specificity so that they can be understood and undertaken by the workforce, and to provide the resources needed for them to successfully accomplish their assignments. As such, HRM techniques, when properly practiced, are expressive of the goals and operating practices of the enterprise overall. HRM is also seen by many to have a key role in risk reduction within organizations.

5) _____

Synonyms such as personnel management are often used in a more restricted sense to describe activities that are necessary in the recruiting of a workforce, providing its members with payroll and benefits, and administrating their work-life needs. So if we move to actual definitions, Torrington and Hall(1987), who published *Human Resource Management*, define personnel management as being: "a series of activities which: first enable working people and their employing organizations to agree about the objectives and nature of their working relationship and, secondly, ensure that the agreement is fulfilled."

4. **Discuss the following questions with your group members.**

   1) If you are an investor, and you find the hourly rate of labor in one place is much cheaper than that of the other, where will you invest? Why?

   2) Some business leaders think there is a negative trend in the way employees behave in recent years — too much entitlement, not enough loyalty, no work ethic, only interested in themselves, and on and on. Do you consider these to be negative trends? Why?

UNIT 7
Business Crisis

1. **Discuss the following questions with your partner.**

   1) Whether you're the owner of a small, local bakery, the manager of a mid-sized call center or president of a large public company, you have one thing in common: You may face a crisis situation. If your business were confronted with the following scenarios, how would you deal with them? Who would you call? What would you say to the newspaper when they called asking for comment? How would you talk with your employees?

   - A gunman enters your retail location and takes the manager and one customer hostage.
   - The local television crew arrives at your business and alleges that your cupcakes sickened an entire kindergarten class.
   - An ex-employee pickets outside your busiest retail location holding a sign that claims your business discriminates against senior citizens.
   - A computer with hundreds of customers' credit card numbers and contact information is stolen from your headquarters.
   - ...

   2) Some expert characterizes most business crises as one of two types: a sudden crisis or a smoldering crisis:

   A sudden crisis is defined as a disruption in the company's business that occurs without warning and is likely to generate new coverage. A Smoldering crisis, meanwhile, is defined as any serious business problem that is not generally known within or without the company, which may generate negative news coverage if or when it goes "public" and could result in a large sum of money in fines, penalties, legal damage awards, unbudgeted expenses, and other costs.

   Try to give some examples of the two types of crises respectively:

Sudden Crises	Smoldering Crises

2. Certain themes arise repeatedly in dealing with organizations that are deciding how far to go in anticipating and managing crises. Too often, faulty assumptions are made about the processes and resources required to manage and communicate the crises. The following are the most common myths about how people look at crises. Work with your group members and discuss why they are taken as myths.

   a. Crises occur only during working hours.

   b. Saying nothing to the media means there's no story.

   c. In a crisis, customers are the only audience that matters.

   d. A crisis always poses a threat — and only a threat.

   e. A crisis manual is all that's required to get the basic procedures clear and in place.

   f. Crisis preparation training is expensive, with no guarantee of return on investment.

   g. A competitor affected by a crisis is good news for my business.

   h. Any publicity is good publicity.

   i. Everyone's a potential enemy when a crisis strikes.

Preview: Crises appear often when they are least expected. The following article gives a warning to business people: when a business is in its prime, they should take precaution against possible dangers. It's natural that people may be so satisfied with success that they turn a blind eye to the hidden crisis. The author himself is of no exception: when he chaired a promising company, the neglect of relevant laws resulted in great loss and nearly the collapse of the company. Fortunately, the company recovered from the financial crisis, thanks to good management. The author drew a lesson from this crisis that good leadership includes skill in handling crises. Still, crisis prevention is the best strategy.

Why Good Times Are the Most Dangerous

*It's easy to get too comfortable, which leaves you unprepared when disaster strikes. That's why the best leaders are always a bit **paranoid**.*

By Keith McFarland

[1] Though managing in tough times can test a leader's **mettle**, the bigger test

often comes when times are good. A crisis, if well-managed, can bring out the best in a company — increasing focus, **intensity**, and commitment. It's when a business gets a comfortable lead that the greatest dangers **lurk: Complacency** creeps in on little cat feet.

[2] When I was in my mid-30s, I became chairman of a promising Los Angeles-based technology company. The business had doubled revenues every year except one for 15 straight years, growing into a national company with 3,500 clients. It had twice made the *Inc. 500*[1] and had even been featured on Inc's cover. We were about to close on some badly-needed venture capital to prepare us for an IPO[2], and we had just inked **alliances** with Mellon Bank[3] and EDS[4]. Times were indeed good, or so we thought.

[3] Then the bottom fell out. One February morning, our CEO handed me a letter from the Business Software Alliance (BSA)[5], the organization empowered by major software companies like Microsoft[6] and Symantec[7] to **prosecute** companies that illegally copy and use their software.

[4] As I scanned the letter, my eyes fell on the words "federal criminal action **pursuant**...fine of up to $250,000 and **imprisonment** of up to five years." They wanted $2 million dollars to settle the **suit** — a fact sure to send our new investors running for the hills. (I later discovered that a few of our employees had, in fact, winked at software-licensing laws.)

[5] Somehow we held the new investor group together while we negotiated a settlement with the BSA — and closed our multi-million dollar funding just before we ran out of cash.

[6] Within weeks of closing our funding, things went from bad to worse. Our largest client, responsible for several million dollars of annual revenue, went into a financial **tailspin**, and we began burning hundreds of thousands of dollars of cash a month. Thirty days later, our bank called in our loans (more than $2 million) and threatened to **sue** us if we didn't pay immediately. And all this bad news wasn't lost on our new investors, who had watched two-thirds of their investment **evaporate** in 90 days. They began to use the word "**attorney**" in our calls with them.

---

1 *Inc. 500*　美国私营企业 500 强
2 IPO Initial Public Offering　首次公开发行股票
3 Mellon Bank　美国梅隆银行，全球领先的资产服务商
4 EDS Electronic Data Systems　电子资讯系统，美国一个全球信息技术服务公司
5 Business Software Alliance (BSA)　美国商业软件联盟
6 Microsoft　美国微软公司，财富 500 强公司之一，总部所在地美国，主要经营软件数据服务
7 Symantec / sɪˈmæntɪk/　美国著名软件公司

[7] Fearing that our company would end up fighting for its survival in court, I booked rooms at a local hotel for our top five executives and hired a **facilitator** to lead us through a discussion of our options. Three **brutal** days of shouting, blaming, and denying ended with the decision to reorganize: I stepped into the CEO role and our former CEO became chairman and focused on trying to replace the lost revenue. We presented the plan at the next board meeting — and the board gave me 90 days to turn the company around.

[8] We spent the better part of two years fighting our way back to financial health. The emotional costs were high: Over a six-month period, we were forced to reduce head count from 300 to 90, and to replace or move to different positions eight of the top 11 executives. But it was worth it. In the four years following the turnaround, the company would grow to more than 2,000 employees.

[9] This experience remains both the high point and the low point of my business career. It was the low point because I had to face the fact that our executive team had become **arrogant** and **complacent**, a fact which resulted in 200 lost jobs, and which required the remaining employees to work day and night to save the company.

[10] It was a high point because I learned over the course of a few months perhaps the most important lesson of leadership: When it counts, people and organizations are capable of far more than we normally imagine. Anyone who has ever successfully navigated a business crisis knows that given good leadership, people rise to the challenge.

[11] For most leaders, the hard part isn't managing a crisis; it's **tapping** that extraordinary **latent** potential between crises, when things are going well. Many of the problems our company encountered could have been avoided entirely, and others could have been more easily handled if we had been willing to question ourselves during the good times.

[12] With the survival of our company at stake, we could no longer avoid the issues which had seemed too sensitive or **intractable** to **confront**. And perhaps most importantly, people in middle management and on the front line started talking openly and **aggressively** about their views of the company's strategy — contributing many valuable **insights**.

[13] We sold the company a couple of years after the turnaround. I decided that never again would I allow a company I was leading to let its guard down during the good times. Since then, I have tried to build some **paranoia** into every business I have run or advised, tried to keep it a little off-balance, hoped to keep it alert as its key assumptions inevitably pass from reliable to dangerously outdated.

65   [14] It seems to me that every company will have to deal with its crises one way or the other: either every day in small preventive **doses**, or every few years in painful, **wrenching collisions** with a changed reality. The former is far preferable.

(931 words)
From *Business Week*

New Words

paranoid /ˈpærənɔɪd/
a. unreasonably or obsessively anxious, suspicious or mistrustful 多疑的

mettle /ˈmet(ə)l/
n. quality of endurance and courage; spirit 忍耐力；勇气；精神

intensity /ɪnˈtensətɪ/
n. exceptionally great concentration; power, or force; strength or depth of feeling 特别强烈的程度、力量或动力；（感情的）强度

lurk /lɜːk/
v. keep out of view, lying in wait or ready to attack 潜伏；埋伏

complacency /kəmˈpleɪsnsɪ/
n. self-satisfaction; quiet contentment 自满；得意

alliance /əˈlaɪəns/
n. a union or an association formed for mutual benefit 联盟；联合

prosecute /ˈprɒsɪkjuːt/
v. institute legal processing against... 起诉；告发

pursuant /pəˈsjuːənt/
a. proceeding from and conformable to; in accordance with 出自并依据……的；与……一致的；依照的

imprisonment /ɪmˈprɪznmənt/
n. the state of being put or kept in a prison 关押；入狱

suit /sjuːt/ (= lawsuit)
n. a claim or dispute brought to a law court for adjudication 诉讼（尤指非刑事案件）

tailspin /ˈteɪlˌspɪn/
n. a state or situation characterized by chaos; panic or loss of control (referred originally to airplanes falling out of control) 混乱；失控状态

sue /sjuː, suː/
v. begin legal proceeding against... 控告；起诉

evaporate /ɪˈvæpəreɪt/
v. cease to exist; disappear 蒸发；消失

attorney /əˈtɜːnɪ/
n. a lawyer appointed to act for another in business or legal matters 代理人；律师

facilitator /fəˈsɪlɪteɪtə/
n. a helper; a person or a thing that makes (an action or process) easy or easier 援助；援手

brutal /ˈbruːtl/
a. extremely violent; not pleasant and not sensitive to people's feelings 激烈的；残酷的；令人不快又无可否认的

arrogant /ˈærəgənt/
a. having or revealing an exaggerated sense of one's importance or abilities 傲慢的；自大的

complacent /kəmˈpleɪsnt/
a. showing uncritical satisfaction with oneself or one's achievements 自满的，得意的

tap /tæp/
v. use or take what is needed from something such as an energy supply or an amount of money; extract or obtain (sth.) from sth./sb. 发掘，开发；自某物／某人处引出或获取（某物）

latent /ˈleɪtənt/
a. hidden, concealed; inactive 潜在的；潜伏的，隐藏的

intractable /ɪnˈtræktəbl/
a. hard to control or deal with 难处理的

UNIT 7 Business Crisis

confront /kənˈfrʌnt/
v. face up to and deal with (a problem or difficult situation) 面对；面临

aggressively /əˈgresɪvlɪ/
ad. forcefully; self-assertively 强有力的；坚持己见的

insight /ˈɪnsaɪt/
n. a sudden clear understanding of something or part of something, especially a complicated situation or idea（对复杂事情的）顿悟，猛醒

paranoia /ˌpærəˈnɔɪə/
n. suspicion or mistrust of people or their actions without evidence or justification 多疑

dose /dəʊs/
n. an amount, especially a quantity of medicine or drug taken or recommended to be taken 剂量

wrench /rentʃ/
v. pull or twist suddenly and violently 猛扭；猛推

collision /kəˈlɪʒən/
n. an instance of one moving object striking violently against another 碰撞；冲突

Phrases & Expressions

bring out
produce sth.; cause to develop; cause to be seen 生产某物；使发挥；使显露

creep in
come in slowly and quietly 慢慢地或无声地进入

venture capital
capital invested in a project in which there is a substantial element of risk, typically a new or expanding business 风险投资

ink... with
sign (a contract) with... 与……签约

wink at
pretend not to notice (sth. bad or illegal) 假装看不见

call in a loan
require someone to pay back borrowed money 讨还借款

be lost on
fail to influence or be noticed or appreciated by sb. 不产生效果；不为注意

step into
start doing something, or become involved in a situation 开始做某事

fight one's way
move forward with difficulty 努力前进，克服困难前进

rise to the challenge
prove oneself able to deal with an unexpected situation, problem, etc. 有随机应变、克服困难、完成任务等的能力

let your guard down
become less cautious, relax and stop worrying about what might happen or what someone might find out 放松警惕

one way or the other
whatever method is used 不是用这种方法就是用那种方法

Exercises

Comprehension

1. Answer the following content questions with your partner.

   1) Why does the author warn managers that crises will likely to happen when companies run well?
   2) According to the article, what are the two usual attitudes toward crises? Which is favored by the author?
   3) In which way does the author consider the crisis is a high point in his business career?
   4) What kind of crisis did the author's company meet? Was it severe or not? Why?
   5) How did the author lead his team to deal with the crisis? Was it a smooth process?
   6) What did the author learn from the crisis they met and how did it influence his further management?
   7) For what reason should the employees on the front line be involved in decision making?
   8) In spite of the obvious danger to the companies, what is the good point of well-managed crises?

2. Do the following exercises and compare your answers with your partner's.

   The following are the main ideas mentioned in the passage with some points unfinished. And they are not arranged in the same order as they appear in the passage. Fill in the blanks and rearrange them properly.

   > a. In every company he managed or advised, he would introduce a system to _____.
   >
   > b. Once a national fast growing private company, the author's company met a crisis when it was _____. To make things worse, _____ and it ran out of money.
   >
   > c. The good way to deal with a crisis is to _____ instead of _____.
   >
   > d. This crisis, though painful, teaches the author a good lesson: _____.
   >
   > e. In order to deal with this crisis, the management decided to _____ and _____ after three-day brutal discussion.
   >
   > f. The crisis is most likely to creep in when _____.
   >
   > The correct order: ☐→☐→☐→☐→☐→☐

Critical Thinking

Work in group to discuss the following questions.

1) When an unforeseen crisis bruises your business, you can either sink or swim, depending on how you communicate with customers and employees. The following are some steps of communication before, during and after a crisis. Discuss with your group members and put them under the proper heading. Some may go under more than one heading.

   a. *Quickly and cautiously communicate with your employees and customers, as well as the community.*

   b. *Assemble a group of employees, if appropriate, to be part of a crisis team.*

   c. *Create a plan for how you would handle a variety of business crises, such as theft, fire, key employee illness or death, loss of a primary supplier or regional catastrophe.*

   d. *Talk with others in your industry about how they handle certain business crises.*

   e. *Maintain contact with media, if appropriate.*

   f. *Appoint a spokesperson to communicate with the media. Be clear and consistent with your message.*

   g. *Communicate about the crisis in as many ways as possible — print, telephone, radio, television or mailings. Focus on any positive outcomes.*

   h. *Work at building a positive relationship with the community and customers, in case you need their support in the future.*

   i. *Put together a plan to rebuild your positive reputation in the community.*

   j. *Regain trust from customers, make good customer service a priority.*

   k. *Put your plan into action — hesitancy and delay will spur rumors and increase anxiety and despair.*

Before a crisis	During the crisis	After the crisis

2) For the majority of companies that have confronted a crisis, the most nerve-wracking aspect of the crisis, other than the event itself, is dealing with the press. The media will pounce on a crisis, so many companies hide behind the shield of "No comment" during a crisis. Do you think it the right thing to do? What is the best strategy to deal with the press?

Vocabulary

1. Use expressions from the text to correct some parts of the following sentences, and then give definitions of the correct expressions.

   1) The company has to deal with its financial crisis one way or around: either to reduce the staff or to cut down their salary.

      correct form: _____ definition: _____

   2) Our company aims to link with the world-famous software company for the exclusive right of its internal net system.

      correct form: _____ definition: _____

   3) Most financial institutions are trying to call for the debt of badly managed companies to prevent great loss.

      correct form: _____ definition: _____

   4) Crises, though difficult to deal with, can bring up the best performance of the employees and promote the development of the company.

      correct form: _____ definition: _____

   5) The bottom fell down of the rubber market when the leading companies declared to cut down prices to 70%.

      correct form: _____ definition: _____

   6) There is a severe punishment in this firm for those who blink at safety regulation.

      correct form: _____ definition: _____

   7) Any complaints among the staff should not be discarded in the management, and dealt with quickly as soon as possible.

      correct form: _____ definition: _____

   8) The newly-founded institutions are trying to struggle their way to rank in *Inc.* 500.

UNIT **7** Business Crisis

   correct form: _____   definition: _____

9) With his 20-year experiences in sales and marketing, Dickson was finally able to serve the role of CEO.

   correct form: _____   definition: _____

10) The threats from overseas competitors have slipped in before many local companies realize them.

   correct form: _____   definition: _____

2. **Complete each sentence with the correct form of the words in capital letters above them.**

   1) INTENSITY

      The plan made by consulting firm aims to _____ commitment to the company so as to raise work efficiency.

   2) COLLISION

      Before the company _____ with the reality, the management should be sensitive enough to update its key assumption.

   3) PARANOIA

      It is a common sense that a good CEO should be always _____ to keep the company from running into crisis.

   4) ALLIANCE

      It is a good idea for the two big companies to _____ in the international market but in fact it is quite difficult to handle.

   5) FACILITATOR

      Though the computer systems have _____ the office work, they have also set barrier in interpersonal communication in workplace.

   6) IMPRISONMENT

      Some workers complained that they were treated like _____ working in a stuffing factory.

   7) ARROGANT

      Irritated by his _____, the local staff wrote to the headquarters, asking the board to transfer him to another company.

   8) COMPLACENT

      This severe problem could have been avoided, but unfortunately, people were

173

indulged in _____ at that time.

9) AGGRESSIVELY

It is a common sense that the _____ in communication usually leads to the breakup of the negotiation.

10) INTRACTABLE

Despite the enormous constraints of a global company, despite the general _____ of life, I need to find new ways to push the limits of business, to make it a force for positive change.

3. **Make collocations connected with business by choosing one word from Column A and another one from Column B. Match each expression with the appropriate definition. Use each word once. The first one has been done for you.**

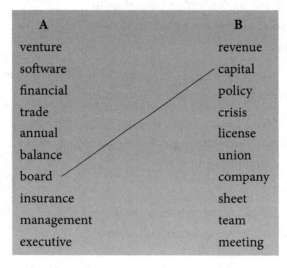

A	B
venture	revenue
software	capital
financial	policy
trade	crisis
annual	license
balance	union
board	company
insurance	sheet
management	team
executive	meeting

1) a document detailing the terms and conditions of a contract of insurance

   insurance policy

   _____

2) a company which is set up to manage a group of properties, a unit trust, and investment fund

   _____

3) the total income of a company or organization and of a substantial nature in each year

   _____

4) group in business or commercial organization with administrative or

managerial powers

5) a conference which the board of directors of company or organization should take part in

6) capital invested in a project in which there is a substantial element of risk, typically a new or expanding business

7) an organization association of workers in a profession, formed to protect and further their rights and interests

8) a statement of the assets, liabilities, and capital of a business at a particular point in time, detailing the balance of income and expenditure over the preceding period

9) a permit from an authority to own or use software

10) a time of intense difficulty or danger in finance

Translation

1. Translate the following paragraphs into Chinese.

   Though managing in tough times can test a leader's mettle, the bigger test often comes when times are good. A crisis, if well-managed, can bring out the best in a company — increasing focus, intensity, and commitment. It's when a business gets a comfortable lead that the greatest dangers lurk: Complacency creeps in on little cat feet.

   It was a high point because I learned over the course of a few months perhaps the most important lesson of leadership: When it counts, people and organizations are capable of far more than we normally imagine. Anyone who has ever successfully navigated a business crisis knows that given good leadership, people rise to the challenge.

2. Put the following passage into English, using the words and phrases given in the box.

| tailspin | evaporate | fall out | latent | ink...with |
| paranoid | venture capital | wink at | confront | creep in |

风险投资的管理者必须保持一点儿多疑的态度，因为管理好上百万元的资金绝不是件容易的事：一个小小的错误就可能会引起巨大的损失。如何选择投资对象、获得稳定的收益确实是他们面临的巨大问题。一些公司为了获得他们急需的投资，无视相关法律，擅自伪造文件、修改账目。因此，风险投资的管理者在签约前需要对有关公司进行深入调查，尽可能排除某些潜在的风险。有时当市场出现暴跌的局面时，投资方的上百万资金可能会在一夜之间消失。在这种情况下，其公司的财务也可能会发生混乱，危机会悄悄地降临。

Handling a PR Crisis

A crisis is a significant business disruption that stimulates extensive news media coverage. The resulting public scrutiny will affect the organization's normal operations. Crises come in all shapes and sizes, from national crises that impact all types of organizations to industry-specific crises. Whatever the type, the way in which you manage a crisis can have a long-lasting effect on your business. Look at the following PR crisis happened to a famous restaurant of the United States and do the tasks in groups.

> On Jan. 23rd, Karen Putz, a hearing-impaired mother of three hearing-impaired children, decided to visit the local steak and shake drive-thru for a milkshake for herself and her 10-year-old son. Since she is unable to use the intercom system, she drove to the payment window to both order and pay. Unbelievably poor customer service then ensued. The end result was that Karen, in front of her 10-year-old son, was denied the opportunity to purchase the milkshakes and was then threatened with police action if she didn't leave the drive-thru immediately.

UNIT 7 Business Crisis

> In the old world of public relations, this event would have gone unnoticed except for Karen's close friends and family. In fact, incidents like this happen every day and for the most part, do go unnoticed by the world at large. But this is the 21st century, and Karen has a blog, in which a Deaf Mom Shares Her World. So that afternoon, she didn't just call her friends and family to complain about the poor service — she wrote a post on her blog.
>
> The next day, she itemized over 80 blogs that had picked up her story. The story was also picked up that night by ABC News and Fox News. Today, approximately three weeks after it happened there are almost 1000 hits on Google when typing in the search words, "Steak and Shake" and "Deaf Mom".
>
> More than that, this story appears in positions #3 through #9 on the front page of Google when searching on the terms "Steak and Shake". Currently, the Steak and Shake site itself holds positions #1 and #2, but if this continues, how long will that last?

Task one: Discuss the following questions about the incident.

- *What might be the reasons for this incident?*
- *Should Steak and Shake attempt to post comments on the blogs that are writing about the story? Why or why not?*
- *Are the deaf mom and her kids better off ignoring bloggers and focusing on traditional methods of reparation? Why or why not?*
- *Is there a third alternative they could try? If yes, what is it?*
- *Without corrective PR action, will the "Steak and Shake incident" develop a legendary status that continues to live on in the blogosphere long after Steak and Shake has revamped its communication equipment?*
- *What lesson should Steak and Shake learn from the incident?*

Task two: Role-play the following situation.

> Steak and Shake responded almost immediately to Karen's complaint and agreed to set up a meeting to hear her concerns. They followed through and met with Karen to discuss the incident and how they can take action to better serve individuals with disabilities in the future. While Karen has continued to update her blog with the progress of her complaint, including the follow-up actions that Steak and Shake has done, most blogs only reference the initial incident, which has seriously tarnished the image of the restaurant. So they are holding a press conference to defend their company.

For executives:

- *To discuss what actions you will take to handle the situation;*
- *To predict what questions the journalists will ask and prepare answers to them;*
- *To explain to the journalists what you are doing to deal with the crisis;*
- *To handle the journalists' questions;*
- *...*

For journalists:

- *To discuss what questions you would like to ask the executives;*
- *To ask probing questions so that you have the true facts about the crisis and find out how the restaurant is dealing with it;*
- *To ask "follow up" questions if you are not satisfied with the answers you've got;*
- *To ask about any information necessary for you to write a powerful and accurate article;*
- *...*

Language Hints

Getting the fact
- Could you give me some details please?
- Something else I'd like to know is...
- Sorry to keep after you, but could you tell me...
- I should be interested to know the fact.
- ...

Giving reasons
- Let me explain. You see, the matter...
- It is like this. You see, there is...
- I believe John is fully justified in saying...
- I think the result warrants that...
- I think there is actually a good case for...
- ...

Reproaching
- I don't know how they could...
- I felt so ashamed of their...
- There is no way to treat a customer.
- I don't think they should forget their responsibility.
- I think it's shocking the way they...
- ...

Making a judgment
- Judging by his words, he must...
- There must be something wrong with...
- Kind of sounds that way.
- It would seem that...
- So far as I can judge, the matter...
- ...

UNIT **7** Business Crisis

Routine Report

Business reports play a crucial role in business practice as most major or decisive actions are based on them. The types of business reports vary with their wide range of functions. Generally speaking, there are three types: Routine Report, Investigation Report, and Feasibility Report.

An ordinary routine report is usually written in a memo form, and is developed in the following ways:

- starting with a summary of the latest development as an instruction;
- presenting the major problem as an illustration;
- discussing the problem presented;
- drawing a conclusion based on the discussion;
- giving recommendation or evaluation if there is any.

Some tips on writing routine report are as follows:

- Use simple tenses.
- Avoid long sentences with hundreds of commas, semicolons and exclamation points.
- Stick to the facts that are available to the reader.
- Give a brief introduction, but a thorough discussion of the context of the problem.
- Don't begin your introduction with a sentence that is either too broad, or too narrow. Be specific.
- Write a conclusion in a brief, concise manner, for your readers are already familiar with everything you talk about.
- Give a numbered list of recommendations if there are any. It gives a quick access to your ideas.
- Don't forget to go back for final revision.

Study the following sample and then do the exercise according to the directions.

To: Kim Jyun Shen, General Director
From: Daisy Steven, Personnel Director
Date: December 28, 2008
Subject: Slimming-down on the Head Office

Introduction

From March to June, with the instruction of the board, we made a slimming-down on the head office in Seattle. The report is on the slimming-down and our recommendations for future alike action.

Illustration

A slow market had led to 3 overseas plants and 1 home branch closed since last December, so the redundancy occurred in the head office in Seattle, as the management team seemed too big with the shrunk production team.

But it would result in the dispute with the Union. After several attempts of negotiation, a solution was made in September that the redundant staffs were to be rearranged in different ways as their pensions and developments could be taken into broadest consideration.

Solution

- Those (seven) aged above 55 were retired with a sum of pension ($ 6,600 per year in the company's service) paid as compensation.
- Those aged between 45 and 54 were sent to take a 5-week training course of new system of management. After finishing the course a test was made and the first 24 (35 all together took the test) were sent to plants to strengthen the management. The rest nine quitted the job with three months salary.

Conclusion

The slimming-down cost time and money, but it is worthy. With the help of the Union, it could be done without too much conflict. It also made staff realize that regular training courses are very important and they are now very eager to take some courses part time.

Recommendation

Such action concerned with the staff's interest needs consultation with the Union beforehand.

1. Look at the case again in "Handling a PR Crisis". You are Anderson, the PR manager of Steak and Shake. Write a report to Mr. Williams, the general manager, telling what the crisis is, how you handle it and what your company should do to avoid such incidents in the future.

2. You are Jeffery Kahn, a Sales Director of WHL Company. Please write a routine report to George Miller, General Director, about drop on the first quarterly sales with the given information. Remember to make some recommendations based on your discussion about the problem.

> WHL Company, produces and sells water heating units mainly in the North, West and Central regions. Due to the global warming weather and the pressing market competition, the sales of the first quarter this year dropped 24% compared with those at the same period last year, which is shown as follows:
>
> | Region | Goal Sales | Actual Sales |
> | --- | --- | --- |
> | The North | 3.4 m. | 2.1 m. |
> | The West | 3.6 m. | 3.2 m. |
> | The Central | 4.7 m. | 3.5 m. |
>
> Nevertheless, the company's products still have a good share because of the established clients and distributors. So it is possible for the company to survive the overstressing market competition as long as it could provide strong support and better after-sales service. But to adjust the global warming trend, the company should shift its products to more types.

Business Expressions

1. In the following boxes there are four words: crisis, emergency, damage, and risk. Match them respectively with the appropriate words in the word bank below, adding "of" or "to" if necessary. Use each word in the word bank once. Then translate the expressions into Chinese.

```
   crisis        emergency        damage        risk
```

confidence property debt adjustment premium amortization stock downside fund decisions atmosphere bearer claim exposure export clause rate capital suit man

1) _____   2) _____
3) _____   4) _____
5) _____   6) _____
7) _____   8) _____
9) _____   10) _____
11) _____   12) _____
13) _____   14) _____
15) _____   16) _____
17) _____   18) _____
19) _____   20) _____

2. In each set of words below, one is different from the others. Find out the different one.

1) A. monopoly   B. outsourcing   C. dominance   D. oligopoly
2) A. breakages   B. sabotage   C. vandal   D. violation
3) A. downsizing   B. streamlining   C. recruitment   D. layoff
4) A. surplus   B. excess   C. surfeit   D. deficit
5) A. aggravation   B. stagflation   C. deflation   D. inflation
6) A. boom   B. recession   C. depression   D. restructuring
7) A. disaster   B. calamity   C. catastrophe   D. fluctuation
8) A. administration   B. takeover   C. merger   D. acquisition
9) A. cyber attack   B. utility outage   C. hacker   D. terrorism
10) A. resilience   B. recovery   C. resuscitation   D. reconstruction
11) A. omen   B. tocsin   C. alert   D. warning
12) A. mitigation   B. lightening   C. saturation   D. relief
13) A. hazard   B. fright   C. threat   D. peril
14) A. disturbance   B. conflict   C. riot   D. interruption

UNIT 7 Business Crisis

3. **Complete the following sentences with the appropriate expressions from the box below.**

smoldering crises	sudden crisis	business fortunes
proactive communication	crisis manager	product recalls
corporate crises	emergency preparedness	customer allegations
extreme events	business continuity	sources of vulnerability

1) Emergency management, _____, and disaster services encompass mitigation, preparedness, response, and recovery related to any kind of disaster, whether natural, technological, or national security.

2) _____ can take the form of plant fires, loss of competitive secrets, workplace violence, product defects, embezzlement and extortion, industrial accidents, sabotage, and natural disasters.

3) We define a _____ as a disruption in the company's business that occurs without warning and is likely to generate new coverage.

4) Ensuring _____ requires a proactive process of identifying essential business functions within an organization and threats to those functions.

5) _____ are defined as any serious business problem that is not generally known within or without the company.

6) High-profile public relations disasters such as various _____, disturbing product tampering incidents have thrown an intense spotlight on the issue of crisis management.

7) As poor crisis management can wreak on _____, a growing percentage of firms have intensified their efforts to put effective crisis management strategies in place.

8) By developing public-private partnerships to deal with interdependencies associated with _____, one should be able to provide substantial benefits to the affected individuals and firms as well as improving the social welfare.

9) Examples of smoldering business crises include indications of significant regulatory action, government investigations, _____, and media investigations.

10) Small businesses can be prepared in the event of a crisis by performing an assessment to determine their most likely _____.

11) When a crisis does erupt, prompt and _____ should be a cornerstone

of any business's crisis containment strategy.

12) Facing crises, a company may employ a risk or _____ who may prepare statistical models, review industry data, or work with consultants to understand how one or more crises could impact the organization.

Specialized Reading

1. Read the passage carefully and then fill in the numbered blanks with the appropriate expressions listed below.

consistent messages	crisis response	maintaining control
course of action	specific messages	natural response
industry-specific crises	early response	flow of information
contact information	the hint of a crisis	precipitate a crisis
the face and voice	manage a crisis	a single spokesperson
newswire service	a central location	a unified internal team
potential crises	full-blown crisis	crisis situations
news coverage	monitoring services	board of directors

Crises come in all shapes and sizes, from national crises that impact all types of organizations to 1) _____. Whatever the type, the way in which you 2) _____ can have a long-lasting effect on your business. Actually, you can anticipate far more than you think. A little forethought and planning can make even the worst crisis more manageable and improve your chances of successful recovery. The key is 3) _____.

Long before a crisis ever occurs there are several steps you can take to ensure that you're ready to react at a moment's notice. To start, establish a crisis communication team. The team will be responsible for creating and executing the 4) _____ and managing the situation as it unfolds. All planning and communications — internal and external — should be dictated by the team. Having 5) _____ is essential to maintaining control, which if lost, is difficult to recover.

Equally important to having a unified team is having 6) _____. While it's difficult to predict how to respond to a crisis that has yet to occur, it's possible to anticipate 7) _____ based on one's business and industry. Focus on known issues that could 8) _____ for your business or organization and create a written document that contains scenarios for 8 to 10 potential crises. Map these scenarios to action steps and 9) _____, and identify who on your team's responsible for executing and delivering each.

Lastly, prepare a communication list of reporters, investors, customers, business partners, advisors, employees, third-party experts, community leaders and anyone else who should be notified during a crisis. Have this list in an easily accessible database, along with 10) _____ for your internal crisis team members, for immediate reference.

When a crisis occurs, the first step is to admit to yourself you've got a problem. It's a 11) _____ to flee during times of distress, but this type of reaction will guarantee doom. Ignoring a problem in the hope that it'll "blow over" will only fuel the fire and increase the chances of a 12) _____. No matter the size or scope of a crisis, it's wise to respond as quickly and as directly as possible.

Gather your crisis team and immediately review your database of scenarios and messages, determining the best 13) _____ based upon the pre-planning you've done. Even if you don't have all the information at hand, you must determine an 14) _____ and communicate it immediately, even if it's only to acknowledge that you're aware of the situation and are investigating it.

Also important to managing a crisis is controlling the 15) _____. This can be achieved by implementing two measures. First, establish a single spokesperson for your business, even if it's you yourself. The spokesperson will be 16) _____ of the organization throughout the crisis, whether talking to the press or internal staff. Having 17) _____ should ensure that the tone and content of what's said is consistent.

A second measure for controlling the flow of information is establishing a central location for news. An organization's website is ideal for this. In fact, well before 18) _____, it's wise for an organization to consider establishing "dark pages" that are engineered specifically for 19) _____ and can be turned on at a moment's notice. Dark pages should initially contain basic information about the company and how it responds to a crisis, such as where to go for updates, key contact information, etc.

Once you've established 20) _____ for communications, you must then consider how, when and to whom you will communicate, based upon the actual circumstances. An important tool in this effort is your 21) _____. Newswires allow for efficient dissemination of news releases and corporate information via wire, fax and e-mail, and ensure that such content reaches all necessary media, investors and public audiences.

While newswires are known mostly for transmitting text-based information, many also offer the ability to create and distribute audio and video messages. During a crisis, using video is an excellent means for a CEO to "personally" communicate with his/her stakeholders, including the 22) _____, at-large executives, customers, business partners and community leaders. Putting a face and voice to a message adds greatly to its impact.

Lastly, many newswire services offer businesses the ability to track 23) _____. In a crisis, it's imperative for a company to be informed about what's being reported in the media and the blogosphere. While it's possible to use the search engines and other resources to track news, doing it without the aid of a monitoring service is daunting, and can result in missed coverage. Therefore, it's recommended that a company consult with its newswire to see what 24) _____ are available.

2. **Read the following passage about small business dealing with its crisis management and then translate the underlined sentences into Chinese.**

"A good image is a terrible thing to lose!" noted Bill Patterson in Public Relations Journal. "It has been said that 30 years of hard work can be destroyed in just 30 seconds." 1) This grim truth is especially evident among small businesses that are rocked by crises, since they are less likely to have the deep financial pockets to weather unpleasant public relations developments. After all, business crises often throw multiple financial blows at companies. 2) Diminished sales as a result of unfavorable publicity, boycotts, etc. are the most widely recognized of these blows, but others can have a significant cumulative impact as well. Added expenses often come knocking in the areas of increased insurance premiums, recall/collection programs, reimbursements, attorneys' fees, and the need to retrieve lost customers through additional advertising.

3) But business consultants and public relations professionals agree that small business enterprises can do a lot to minimize the damage done by sudden flare-ups of bad news, provided they adhere to several fundamental rules of behavior.

Small businesses that are faced with public relations crises are far more likely to escape relatively unscathed if they can bring two weapons to bear: (1) a solid record as a good citizen, and (2) an already established crisis management strategy.

"Before the crisis, it is important to build good will and good relations on a daily basis," said media consultant Virgil Scudder in an interview with Communication World. "The way you are treated in a crisis, by the media and the public, will be determined in part by what they think of you at the beginning of the crisis situation." Writing in Public Relations Journal, Bill Patterson offered a similar assessment of the importance of building a "reservoir of good will" in the community: 4) <u>"The most important rule in defending, preserving, or enhancing a reputation is that you work at it all year long, regardless of whether or not a crisis strikes."</u>

5) <u>The other vital component of crisis management preparation is the creation of an intelligent and forceful strategy for dealing with various crises if they do occur.</u> "For many executives, a crisis is something that happens to someone else," wrote Patterson. "It is a distant thought that can quickly be relegated to the back of the mind, replaced by concern for profit and productivity." But business owners and managers who choose to put off assembling a CMP (Crisis Management Plan) do so at significant risk. Indeed, the hours and days immediately following the eruption of a crisis are often the most important in shaping public perception of the event. A company that has a good CMP in hand is far more likely to make good use of this time than one that is forced into a pattern of response by on-the-spot improvisation, or one that offers little response at all in the hopes that the whole mess will just go away.

1) _____

2) _____

3) _____

4) _____

5) _____

3. **Discuss the following questions with your group members.**

   1) What are the important things we should consider when crises do occur?
   2) What positive effects can a crisis have on a business if the crisis is handled successfully?

UNIT 8
Business Ethics

1. **Discuss the questions below with your partner.**

   1) What do you think contribute to good corporate reputation?

   2) According to a Millennium Poll on Corporate Social Responsibility:
      - 90 per cent of respondents believe that companies should focus on more than profitability;
      - 60 per cent said that they form an impression of a company based on its social responsibility;
      - 40 per cent responded negatively to or said they talked negatively about companies that they perceived as not being socially responsible.

      Which of the above do you belong to? Justify your answers.

   3) If businesses exist to be profitable, what benefit does ethics offer to business leaders? To what degree is ethical behavior profitable?

   4) If business ethics isn't as strong as it should be, what's the reason for the problem? Who should be responsible for delivering the improvements? And how should it be done?

2. **Work with your group members on the following questions.**

   The following are the business ethics scenarios happening in organizations almost every day. How do you look at them? Do you think they conform to the basic rules of society? why do you think so? What other cases can you add to the list?

   - Bribing the important officials in order to win a contract.
   - Spying on competitors' R&D information or bribing their employees.
   - Surfing the Internet shopping for personal items on company time.
   - Sharing important company information with a competitor for potential gain.
   - Misrepresenting the quality or functionality of an advertised sale item.
   - Taking office supplies home to stock one's home office.
   - A finance officer accounts questionably for purchases and expenditures.
   - ...
   - ...
   - ...

Preview: Business ethics, a system of moral principles applied in the commercial world, provide guidelines for acceptable behavior by organizations in both their strategy formulation and day-to-day operations. An ethical approach is becoming necessary both for corporate success and a positive corporate image. In the following passage, the author, based on his personal experience, has explained the important role of business ethics in the management and daily operation of business. Business ethics, in his point of view, can enhance the loyalty and morale among employees. The author fell in a dilemma of profits or ethics, but he finally chose ethics over profit and succeeded in leading his company over many crises. He believes that if a company wants to keep the momentum in the long run, the management should stick to the basic moral principle and set moral standards for all the staff.

Integrating Ethics at the Core

Building your company on an ethical basis isn't easy. But staying true to your principles will make you stronger in the long run.

By Vivek Wadhwa

[1] Entrepreneurship is a **fascinating** journey along **treacherous** paths. You'll find tough choices at every **juncture**. And while business decisions usually have clear consequences and **outcomes**, ethical decisions are always hard. Making the right choice doesn't necessarily make success, but ethical **lapses** almost always lead to failure.

[2] I've learned that no matter what the consequence, doing what's ethical and right is always the best long-term strategy. So business leaders must be proactive in setting and enforcing ethical standards and values for their companies.

[3] When I look back at the first half of my career, I realize how naive I was about the business world. I used to believe that corruption was only a Third-World ill. Having worked for top American corporations and a technology startup in which ethics and **integrity** were values we lived by, I had no reason to think differently.

[4] Then I became a tech CEO and got to see the world from a different point of view. I once needed to negotiate a distribution deal with a company that controlled market access to my products. The company's CEO demanded that I give his **spouse** partial **ownership** of my business in return for his support. Making the stock gift would lead to millions. Not making it would **forfeit** the business opportunity.

[5] I was totally **dumbfounded**. In other parts of the world, things like this are

common business practice, but we were in America — and I was dealing with a public company. After extensive **soul-searching**, I decided that I would rather **sink** my new startup than compromise my values.

[6] I declined the deal. My team was forced back to the drawing board to develop new technologies. Eventually, we built a company with better products for a larger market, and we were able to raise millions from top investment firms.

[7] A key to achieving success is to assemble a strong and stable management team, and we did a great job at recruiting the very best. But just as the company was taking off in a big way, I heard whispers about sexual **harassment**.

[8] After investigating, I found a potential problem with one of my senior executives. Losing an executive so critical to our operations would be a major **setback**, yet I couldn't tolerate a situation like this. So I decided to accept his immediate **resignation**.

[9] The company lost significant **momentum**, and **morale** took a hit, but we survived. Later, I was made aware of other ethical **breaches** by the same executive. If I hadn't made this decision, the **fallout** would likely have cost me the company.

[10] I was in **precarious** health, yet I had to decide whether to fight an ugly battle or **concede**. At stake was ownership in a company that my employees had worked hard to build. And the financial investment that saved us came from my friends and our executive team, not the venture capitalists.

[11] My wife encouraged me to fight, no matter what the cost. She knew that giving in would be easier for me in the short term. But I would have lived with regret for the rest of my life if I didn't do what was right.

[12] Over a period of months, investors who held board seats made one questionable move after another. It seemed to me that they had completely forgotten about **fiduciary** duty and proper corporate governance. I saw first-hand what happens when people who are normally ethical start making all decisions from the **perspective** of their **pocketbooks**. It's a slippery slope.

[13] My experiences may be unique, but corporate scandals seem to be **pervasive**. It seems that every month brings another **spectacular** fall. Big companies get all the press attention, but I have no doubt that the problems are widespread.

[14] Is there a better way?

[15] Corporate executives and small-business owners need to realize that business ethics need to be carefully sewn into the **fabric** of their companies. They need to start by

spelling out and communicating their values. Then they need to lead by example.

[16] Corporate culture is built from the top down. Employees embrace the ethics and values of their leaders. You simply can't have one set of standards for management and another for staff. And every executive and employee needs to be held **accountable**.

[17] When a mistake is made, it's better to deal with the immediate fallout rather than allowing it to build its own momentum. A corporate culture that doesn't allow for mistakes is **destined** for disaster. The best strategy is to encourage employees to come clean and learn from their errors. The worst is when employees are pressured to hide information. A company can usually survive short-term **snags**. But covering up a problem is likely to create even bigger problems later on. No truth remains hidden forever.

[18] The best organizations build ethics into their management and **compensation** systems. They **reinforce** corporate values by making these an integral part of how success is measured and rewarded. Performance reviews and **bonuses** tied to corporate goals can be very effective.

[19] As businesses grow, corporate boards take on increasing importance. Laws and Securities & Exchange Commission[1] rules govern how public-company boards must operate. But in private industry, things aren't that clear.

[20] In tech, venture firms often demand a majority of board seats as a condition for their investments. Conflicts **invariably** arise. Attorney Reid Phillips of law firm Brooks Pierce argues that the majority of directors should be independent. Otherwise, the board simply serves **insiders** — typically management and venture capitalists.

[21] The fact is, venture capitalists are usually motivated by quick, short-term profits. Management typically wants high salaries, perks, and more stock options. Independent directors are needed to protect the interests of all shareholders, because ultimately, it's the board that needs to enforce the corporation's ethical standards.

[22] The bottom line is that there are no **shortcuts** to creating an ethical organization. The challenges are different at every stage of the game, and it only gets harder. But if you do everything right, you will have laid the foundation for a **sustainable** and successful business.

(1052 words)
From *Business Week*

---

1 Securities & Exchange Commission 美国证券交易委员会

New Words

fascinating /ˈfæsɪneɪtɪŋ/
a. extremely interesting 迷人的，醉人的

treacherous /ˈtretʃərəs/
a. marked by unforeseen hazards; dangerous or deceptive 变化莫测的；危险的；欺骗性的

juncture /ˈdʒʌŋktʃə/
n. a particular point in events or time 时刻；关键时刻

outcome /ˈaʊtkʌm/
n. effect or result of an event, or of circumstances 结果，成果

lapse /læps/
n. slight error in speech or behavior 错误，过失

integrity /ɪnˈtegrɪtɪ/
n. the quality of being honest and having moral principles 正直，诚实

spouse /spaʊs/
n. a husband or wife 配偶（指夫或妻）

ownership /ˈəʊnəʃɪp/
n. the right or status of owning sth. 所有权；物主身份

forfeit /ˈfɔːfɪt/
v. (have to) lose or give up (sth.) as a consequence of or punishment for having done sth. wrong, or in order to achieve sth.（因做错事或为得到某事物）失去或放弃（另一事物）

dumbfound /dʌmˈfaʊnd/
v. fill with astonishment and perplexity; confound 充满惊讶与不解；迷惑

soul-searching /ˈsəʊlˌsɜːtʃɪŋ/
n. self-reflection, deep and anxious consideration of one's emotions and motives or of the correctness of a course of action 真挚的自我反省；深思

sink /sɪŋk/
v. bring to a low or ruined state; defeat or destroy 使进入低下或被毁的状况；击败或破坏

harassment /ˈhærəsmənt/
n. being troubled or annoyed continually 烦扰；骚扰

setback /ˈsetbæk/
n. a problem that delays or prevents progress, or makes things worse than they were 挫折，顿挫

resignation /ˌrezɪgˈneɪʃən/
n. an act of giving up a position or retiring 辞职

momentum /məʊˈmentəm/
n. positive motion; the ability to keep increasing, developing, or being more successful 动力；势头

morale /məˈrɑːl/
n. the confidence, enthusiasm and discipline of a person or group 士气；民心

breach /briːtʃ/
n. breaking or neglect (of a rule, duty, agreement, etc.) 违反；忽视；破坏（规则、职责、契约等）

fallout /ˈfɔːlˌaʊt/
n. the results of a particular event, especially when they are unexpected（尤指一特殊事件预料不到的）附带影响或结果

precarious /prɪˈkeərɪəs/
a. uncertain; unsafe 不稳定的

concede /kənˈsiːd/
v. surrender or yield 让步

fiduciary /fɪˈdjuːʃərɪ/
a. involving trust and confidence especially with regard to the relationship between a trustee and a beneficiary 基于信用的；信托的；受信托的

perspective /pəˈspektɪv/
n. subjective evaluation of relative significance; a point of view 相对重要的客观评估和评价；观点，看法

pocketbook /ˈpɒkɪtˌbʊk/
n. one's financial resources; wallet, purse 经济来源；钱袋，皮夹

pervasive /pɜːˈveɪsɪv/
a. present and perceived everywhere; pervading 无处不在的，遍布的

spectacular /spekˈtækjʊlə/

UNIT 8 Business Ethics

a. impressive or extraordinary; very sudden, unexpected 引人注目的；与众不同的；轰动一时的；惊人的

fabric /ˈfæbrɪk/
n. an underlying structure or set of expectations 一种复杂的基础结构

accountable /əˈkaʊntəbl/
a. responsible; expected to give an explanation 应负责的，有责任的；可解释的

destined /ˈdestɪnd/
a. seeming certain to happen at some time in the future 注定的

snag /snæg/
n. an expected or hidden obstacle or drawback 阻碍，障碍

compensation /ˌkɒmpenˈseɪʃən/
n. sth. typically money, awarded to someone as a recompense for work or for loss, injury, or suffering 补偿，赔偿

reinforce /ˌriːɪnˈfɔːs/
v. give more force or effectiveness to; strengthen 增强，加强

bonus /ˈbəʊnəs/
n. payment or gift added to what is usual or expected, in particular 奖金；红利

invariably /ɪnˈveərɪəblɪ/
ad. in every case or on every occasion; always 不变地；总是

insider /ɪnˈsaɪdə(r)/
n. a person within a group or organization or a person with privileged knowledge 内部的人；会员；知道内情的人；权威人士

shortcut /ˈʃɔːtkʌt/
n. an alternative route that is shorter than the one usually taken, often refers to omitting a key element to make things simpler 捷径

sustainable /səˈsteɪnəbl/
a. able to continue for a long time 可持续的

Phrases & Expressions

stay/be true to your principles/beliefs
behave according to the principles that you claim to believe in 忠实于原则/信仰

in the long run
during a long course of time (rather than short-term); in the final analysis or outcome 从长远看；从最终结果来看

look back
think of the past, recall 回顾，回想

in return for
as a payment for sth.; in exchange for 以……为报答，回报，回礼

take off in a big way
improve or increase dramatically; make a start on a large scale 大规模地开始

in ... health
in a condition of body or mind 处于……身体状态

give in
yield or surrender 屈服，让步

in the short term
in the near future 短期

slippery slope
(BrE.infml.) used to talk about a process or habit that is difficult to stop and which will develop

into something extremely bad〈英，非正式〉（恶习等）无法克制以致严重后果

spell out
make clear and easy to understand; explain in detail 使清楚易懂；详细解释

lead by example
show the people you are in charge of what you want them to do by doing it yourself 身体力行，起带头作用

allow for
take a possibility into account 考虑到某种可能性；考虑到客观情况

come clean
finally tell the truth about something you have been hiding 坦白交代，承认

cover up
put sth. on, over or around sth., especially in order to conceal or disguise it; hide or deny the fact of an illegal action 掩盖；隐瞒

later on
afterwards 稍后；以后

take on
begin to have (a particular quality, appearance, etc.); assume sth. 呈现（某种性质、样子等）；装成某事物

stock option
a right to buy or sell specific securities or commodities at a stated price within a specified time 优先认股权，在规定的时间内以规定的价格买卖具体证券或商品的权利

bottom line
the main or essential point 要点，关键之处

lay the foundation for
provide the conditions that will make it possible for something to be successful 为……打基础

Exercises

Comprehension

1. Mark the following statements with T (true) or F (false) or NM (not mentioned) according to the passage. Discuss with your partner about the supporting points for each statement.

    1) _____ The decision of not giving the stock to an important person as a gift turned out to be right for the author's business.

    2) _____ The company suffered a lot from losing the executive, and the author felt regret.

    3) _____ The author's wife, employees, and investors give him great help in his difficult time.

4) _____ In business, it is hard for people to stick to ethical principles.

5) _____ Once employees do anything ethically wrong, employers should fire them at once.

6) _____ There should be the same standards of ethics for both the leaders and the employees.

7) _____ A private company, with few people to control, can build ethic systems moreeasily than a public company.

8) _____ The author claims that no ethical standards definitely means no success.

2. The following questions are meant to help you have a better understanding of the organization of the text. Now write down your answers.

   1) What makes the beginning of the text effective?

   2) What is the whole point of the text?

   3) What is the author's point in telling about his personal experience?

   4) Is the last paragraph a good ending for the whole article? why or why not?

Critical Thinking

Work in group to discuss the following questions.

1) Traditionally, Chinese people look down upon business people in terms of ethics and morality. In the Chinese language, many derogative phrases and idioms, such as "无商不奸", "商人重利轻离别", are adopted when referring to business people. Do you think it's a bias against business people? Why or why not?

2) Read the following case about an ethical dilemma and discuss the questions below it.

> Jonica Gunson is the environmental compliance manager for a small plastics manufacturing company. She is currently faced with the decision whether or not to spend money on new technology that will reduce the level of a particular toxin in the wastewater that flows out the back of the factory and into a lake.
>
> The factory's emission levels are already within legal limits. However, Jonica knows that environmental regulations for this particular toxin are lagging behind scientific evidence. In fact, a scientist from the local university had been quoted in the newspaper recently, saying that if emission levels stayed at this level, the fish in the lakes and rivers in the area might soon have to be declared unsafe for human consumption.
>
> Further, if companies in the region don't engage in some self-regulation on this issue, there is reason to fear that the government backed by public opinion may force companies to begin using the new technology, and may also begin requiring monthly emission level reports (which would be both expensive and time consuming).
>
> But the company's environmental compliance budget is tight. Asking for this new technology to be installed would put Jonica's department over-budget, and could jeopardize the company's ability to show a profit this year.

- What motives would the company have to install the new technology?
- What motives would the company have to delay installing the new technology?
- Why might the companies in this region *prefer* the government to impose new regulations?
- Does business ethics pay in the face of ruthless competition? Why or why not?
- How could the company gain by installing the new technology?

Vocabulary

1. **Match the words in Column A with the words in Column B to make collocations as they appear in the text.**

A	B
market	company
sexual	lapse

UNIT 8 Business Ethics

business	practice
common	capitalist
corporate	system
stock	access
management	harassment
ethical	culture
venture	opportunity
public	option

2. Link each verb on the left with a noun on the right to make collocations. Then complete the sentences below using the collocations. You may have to make some changes to fit the grammar of the sentences.

A	B
accept	team
protect	resignation
set	success
achieve	standards
forfeit	interest
lose	momentum
assemble	foundation
lay	opportunity

1) She's just started up a new company; I hope she will _____ in the long run.

2) If you don't return the article to the shop within a week, you _____ of getting your money back.

3) It is critically important to _____ at the start of a business and enforce them in daily operation.

4) As a tech CEO, Mr. Green has absolute right to _____ for the solution of some technological issues.

5) A set of contracts was signed to _____ of their own company.

6) The investigation commission will not _____ from the accused president until he proves to be guilty.

7) The regulations lacking in rewarding system will lead to failure because the staff under it will _____.

199

8) The 10-year experiences in big company enable him to _____ for his further development.

3. The underlined words are wrongly used in the following sentences. Choose a proper word or phrase from the box to replace each.

| pervasive | compensation | precarious | accountable | concede | momentum |
| morale | setback | | spectacular | treacherous | breach | invariably |

1) The rumor goes in the company that the newly elected manger has been making a <u>faithful</u> plan of getting partial ownership.

2) It is widely accepted that <u>virtue</u> of employees are boosted by simply telling them how valuable their work is.

3) It is a major <u>drawback</u> to our hopes of reaching an agreement between employees and management.

4) The struggle for human rights in the company is gaining <u>push</u> every day.

5) The new decision of cooperating with a foreign company represents a <u>damage</u> of our independent ownership and management.

6) Our financial situation is still <u>stable</u> despite all the efforts we have made.

7) There are <u>penetrating</u> doubts among all the staff about the executive's decision.

8) The news that a world-famous company applied for bankruptcy caused a <u>grand</u> fall in the stock market.

9) The union is seeking <u>comfort</u> for two factory workers who were dismissed last week.

10) A strike by some ten thousand bank employees has ended after the government <u>adopted</u> some of their demands.

4. Use the given phrases to make sentences that complete the following dialogues.

1) take on

a. What do you think about the reform in promotion and salary?

_____

b. The company is turning from loss to profit; how do you look at the role of the corporate board in this turning?

_____

UNIT **8** Business Ethics

2) give in

   a. When it comes to public interest, which should enjoy the priority: business gain or environment protection?

   _____

   b. Suppose your business is facing great difficulties, what should you do?

   _____

3) live by

   a. Why has the company survived more than two hundred years and enjoyed high reputation?

   _____

   b. The company is on the verge of bankruptcy; how will the workers survive if they are laid off?

   _____

4) look back

   a. What should a businessman do to prevent any possible mistake?

   _____

   b. You have made great success in your business, what will you do next?

   _____

5) allow for

   a. What should a manager do to avoid a disasterous outcome in operation?

   _____

   b. Why should we prepare so carefully for negotiation with a Japanese company?

   _____

6) cover up

   a. Why did the former manager resign from the post? It must have something to do with the business scandal.

   _____

   b. What happened after the new director took the charge? There is no relevant report in newspapers.

   _____

Translation

1. Translate the following paragraphs into Chinese.

   I was in precarious health, yet I had to decide whether to fight an ugly battle or concede. At stake was ownership in a company that my employees had worked hard to build. And the financial investment that saved us came from my friends and our executive team, not the venture capitalists.

   My wife encouraged me to fight, no matter what the cost. She knew that giving in would be easier for me in the short term. But I would have lived with regret for the rest of my life if I didn't do what was right.

   Over a period of months, investors who held board seats made one questionable move after another. It seemed to me that they had completely forgotten about fiduciary duty and proper corporate governance. I saw first-hand what happens when people who are normally ethical start making all decisions from the perspective of their pocketbooks. It's a slippery slope.

2. Put the following passage into English, using the words and phrases given in the box.

integrity	juncture	setback	lead to	in the long run
sustainalble	forfeit	in the short term	bottom line	lay the foundation for

   商业道德应当成为企业的核心价值观,企业要持续发展,必须严格遵守法律、法规以及商业道德。创立并经营一家有道德规范的公司并不像你想象的那么容易,你要面对许多商业挑战,在每一个关键时刻都必须做出正确的、符合商业道德的选择。公司遵守道德规范的关键是要有强烈的社会责任感,要始终诚实正直。遵循道德规范有时可能会使公司失去某些获利的机会,甚至会使其业务发展暂时受挫。但是遵守商业道德规范能为公司带来好的声誉,从而为其今后的长远发展打下坚实的基础。

Ethics Challenges

Managing ethics in the workplace holds tremendous benefit for leaders and managers, benefits both moral and practical. This is particularly true today when it is critical to understand and manage highly diverse values in the workplace. Look at the following situation and work through the required steps.

Step 1: Work in pairs on the situation below to ensure that you understand it, and then figure out the solution to the problem.

Step 2: Work in groups of 4-6. Share the results of your pair work and prepare an oral report based on your further discussion.

Step 3: Group representatives present the reports to the class.

MANAGEMENT'S DILEMMA

You are on the management team of a rapidly growing, privately-held apparel company that had $80 million in sales last year and is projecting $150 million for next year. Your company has succeeded by targeting a niche market that will pay more for fashionable styles, making the speed and flexibility of operations more important than the price. Your company is also unique in its employee policies. Poor working conditions are common at many apparel factories in your country and abroad, and the industry is besieged by public criticism of labor practices. Yet a fundamental tenet of your company is the belief that apparel manufacturing should be profitable without exploiting workers. Management has worked hard since the company's inception to treat employees as well as possible, and it has developed a reputation for these efforts.

This summer your team found the company could not keep pace with orders. You added a second shift and hired 1,000 new sewers to staff it, bringing the total number of sewers to 3,000. During the summer months, all employees worked fulltime (eight-hour shifts, five per week) and often overtime to meet sales needs and replenish dwindling inventories.

It is now September, and it has become clear that the company's inventory is growing too large. Sales across the industry are usually slow during winter months, and you know the company must slow its production. Therefore, you must determine how to reduce your actual production over the next 20 weeks to only two-thirds of full capacity. Wages for sewers are not based on the number of hours they work, but on the number of pieces they sew. The efficiency of production at your company is partly responsible for the high wages workers earn. Typical industry practice in your country and abroad is to lay off excess labor for the winter season, with no severance pay or other assistance and no promise of rehire. Many of your sewers have lost their jobs elsewhere during the slow season for several years. However, if your company made such a move it would contradict the company's philosophy regarding the treatment of employees as valued partners. Laying workers off seems like it would be a significant defeat in this respect, with possible repercussions in employee motivation and public relations. Also, your team has invested several thousand dollars in training each employee, and you are concerned that new sewers may not be skilled enough to meet the steep climb in orders anticipated in the spring. If workers are laid off, there is no guarantee that you will be able to rehire the same people in the spring. However, the company cannot afford to pay workers to do nothing for 20 weeks, and many workers will likely return to the company if they fail to match your wages or working conditions elsewhere.

How should your management team address the company's excess labor problem during the upcoming period of slow sales? Be specific in your recommendations. For example, if you recommend layoffs, state exactly how many workers will be affected, how you will determine which workers will be affected, and how this cuts production appropriately. Keep in mind, there is no union and there are no other specific policies or agreements that mandate the basis (e.g., seniority) for prioritizing which sewers might be affected by your decision.

Language Hints

Expressing comparison
- On balance, your suggestion is more acceptable.
- All in all, I feel his ideas are more practical.
- ...

Trying to persuade somebody
- It is a pity that we can't compromise on it.
- Perhaps you should think before you decide.
- Are you quite sure you've taken

everything into account?
- How can I persuade you to accept the offer?
- It's all right in theory, but in practice it may not work.
- ...

Correcting information
- Sorry, I think you misunderstood what I said.
- Sorry, that's not quite right.
- I'm afraid you don't understand what I'm saying.
- That's not quite what I had in mind.
- That's not what I meant.
- ...

Asking for Contributions
- We haven't heard from you yet, (name of participant).
- What do you think about this?
- Would you like to add anything, (name of participant)?
- Has anyone else got anything to contribute?
- Are there any more comments?
- ...

Stating you have no opinion
- I've no strong feelings about the matter.
- I can't say I have any particular views on the matter.
- It is not something I've considered a great deal, I'm afraid.
- ...

Commenting
- That's interesting.
- I never thought about it that way before.
- Good point!
- I get your point.
- I see what you mean.
- ...

Newsletter Articles

It is a common practice for corporations or companies to publish their own newspapers or magazines, often called company newsletters or in-house journals. Newsletters include articles with a variety of information, telling their readers what is happening in their company. They also carry updated information on the company's products/services, personal details of appointments, promotions, retirements, marriages and horrors, etc. What's more, they often mean to encourage and print correspondence and contributions from staff members. Obviously, the aim of such publication is to promote good industrial relations by providing a channel of communication between management and workers and to give all members of the workforce a sense of being kept informed and involved in the well-being of the organization.

A newsletter is usually short and informative, so its articles should be brief and readable. It normally consists of four parts:

- Headline — be appropriate and snappy;
- Introduction — give the main gist of the article (who? what? where? when?);
- Main body — be short and self-contained in an interesting and punchy style;

  Close — repeat the main message again, summarizing or including a quotation from a key person.

To promote readership for the company newsletter, remember to:

use short and concise sentences;

write in a clear and logical manner; and

make the story interesting to read.

Study the following sample and do the exercises according to the directions.

Sample

Hundred Managers at Group Conference

More than one hundred directors and managers converged on American Airlines at the end of August for the biggest ever American Airlines management conference.

Every U.S. branch and subsidiary company was represented, with key staff and managers, joining with American Airlines for the first ever conference of this type.

Held at the city's Shangri-La Hotel, the one-day event brought together regional directors, general managers, industrial managers, and senior personnel in sales, transport and warehousing.

The five-hour session included a report on the company's successful first half and a review of performance to date against the targets set for the year.

UNIT **8** Business Ethics

1. Look at again the situation in "Ethics Challenges", and suppose your group to be the board of directors of your company. You held a meeting, discussed and agreed on the solution to the company's excess labor problem. Please write a short article for your company's newsletter based on the real results of your group discussion.

2. You are assistant to the editor of your company newsletter, and have been informed that one of your e mployees is leaving shortly. Please write an article for your newsletter with the help of the following information.

   - Cathy Wong — joined personnel 2004 — promoted to secretary 2006;
   - ... popular staff member — cheerful — outgoing — conscientious — helpful (quoted from employer);
   - ... upgraded qualifications — evening course for LCCI Private Secretary Certificate;
   - ... met Mathew Smith (a new sales rep) 3 months ago — love at first sight — quickly engaged — leave for Toronto, Ontario (Marthew's birthplace) in 2 months' time;
   - ...wish every happiness.
   - ... Mr Peter Boon, Personnel Director

   ...Miss Cathy after being with the company for so long, ... hope...a replacement... proves... conscientious as she...

3. You work for Foley Press, publishers of school and college textbooks. Your company is employing more people all the time, but the canteen remains desperately understaffed, and too small for your requirements. So your office manager, Mrs. Mary Macmahon, asked you to write an article for the staff newsletter to obtain staff cooperation in helping to keep the canteen service running as smoothly as possible. Add some of your own ideas in addition to the following suggestions from the canteen management.

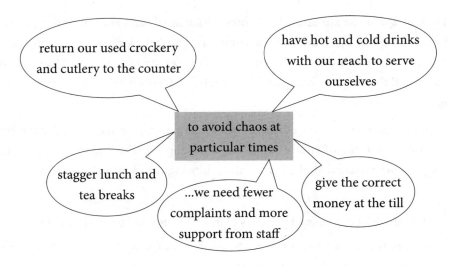

Business Expressions

1. Combine the words from the two columns A and B to make expressions connected with business ethics. Use each word once and add the word *of*, or hyphen(-) if necessary. Then translate the expressions into Chinese.

A	B
double	scandal
pad	market
corruption	virtue
conventional	duty
statutory	dealing
professional	dilemmas
moral	accountability
standards	ethics
gray	interest
whistle	morality
express	obligation

UNIT 8 Business Ethics

code	behavior
conflict	blower
ethical	provisions
bounden	bills

1) _____
2) _____
3) _____
4) _____
5) _____
6) _____
7) _____
8) _____

9) _____
10) _____
11) _____
12) _____
13) _____
14) _____
15) _____

2. **Complete the following sentences by translating the expressions in the brackets.**

   1) The charge in the present case is one of _____ (贪污受贿).

   2) There should be _____ (一套商业行为守则) which indicates how clients are to be served.

   3) Having not informed his superiors of his decision, he was accused of _____ (违反了行业规矩).

   4) As an investor, you can _____ (问心无愧地挣钱), helping companies develop products to save the environment by choosing to invest in them.

   5) Aimed at business people who want to find ways to adopt environmentally sustainable business practices, the three-day event drew attendees from a wide range of businesses who are looking for ecologically friendly practices they could adopt to _____ (抚慰他们的良心).

   6) The independent director of the bank is required to _____ (有良好的职业操守) and moral ethics, be familiar with trust principles and trust operating rules and have adequate time and energy to perform his duties.

   7) Our reputation for integrity is our most important asset. We will not do anything to _____ (损害公司的诚信) or risk damage to our reputation in return for financial gain or any reason.

   8) The salespeople who are assumed to _____ (品行不端) and poor education can hardly get long-lasting success in their business.

   9) The training programme helps the chief executive to hone their creative

instincts and ＿＿＿＿＿＿ (灌输道德观念) and cultural ethics in their business organizations.

10) Ultimately, Government, as sole owner of Royal Mail Group, cannot ＿＿＿＿＿＿ (推卸责任/逃避责任) for the shape of the network.

11) Robinson filed a petition for bankruptcy last year. In the bankruptcy proceeding he sought to ＿＿＿＿＿＿ (履行义务) to his former wife arising from the divorce decree.

12) Where companies fail or refuse to ＿＿＿＿＿＿ (遵守义务) to consumers, the bonds provide fair and effective recourse. Consumers, through the Consumers' Bureau, can make claims against these bonds to recover losses.

13) A bank lost several million pounds ＿＿＿＿＿＿ (由于一次缜密的计算机诈骗).

Specialized Reading

1. Working with integrity is an important ethical feature. Read the following passage and choose the correct statement from A-F to fill in each gap marked with 1-6.

> A. Employees expect supervisors and managers to set an example
> B. Business ethics is never going to be successfully regulated
> C. Distinguish between compliance and ethics
> D. It would be nothing more than just a reminder
> E. Ethics training in and of itself is very important
> F. Set your goals in conjunction with your team members

In response to the increasing number of corporate and accounting scandals, some experts believe that the responsibility for maintaining an ethical environment is up to management. "＿＿1)＿＿. There are bad people who are always going to want to do bad things," says Martin L. Taylor, vice president of organizational services for the Institute for Global Ethics. You can set a standard for good behavior. Experts offer the following advice on creating a climate of integrity:

Set an example through strong leadership. "Ethics programs are generally aimed at employees when it's management who are the ones in trouble," says Taylor. ＿＿2)＿＿. Perhaps that's why half of the employees surveyed in a study sponsored by the Ethics Officer Association and the American Society of Chartered Life Underwriters & Chartered Financial Consultant admitted to acting unethically or illegally while on the job. Approximately 60%, however, believed that ethical dilemmas are an avoidable consequence of doing business.

Set realistic goals. "____3)____," urges Kelly. "Don't sit in your office with a calculator and a spreadsheet and think about what's going to make your stockholders and you happy. Get down in the field with the people who are talking to the customers and find out what goals are realistic."

Provide training. 71% of those polled believed serious commitment by management to address ethical issues would help with the problem. "____4)____, but it's got to be in the context of an overall program," advises Michael Schlein, deputy director for public affairs at Citigroup. "If you just have the ethics training, I don't think you'd be accomplishing very much. ____5)____, but it won't change a culture," he says.

____6)____. "You can pass all the laws, all the reforms, all the structural changes, but when it comes right down to it," offers Marianne Jennings, professor of legal and ethical studies at the College of Business of Arizona State University, "ethics is about being forthright even when the law allows you to be less than forthright."

2. **Read the passage concerning theories of ethical issues and answer the following questions.**

Philosophers disagree about the purpose of a business in society. For example, some suggest that the principal purpose of a business is to maximize returns to its owners, or in the case of a publicly-traded concern, its shareholders. Thus, under this view, only those activities that increase profitability and shareholder value should be encouraged. Some believe that the only companies that are likely to survive in a competitive marketplace are those that place profit maximization above everything else. However, some point out that self interest would still require a business to obey the law and adhere to basic moral rules, because the consequences of failing to do so could be very costly in fines, loss of licensure, or company reputation. The economist Milton Friedman, an American Nobel Laureate economist and public intellectual, was a leading proponent of this view.

Other theorists contend that a business has moral duties that extend well beyond serving the interests of its owners or stockholders, and that these duties consist of more than simply the law. They believe a business has moral responsibilities to so-called stakeholders, people who have an interest in the conduct of the business, which might include employees, customers, vendors, the local community, or even society as a whole. They would say that stakeholders have certain rights with regard to how the business operates, and some would even suggest that this even includes rights of governance.

Some theorists have adapted social contract theory to business, whereby companies become quasi-democratic associations, and employees and other stakeholders are given voice over a company's operations. This approach has become especially popular subsequent to the revival of contract theory in political philosophy, which is largely due to a professor of political philosophy at Harvard University John Rawls' *A Theory of Justice*, and the advent of the consensus-oriented approach to solving business problems, an aspect of the "quality movement" that emerged in the 1980s. Professors Thomas Donaldson (a Professor in Ethics and Law at the Wharton School, University of Pennsylvania) and Thomas Dunfee (a professor of Wharton Legal Studies and Business Ethics Department) proposed a version of contract theory for business, which they call Integrative Social Contracts Theory. They posit that conflicting interests are best resolved by formulating a "fair agreement" between the parties, using a combination of (1) macro-principles that all rational people would agree upon as universal principles, and (2) micro-principles formulated by actual agreements among the interested parties. Critics say the proponents of contract theories miss a central point, namely, that a business is someone's property and not a mini-state or a means of distributing social justice.

1) Which of the following statements (A-H) would Milton Friedman support?

_____

2) Which of the following statements (A-H) would Professors Thomas Donaldson and Thomas Dunfee advocate?

_____

A. In spite of the pursuit of self-interest, a business should conform to basic moral rules.

B. It can be a heavy loss for a business that fails to obey the law and adhere to moral rules.

C. Companies that survive in the fierce competition are those that put profit maximization above all.

D. The moral duties of a business should serve the owners and customers as well.

E. Moral duties are composed of simply obeying the law.

F. A business is a personal property and should not be used to distribute social justice.

G. Interest groups should resolve their conflicts by means of some fair agreements.

H. Integrative Social Contracts Theory is meant to protect every party's interest.

3. **The following guidelines ensure the ethics management program is operated in a meaningful fashion. Read the statements A-N carefully and put them respectively under the five Guidelines in a correct order.**

   1) Recognize that managing ethics is a process.

   _____
   _____

   2) The best way to handle ethical dilemmas is to avoid their occurrence in the first place.

   _____
   _____

   3) Make ethics decisions in groups, and make decisions public, as appropriate.

   _____
   _____

   4) Integrate ethics management with other management practices.

   _____
   _____

   5) Note that trying to operate ethically and making a few mistakes is better than not trying at all.

   _____
   _____

   A. It's the trying that counts and brings peace of mind — not achieving an heroic status in society.

   B. Values are discerned through the process of ongoing reflection.

   C. Some leaders may fear sticking their necks out publicly to announce an ethics management program, which is extremely unfortunate.

   D. All organizations are comprised of people and people are not perfect.

   E. Therefore, ethics programs may seem more process-oriented than most management practices.

F. Ethics is a matter of values and associated behaviors.

G. Ethics programs do produce deliverables, e.g., codes, policies and procedures, budget items, meeting minutes, authorization forms, newsletters, etc.

H. When developing the values statement during strategic planning, include ethical values preferred in the workplace.

I. When a mistake is made by any of the organizations, the organization has a long way to fall.

J. However, the most important aspect from an ethics management program is the process of reflection and dialogue that produces these deliverables.

K. Their development sensitizes employees to ethical considerations and minimizes the chances of unethical behavior occurring in the first place.

L. That's why practices such as developing codes of ethics and codes of conduct are so important.

M. This usually produces better quality decisions by including diverse interests and perspectives, and increases the credibility of the decision process and outcome by reducing suspicion of unfair bias.

N. When developing personnel policies, reflect on what ethical values you'd like to be most prominent in the organization's culture and then design policies to produce these behaviors.

4. Discuss the following questions with your group members.

1) In the workplace there are always some myths about business ethics. Some of these myths arise from general confusion about the notion of ethics. Other myths arise from narrow or simplistic views of ethical dilemmas. Look at the following myths and discuss how you counter them.

- *Our employees are ethical so we don't need attention to business ethics.*
- *Business ethics is a matter of the good guys preaching to the bad guys.*
- *Ethics can't be managed.*
- *Business ethics and social responsibility are the same thing.*
- *Managing ethics in the workplace has little practical relevance.*

2) An increasing number of companies require employees to attend seminars regarding business conduct and some even require their employees to sign agreements stating that they will abide by the company's rules of conduct. Do you think it fair? Give your reasons.

UNIT 9
International Trade

1. Discuss the following questions with your partner.

   1) Why is international trade important to a country's economy?

   2) What are Mainland China's major trading partners?

   3) What are generally regarded as the three pillars of the world economy?

2. Work in groups. Try to name the leading countries of the following sectors.

Sectors	Leading exporters	Leading importers
crude oil		
coal		
cotton		
rice		
corn		
beef		
wood		
dairy products		
iron ore		
textile products		
cars		

Preview: Exports are one of the three major parts of U.S. economic growth, but they are receiving less attention than the other two, namely, consumer spending and business outlays. However, export growth is especially critical for the country's economy and for manufacturing in that exports account for a large share of overall output and corporate receipts. Furthermore, U.S. exporters are expecting further increases as they take advantage of globalization in an international climate that was, at the time of this writing, witnessing cheaper energy and the dollar's steady decline, two favorable factors for U.S. exporters.

Exports Are Giving the Economy a Surprise Lift

By James C. Cooper

[1] The three **pillars** of U. S. economic growth this year have been consumer spending, business **outlays** for new buildings and equipment, and exports. They have supported the economy strongly through $70-per-barrel oil, $3-per-gallon gasoline, interest rate **hikes**, and a housing **recession**. Each pillar was crucial, yet a demand by U.S. consumers and businesses tends to get most of the attention, while foreign demand often gets pushed into the background. It shouldn't be. As globalization opens an ever-wider array of opportunities, U.S. exports are playing an essential role in powering overall output, employment, and profits.

[2] Just look at the latest report on U.S. international trade. Most of the notice, as usual, was on the import side of the **balance**. The impact of cheaper oil on overall imports helped to narrow the monthly trade gap to $64.3 billion in September from $69 billion the previous month, one of the largest declines on record. Receiving less attention: Exports are on a tear this year. Overseas shipments of goods and services in September **posted** a solid 0.5% increase from August, and they are up 15.8% from a year ago.

[3] Exports of goods, which **comprise** 70% of foreign shipments, have been especially strong. Real exports of goods, which are **adjusted** for price changes, jumped 1.3% from August and have grown 15.7% from a year ago — the fastest annual growth rate in nine years. The gains have been broad, **spanning** product sectors and geographic regions. Shipments to European and Pacific Rim countries have **accelerated** sharply over the past year, and capital goods continue to lead the gains.

[4] The enormous **thrust** exports have provided to economic growth is somewhat hidden in the gross domestic product data. That's because foreign trade's contribution to GDP[1] is the net of exports minus imports. On balance, the widening trade **deficit** has **subtracted** from growth. But take a look at only the export side of the **ledger**. Shipments abroad added 0.7 percentage points to the economy's 3.2% growth rate, and

---

1 GDP (Gross Domestic Product)　国内生产总值

the **fillip** has been even greater this year. In fact, exports have **contributed** as much to GDP growth as capital spending by businesses.

[5] In addition, note that exports are accounting for an ever-larger share of overall U.S. output. After falling during the global **downturn** earlier in the decade, the share of total production of goods being shipped abroad has **surged** to a record 17.6% as of the third quarter, up from a low of 13.7% only three years ago.

[6] That greater share is a **by-product** of globalization, which is also evident in the accelerating volume of U.S. trade — exports plus imports — over the past three years. It also shows up in the increasing percentage of profits of U.S.-based corporations that is coming from their overseas operations. During the same three years, that share of **corporate receipts** has averaged 25.3%, up. Although there are no official data, it's a good bet export-related profits are making a greater contribution to the bottom line as well.

[7] The benefits of strong foreign demand are providing an especially important source of support to the economy right now as the housing downturn takes its biggest bite out of growth. U.S. manufacturing is the key **beneficiary**. Domestic demand for factory goods has slipped, reflecting the softness in construction supplies and the recent **cutbacks** in the auto industry. The weakness in both of these areas has put a **drag** on industrial output and jobs in recent months, but exports have helped to keep factories **humming** at high rates of capacity **utilization**.

[8] Exports are almost certain to continue to grow strongly in the coming year, and it's easy to see why. In the very near term, for example, the index of export orders in the industrial sector **compiled** by the Institute for Supply Management[1] posted a big rise in October to its highest level since January.

[9] Further ahead, and more fundamentally, favorable economic and financial forces are in place to keep economies overseas growing strongly in the coming year. Although interest rates outside the U.S. continue to rise, most notably in the euro zone, global financial conditions remain relatively easy and support growth. In both the euro zone and Japan, for example, the central banks' **inflation**-adjusted policy rates remain well below those in America. Also, the narrow difference between **yields** on government and corporate **bonds** indicates that global credit markets see little risk in lending, suggesting a climate that will **accommodate** borrowing.

[10] What's different about growth outside the U.S. now, compared with past

---

1 Institute for Supply Management   美国供应管理协会

business cycles, is that it is being driven more by **homegrown** demand and less by exports, especially to America. That independence will give foreign growth more staying power as the U.S. economy slows. Earlier **upswings** overseas, such as Germany's and Japan's in the late '90s, were cut short precisely because export growth slowed and those countries lacked solid domestic demand to fall back on.

[11] This time, although third-quarter growth in the euro zone slowed to a 2.1% annual rate after averaging a strong 3.5% **clip** in the first half, both Europe and Japan still **boast** solid corporate sectors, improving labor markets, and healthy financial markets. Much the same is true across the Pacific Rim. As a result, U.S. exports to Europe in the third quarter are up 20.7% over the past year, the fastest annual growth rate in more than a decade. The increase to all Pacific Rim countries has nearly doubled, to 15.2% from 8.7% last year. Those two regions account for about half of all U.S. exports, and other areas show strong growth as well.

[12] In addition, energy-importing economies worldwide will benefit from the **dip** in oil prices in ways that will do even more to **bolster** demand at home. Cheaper energy will lower production costs, helping to shore up profits. It will lift the confidence of businesses and consumers and cut overall inflation, boosting the purchasing power of consumers' incomes.

[13] The other reason to expect further gains in U.S. exports is the dollar's decline. Its dip seems likely to continue given the still-**yawning** American trade deficit and the narrowing spread between U.S. and foreign short-term interest rates. That tighter spread tends to decrease the attractiveness of dollar-based **securities** as investments.

[14] From its peak in early 2002 through October this year, the real trade-weighted dollar has dropped 14.3%, and it fell further against most **currencies** in November. In particular, the **greenback** has **grudgingly** but steadily made competitive gains against the Chinese yuan as China continues its baby steps toward greater currency flexibility.

[15] Clearly, globalization creates both challenges and opportunities. The emergence of greater U.S. competitiveness in a growing world economy is one opportunity that many American exporters are taking advantage of. And the timing is especially favorable — when the economy can use the extra support.

(1133 words)
From *Business Week*

New Words

pillar /ˈpɪlə/
n. a slender, freestanding, vertical support; a column; an element supporting another component 柱子，支柱；栋梁

outlay /ˈaʊtleɪ/
n. spending, esp. to help future developments in a business, etc. 花费，开支（尤指有助于公司进一步发展的）

hike /haɪk/
n. an often abrupt increase or rise 突然的或急剧的上升，上涨；增加

recession /rɪˈseʃən/
n. an extended decline in general business activity, typically three consecutive quarters of falling real gross national product 衰退（经济活动普遍而持续地衰败，尤指三个连续季度的国民生产总值的下降）

balance /ˈbæləns/
n. balance sheet, written record of money received and paid out, showing the difference between the two total amounts 资产负债表；资金平衡表（显示收支总差额的记录）

post /pəʊst/
v. announce sth. publicly or officially, especially financial information or a warning 发布，公布，宣布（尤指财经信息或警告）

comprise /kəmˈpraɪz/
v. consist of; contain; be composed of 由……构成；由……组成

adjust /əˈdʒʌst/
v. change slightly, esp. in order to make it more correct, effective, or suitable 调整，调节，校准；使适合

span /spæn/
v. cover a range of things; include 横跨，跨越

accelerate /ækˈseləreɪt/
v. move more quickly, or to make (something) happen faster or sooner 加速；促进

thrust /θrʌst/
n. a forceful shove or push 猛推；推力

deficit /ˈdefɪsɪt/
n. inadequacy or insufficiency 不足；缺乏

subtract /səbˈtrækt/
v. remove (a number) from another number 减去；减

ledger /ˈledʒə/
n. a book in which the monetary transactions of a business are posted in the form of debits and credits 分类账

fillip /ˈfɪlɪp/
n. stimulus or incentive; encouragement 刺激；激励，鼓励

contribute /kənˈtrɪbjuːt/
v. help bring about a result; act as a factor 贡献；促成……

downturn /ˈdaʊntɜːn/
n. a reduction in the amount or success of something, such as a country's economic activity 低迷时期

surge /ˈsɜːdʒ/
v. increase suddenly and greatly 猛冲；激增

by-product /ˈbaɪˌprɒdʌkt/
n. something that is produced as a result of making something else, or something unexpected that happens as a result of something 副产品

corporate /ˈkɔːpərɪt/
a. of or belonging to a corporation 法人团体的；公司的

receipt /rɪˈsiːt/
n. a quantity or amount received 收入；收到的数量

beneficiary /ˌbenɪˈfɪʃərɪ/
n. one who receives a benefit 受益人

cutback /ˈkʌtbæk/
n. decrease; curtailment 缩减，削减，减少

drag /dræg/
n. something that impedes or slows progress; a drawback or burden 阻碍；妨碍或减慢进程的事物；劣势

hum /hʌm/
v. be in a state of busy activity 活跃；忙碌

utilization /ˌjuːtɪlaɪˈzeɪʃən/
n. putting into use, especially finding a

UNIT 9 International Trade

profitable or practical use 利用

compile /kəmˈpaɪl/
v. gather into a single book 编辑；汇编

inflation /ɪnˈfleɪʃən/
n. a generous continuous increase in prices 通货膨胀

yield /jiːld/
n. a profit obtained from an investment; a return （投资等的）利润；收益

bond /bɒnd/
n. a certificate of debt issued by a government or corporation guaranteeing payment of the original investment plus interest by a specified future date 债券

accommodate /əˈkɒmədeɪt/
v. allow for, give consideration to; make suitable; adapt 允许；考虑；使适应；使符合

homegrown /ˈhəʊmˈɡrəʊn/
a. made or produced in your own country, town etc. 本国（或本地）制造的

upswing /ˈʌpswɪŋ/
n. an upward swing or trend 增长，向上的趋势；兴隆

clip /klɪp/
n. curtailment 缩减

boast /bəʊst/
v. possess (sth. to be proud of) 有（引以为荣的事物）

dip /dɪp/
n. a sharp downward course; a drop 下降

bolster /ˈbəʊlstə/
v. support or prop up; buoy up 支撑；鼓舞

yawning /ˈjɔːnɪŋ/
a. gaping open 裂开的；距离大的

security /sɪˈkjʊərətɪ/
n. a document indicating ownership or creditorship; a stock certificate or bond 有价证券；标明所有权和债权的文件；股票证书或证券

currency /ˈkʌrənsɪ/
n. the money in use in a particular country at a particular time 货币，通货

greenback /ˈɡriːnbæk/
n. a note of U.S. currency 美钞

grudgingly /ˈɡrʌdʒɪŋlɪ/
ad. unwillingly; reluctantly 不情愿地，勉强地

Phrases & Expressions

as usual
as commonly or habitually happens 照常

on record
(of facts, events, etc.) noted or recorded, esp. officially （指事实、事件等）记载下来的；（尤指）正式记录的

on a tear
(be) improving or advancing rapidly 快速发展

Pacific Rim
the countries and landmasses surrounding the Pacific Ocean, often considered as a socioeconomic region 太平洋圈；环太平洋国家和地区

capital goods
goods, such as machinery, used in the production of commodities; producer goods 资本货物

on balance
in summary 总而言之

account for
form the total of 占总数的数量或比例

show up
become visible; make sth. become visible; arrive at （使）看得见；变得明显；显现出来

bottom line
the amount of money that is a profit or a loss after everything has been calculated 最终赢利（或亏损）；损益表底线

at rates of
at the speed of 以……的速度

credit market
the environment in which the issuance and trading of debt securities occurs 信贷市场

cut short
stop or reduce prematurely 提前缩减

fall back on
go to sb. for support or use sth. when in difficulty 有困难时（能）求助于某人；依靠某事物

shore up
support 支持

in particular
especially 特别是，尤其是

take advantage of
put to good use; avail oneself of 利用

Exercises

Comprehension

1. Answer the following questions with your partner.

   1) What are the three pillars of U. S. economic growth this year?

   2) Why does the author mention "$70-per-barrel oil, $3-per-gallon gasoline, interest rate hikes, and a housing recession"?

   3) What is the impact of cheaper oil on overall imports?

   4) Why is the enormous thrust exports have provided to economic growth is somewhat hidden in the gross domestic product data?

   5) What is the driving force behind the ever-increasing volume of the U.S. trade?

   6) According to the author, what contributes more to growth outside the U.S.?

   7) What's the attitudes of the author toward the growth and future of the U.S. exports?

8) What's the author's purpose of writing of this passage?

2. Match the headings on the right column with their equivalent numbered paragraphs on the left column, and then compare your answers with your partner's.

Paragraphs	Main ideas
Para. 1	A. U.S. exports provide a very important source of support to the economy, and to manufacturing in particular.
Para. 2	B. Europe and Pacific Rim countries account for half of all U.S. exports.
Para. 3	C. U.S. exporters are making good use of globalization.
Para. 4	D. The international climate favors further U.S. export growth.
Para. 5	E. Cheaper energy is important to the U.S. economy.
Para. 6	F. Exports have been especially strong and wide-ranging.
Para. 7	G. Little attention is paid to exports, one of the three pillars of U.S. economy.
Para. 8	H. Foreign countries' domestic demand is a driving force for their own economies.
Para. 9	I. The dollar's decline facilitates further U.S. export growth.
Para. 10	J. The dollar's depreciation against RMB helps with U.S. export growth.
Para. 11	K. Exports are a result of globalization and play a role in increasing corporate profits.
Para. 12	L. Export orders will continue to grow in the future.
Para. 13	M. Attention to imports outweighs that to exports, which posted a solid increase.
Para. 14	N. Exports are accounting for a larger share of the overall U.S. output.
Para. 15	O. Exports actually contributed much to GDP growth.

Critical Thinking

Work in group to discuss the following questions.

1) How can you benefit directly from trading globally in your daily life?
2) In some countries, especially the developed countries, although a strong majority of people views trade, in principle, as something positive and as having significant benefits for their economy, they also have major reservations about how trade

has been put into practice. Do you know what these people are concerned about?

3) Name a few countries that excel in international trade and discuss their competitive edges.

Vocabulary

1. Read the following phrases and decide if the words make sense together. If they do, write "yes" on the line. If they don't, write a new word to replace the underlined word.

    1) <u>balanced</u> receipts   _____
    2) <u>lead</u> the gains   _____
    3) <u>hard</u> demand   _____
    4) <u>put out</u> a big rise   _____
    5) <u>solid</u> financial market   _____
    6) <u>span</u> the regions   _____
    7) <u>home</u> turndown   _____
    8) <u>do</u> a major contribution to _____
    9) <u>cut</u> a trade gap   _____
    10) <u>have</u> a drag on   _____
    11) <u>boosting</u> the purchasing power _____
    12) <u>dollar-founded</u> securities _____

2. Make collocations connected with business by choosing one word from Column A and one from Column B. Match each expression with the appropriate explanation.

A	B
global	outlays
business	bond
capacity	risk
housing	deficit
investment	downturn
capital	utilization
corporate	recession
trade	goods

UNIT 9 International Trade

1) the use of the amount that something can produce
   _____

2) net disbursements for administrative expenses and for loans and related costs and expenses
   _____

3) property or equipment, such as machinery, used in the production of commodities
   _____

4) weakness in the housing market
   _____

5) an excess of imports over exports
   _____

6) a negative change in the world economy, such as from expansion to recession
   _____

7) uncertainty about the future benefits to be realized from an investment
   _____

8) a debt security issued by a corporation, as opposed to those issued by the government
   _____

3. Study the following groups of words, and then choose the proper words to fill in the blanks. Change the form where necessary.

   1) economy   economical   economic   economist   economically
      a. He is the _____ who developed new _____ theories regarding the effects of deficit spending.
      b. The company possesses a modern, _____ heating system.
      c. If the natural resources are used _____, we can certainly slow down the present drain on the limited energy supply.
      d. We'd better learn to practice _____ in making out the household budget.

   2) product   production   produce   productive   productivity
      a. Is history the _____ of impersonal social and economic forces?
      b. This country is famous for its large output of farm _____.

c. Well, _____ isn't about doing a lot of stuff. It's about getting the important stuff done.

d. The company was recently criticized for its policies _____ of much harm.

3) consume   consumption   consumptive   consuming   consumer

a. Industrialized countries should do their best to reduce energy _____.

b. The _____ price index this year has been rising steadily.

c. Luxury industry is largely based on extravagant _____ activities on the part of _____.

4) essence   essential   essentially   essentialize   essentialization

a. All his life philosophy is _____ by a single sentence, "seize the day."

b. We should try to make clear the _____ difference between these two management systems.

c. Being thoughtful of others is the _____ of politeness.

d. The studio had all the _____ like heating and running water.

5) benefit   benefactor   beneficiary   beneficent   beneficial

a. To everyone's surprise, the _____ of the charity fund was none other than the young son of a local business tycoon!

b. This business guide is of great _____ to the newcomers.

c. This suburb has been the accidental _____ of a large restoration program.

d. To me, the issue is whether the medical practice of polypharmacy is a truly _____ practice both to the individual patient but also to society.

6) receive   reception   receipt   receptive

a. A hilarious _____ was held to celebrate the marriage of the two multinational corporations.

b. Due to effective management, the theme park enjoys good cash _____.

c. At the crucial moment, the CEO _____ the full weight of unfavorable remarks from the press.

7) note   notify   notification   notice   notable

a. It is almost impossible for the speculators of the stock market to react promptly at such short _____.

b. Please _____ the change in the enthusiasm of the personnel, which is the life of any enterprise.

   c. A _____ quantity of new university graduates have expressed their heartfelt gratitude for those employers who kindly gave them instructions when they worked as interns.

   d. Payments should be sent with the written _____.

8) recess   recession   recessionary   recessive   recessionarily

   a. We should concentrate on sharply reducing interest rates to pull the economy out of _____.

   b. Reduced interest rates would help ease _____ pressures in the economy.

   c. When formal meetings or court cases _____, they stop temporarily.

   d. It couldn't be worse than advocating higher taxes and _____ tight budgets — both of which will eliminate jobs, growth and consumer demand.

Translation

1. **Translate the following paragraphs into Chinese.**

   The three pillars of U. S. economic growth have been consumer spending, business outlays and exports. They have supported the economy strongly through high energy prices and a housing recession. Each pillar was crucial, yet a domestic demand tends to get more attention, while foreign demand often gets pushed into the background. As a matter of fact, in the course of globalization, exports are playing an essential role in powering employment and profits. Domestic demand for factory goods has slipped in recent months, which results in a drag on overall industrial output, but steady growth in exports has helped to keep factories humming at high rates of capacity utilization. In addition, the greenback has grudgingly but steadily made competitive gains against the Chinese yuan as China continues its steps toward greater currency flexibility. Undoubtedly, this facilitates further increase in U.S. exports.

2. **Put the following passage into English, using the words and phrases given in the box.**

hum	manufacturing	pillar	trade deficit	fillip
dip	purchasing power	currency	fall back on	shore up

出口是许多国家的一个经济支柱。当这些国家国内购买力下降或有限时，

往往会利用出口来扶持经济的发展。甚至一些经济巨头也极力限制进口，鼓励出口以支持经济的发展。在这两种情况下，国内的生产商得到了保护，他们可以免受来自国外制造业的竞争，而同时由于出口大增使得硬通货大量流入本国。 在极端的情况下，有些国家还为企业制定了严格的出口限额，促使营销人员带着"成者王，败者寇"的营销计划奔赴国外推销自己的产品。还有的国家则有意识地削弱本币的币值以鼓励国外企业购买本国的产品，如美国和日本就相互指控对方运用此策略进行贸易。值得一提的是，当政府开始注意到不断增长的贸易赤字和一蹶不振的外汇储备时，向海外市场营销就可能不再是一种可以选择的事情，而是一项必须执行的命令。

Establishing Business Relations

It is possible to build a good relationship with a client or a supplier if he/she feels confident that you are able to meet their expectations. In order to develop this confidence, you will need to know your client/supplier on a friendly, yet professional level, and work hard to develop and maintain the relationship. Read the sample dialogue, and then refer to the related information and role-play the situations with your partner. Remember to reverse your roles.

Sample dialogue

A: Good morning. My name is Mr. Brown. I'm from Australia. Here is my card.

B: Thank you. I'm pleased to meet you, Mr. Brown. My name is Kathy Perless, the representative of Green Textile Import and Export Corporation.

A: Pleased to meet you too, Ms. Perless. I travel a lot every year on business, but this is my first visit to your country. I must say I have been much impressed by your friendly people.

B: Thank you for saying so. Have you seen the exhibition halls? On display are most of our products, such as silk, woolen knitwear, cotton piece goods, and garments.

UNIT 9 International Trade

> A: Oh, yes. I had a look yesterday. I found some of the exhibits to be fine in quality and beautiful in design. The exhibition has successfully displayed to me what your corporation handles. I've gone over the catalogue and the pamphlets enclosed in your last letter. I've got some idea of your exports. I'm interested in your silk blouses.
>
> B: Our silk is known for its good quality. It is one of our traditional exports. Silk blouses are brightly colored and beautifully designed. They've met with great favor overseas and are always in great demand.
>
> A: Some of them seem to be of the latest style. Now I've a feeling that we can do a lot of trade in this line. We wish to establish relations with you.
>
> B: Your desire coincides with ours.
>
> A: Concerning our financial position, credit standing and trade reputation, you may refer to Bank of Hong Kong, or to our local Chamber of Commerce or inquiry agencies.
>
> B: Thank you for your information. As you know, our corporation is a state-operated one. We always trade with foreign countries on the basis of equality and mutual benefit. Establishing business relations between us will be to our mutual benefit. I have no doubt that it will bring about closer ties between us.
>
> A: That sounds interesting. I'll send a fax home. As soon as I receive a definite answer, I'll make a specific inquiry.
>
> B: We'll then make an offer as soon as possible. I hope a lot of business will be conducted between us.

Lenovo Group is an innovative, international technology company formed by former Lenovo Group and IBM Personal Computing Division. As a global leader in the PC market, Lenovo develops, manufactures and sells the most reliable, safe and easy-to-use technology products, provides professional, high-quality services, and helps global clients and partners to achieve their success. Headquartered in Raleigh, North Carolina, Lenovo has principal operations in Beijing and Raleigh. The company employs more than 19,000 people worldwide. Lenovo's sales network is spreading around the world, with the market share of its PC ranked third globally.

Taizhou Evergreen Gifts Co., Ltd is one of the leading manufacturers in China specializing in producing various houseware and gift items. The materials we use range from glass, aluminums, stainless steel to wood. Our houseware products cover fruit bowls, vases, fountains, etc. Our gift products cover photo frames, candle holders, chess sets, etc. Our goal is to brighten your home and life. With the help of service follow-up system experienced by our Australia joint-venture partner, we have gained high popularity among all our customers from Europe, USA, South America, Middle East, Asia, Africa, etc. with a turnover increasing 80% on average per year. We are located in Jiaojiang, Taizhou city, about 180 kilometers south from Ningbo in Zhejiang province, which has many sea liners to the main international port.

Situation 1: The Seller Contacts the Buyer Directly

Seller: David Lee

- A sales manager of Lenovo Group
- Want to export the products
- Know a prospect's information from the Guangzhou Trade Fair being held now
- Call to the prospect in the hotel
- Want to meet the prospect and show him the products catalog
- Leave the catalog at the front desk of the hotel
- Invite the prospect to contact him by fax or e-mail
- ...

Potential buyer: Mr George

- Hear of the seller's company
- See the sample products in the Trade Fair
- Be kind of interested in the products
- Want more information about the seller's company
- Be too busy now to talk with the seller in details
- Leave for his country next morning
- Want the seller to contact their agent directly
- ...

Situation 2: The Buyer Contacts the Seller Directly

Buyer: Bob Johnson

- Be from the United States
- Know about company A from the advertisement
- Be interested in their product
- Call company A
- Ask the operator to get him through to their Export Sales Manager
- Ask for a meet with the manager

Next day:

- Receive the seller in the hotel
- Ask for the detailed information about the products
- Want to have more information about the company
- Promise to place an order soon if everything goes smoothly
- ...

Seller: David Lee

- Export Sales Manager of Evergreen Gifts Co Ltd.
- Receive the phone
- Thank Bob for his interest in their products
- Agree to meet with Bob in Hilton Hotel
- Decide on the date and time for meeting

Next day:

- Go to meet the buyer in his hotel
- Ask about the buyer's feelings of the visit to the country
- Tell about the company's export businesses with other countries
- Promise to offer the best prices and services
- Express the sincere hope to build a long-term relationship between the parties
- ...

UNIT 9 International Trade

Language Hints

Sample questions on the phone
- When will you be available?
- What's the best time to meet you?
- When will you be free?
- When will you have time?
- May I know your hotel's name and room no.?
- Would you please spare us just 10 minutes? It will only take you 10 minutes, any time will be fine with us.
- Can we leave our catalog at the front desk?
- Can you come to meet me at my hotel?
- ...

Ending telephone calls
- Thanks for giving us the chance, and it's my pleasure to have talked with you. Wish you have a good stay here and have a good trip!
- Good, I'll be waiting and see you tomorrow morning.
- Thanks for (your) calling, bye.
- ...

A Letter of Establishing Business Relations

It is of vital importance for businesses to enter new markets and establish new connections. To achieve that purpose, writing a business letter to the party concerned is a useful and effective way. It could be written by either the seller or the buyer. A letter of establishing trade relations usually consists of the following parts:

- Inform the party concerned about your source of information regarding their firm, i.e., how you get to know their company, such as by advertisement, from the Commercial Counselor's Office or from the Chambers of Commerce, etc.;
- Explain your intention to establish business with them;
- Introduce your business scope. You may also enclose some brochures, catalogues or price list for their information;
- Express your hope for cooperation and an early reply.

Such letters should sound courteous, sincere and polite, but do not have to sound overmodest. If yours is the first letter, try to make a good impression on the correspondent.

Study the following sample letter and then write a letter according to the situations.

Johnson Supply Corporation
376 Sutton Street
San. Francisco, California
U.S.A.

Our Ref. No. EC89/4706

July 27, 2008

China National Light Industrial Products

Import & Export Corporation

82 Dong An Men Street

Beijing, China

Attention: Mr. Li Qun

Dear Mr. Li,

<u>Seeking the possibilities of establishing business relations</u>

We heard from China Council for the Promotion of International Trade that you are in the market for light industrial products.

We specialize in international trade, but we have no contact with your company. As being interested in selling light industrial products, we address this letter to you in order to enter into direct business relations with you at an early date.

We are looking forward to receiving your details and prices of various kinds of light industrial products you would be interested in selling, and shall be glad to study the sales possibilities in our market.

On the other hand, please favor us with a list of those products you are interested in obtaining from here, so that we might give you all the necessary information regarding supply possibilities.

We look forward to your early reply.

Yours truly,

J. L. Hudson

J. L. Hudson

Purchasing Manager

UNIT 9 International Trade

1. Use the information given in "Establishing Business Relations" to write a letter to either company, expressing your hope of establishing business relations with them. Add anything necessary.

2. John Brown is the Purchasing Manager of an American company—King Clothing Inc. (56 George Road, Rockville, LA 766565, U.S.A.). His company mainly imports clothes and sells in U.S. market. On May 8, he attended the Guangdong International Trade Fair. He was very interested in the silk garments displayed by a Chinese company—Jintai Clothing Inc. After discussing with the General Manager, Mr. Li Lin of the company, he decided to establish business relationship with that company. Draft a letter to Jintai Clothing Inc. (48 Furong Road, Kaifu District, Changsha, China).

Business Expressions

1. Match the English expressions in the left column to their Chinese equivalents in the right column.

English expressions	Chinese equivalents
1) foul Bill of Lading	a. 到岸价（成本加运费、保险费价）
2) fair average quality	b. 国内发票
3) price indication	c. 不清洁提单
4) to take delivery of goods	d. 允许装卸时间
5) CIF-cost, insurance and freight	e. 成本加运费价（离岸加运费价）
6) original BL	f. 大路货（一般品质）
7) Fragile-with care	g. 期货价格
8) spot price	h. 光票
9) C&F-cost and freight	i. 指示性价格
10) shipping invoice	j. 离岸价（船上交货价）
11) laying days	k. 提货单
12) FOB-free on board	l. 装箱单

13) inland invoice				m. 提货
14) to be cased				n. 用木箱包装
15) delivery order				o. 正本提单
16) forward price				p. 现货价格
17) Packing list				q. 小心易碎
18) clean bill				r. 装运单 / 载货单

2. Give the Chinese equivalents of the following English expressions.

English expressions	Chinese equivalents
1) letter of indemnity	
2) in defective condition	
3) special preferences	
4) unfavorable balance of trade	
5) import quotas	
6) most-favored nation treatment	
7) clearance of goods	
8) counter offer	
9) subject to sellers confirmation	
10) submission of tender	
11) assembling on provided parts	
12) certificate of origin	

3. Translate the following Chinese expressions into English.

1) 小心搬运
2) 防止潮湿
3) 外汇倾销
4) 卸货港
5) 进口许可证
6) 实盘
7) 参考价
8) 习惯做法
9) 有效期限

10) 招标
11) 来料加工
12) 品质检验证书

Specialized Reading

1. **Read the following passage about implications of international trade and do the multiple choice exercises.**

    International trade has social and cultural dimensions. We must remember the cultural and social implications of trade.

    Let's consider an example from history. In the Middle Ages, Greek ideas and philosophy were lost to Europe when hordes of barbarians swept over the continent. These ideas and that philosophy were rediscovered in the Renaissance only as a by-product of trade between the Italian merchant cities and the Middle East. (The Greek ideas that had spread to the Middle East were protected from European upheavals.) Renaissance means rebirth: a rebirth in Europe of Greek learning. Many of our traditions and sensibilities are based on those of the Renaissance, and that Renaissance was caused, or at least significantly influenced, by international trade. Had there been no trade, our entire philosophy of life might have been different.

    Fernand Braudel, a French historian, has provided wonderful examples of the broader implications for trade. For instance, he argues that the effects of international trade specifically Sir Walter Raleigh's[1] introduction of potato into England from South America in 1588, had more long-run consequences than did the celebrated 1588 battle of the English navy and Spanish Armada.

    1) When did Greek philosophy lose its position in Europe?

        A. In the Renaissance.   B. During the French Revolution.

        C. In the Middle Ages.   D. After the rebirth of Greek learning.

    2) According to the passage, Renaissance refers to _____.

        A. a revival of Greek learning in Europe

        B. a revival of Italian philosophy in the Middle East

        C. a rebirth of Greek ideas in the Middle East

        D. a rebirth of French philosophy in Europe

---

1 Sir Walter Raleigh: British explorer, poet and historian

3) The author used an example from history to illustrate that _____.

   A. international trade can help to spread great ideas

   B. many of western traditions are based on those of renaissance

   C. the entire philosophy of life would be totally different without trade

   D. renaissance is a by-product of the international trade

4) What has the article laid stress on with regard to international trade?

   A. Its economic influence.   B. Its military implications.

   C. Its technical issues.   D. Its cultural aspect.

5) Introduction of the potato into England is compared with a famous 1588 battle for the purpose of _____.

   A. discussing interaction between military influence and trade

   B. stressing long-term effect of international trade

   C. emphasizing the long-run consequences of war

   D. explaining importance of international trade

6) The origin of the article probably comes from _____.

   A. a chapter dealing with social difference

   B. a book concerning economics

   C. a book on ancient ideas and philosophy

   D. a history book

2. **Read the following passage and mark the statements with T(true) or F(False).**

   Traditionally trade was regulated through bilateral treaties between two nations. For centuries under the belief in Mercantilism most nations had high tariffs and many restrictions on international trade. In the 19th century, especially in Britain, a belief in free trade became paramount and this view has dominated thinking among western nations for most of the time since then. In the years since the Second World War, multilateral treaties like the GATT[1] and World Trade Organization have attempted to create a globally regulated trade structure.

   Free trade is usually most strongly supported by the most economically powerful nations in the world, though they often engage in selective protectionism for those industries which are politically important domestically, such as the

---

1 GATT: General Agreement on Tariffs and Trade　关税和贸易总协定

protective tariffs applied to agriculture and textiles by the United States and Europe. The Netherlands and the United Kingdom were both strong advocates of free trade when they were economically dominant. Today the United States, the United Kingdom, Australia and Japan are its greatest proponents. However, many other countries (such as India, China and Russia) are increasingly becoming advocates of free trade as they become more economically powerful themselves. As tariff levels fall there is also an increasing willingness to negotiate non tariff measures, including foreign direct investment, procurement and trade facilitation. The latter looks at the transaction cost associated with meeting trade and customs procedures.

Traditionally agricultural interests are usually in favor of free trade while manufacturing sectors often support protectionism. This has changed somewhat in recent years, however. In fact, agricultural lobbies, particularly in the United States, Europe and Japan, are chiefly responsible for particular rules in the major international trade treaties which allow for more protectionist measures in agriculture than for most other goods and services.

During recessions there is often strong domestic pressure to increase tariffs to protect domestic industries. This occurred around the world during the Great Depression leading to a collapse in world trade that many believe seriously deepened the depression.

The regulation of international trade is done through the World Trade Organization at the global level, and through several other regional arrangements such as MERCOSUR[1] in South America, NAFTA[2] between the United States, Canada and Mexico, and the European Union between 27 independent states. The 2005 Buenos Aires talks on the planned establishment of the Free Trade Area of the Americas (FTAA) failed largely due to opposition from the populations of Latin American nations. Similar agreements such as the MAI (Multilateral Agreement on Investment) have also failed in recent years.

1) _____ Trade has always been regulated through multilateral treaties like the GATT and World Trade Organization.

2) _____ For centuries, a belief in free trade has been accepted by most nations as a very important view.

---

1 MERCOSUR: a trade association, consisting of Argentina, Brazil, Paraguay, and Uruguay
2 NAFTA: North American Free Trade Agreement

3) _____ Economically powerful nations often protect some industries through protective tariffs.

4) _____ More and more countries are increasingly becoming advocates of free trade as they become more economically powerful themselves.

5) _____ Many countries agree to take measures to remove the trade tariffs.

6) _____ In recent years manufacturing industries are increasingly in favor of trade protectionism.

7) _____ Many people think the world trade seriously deepened the Great Depression.

8) _____ The regulation of international trade is mainly done through the World Trade Organization at the global level.

3. **Discuss the following questions with your group members.**

   1) Running a trade deficit is not necessarily bad, since the country is consuming (importing) more than it is producing (exporting). Personally, do you want to be a debtor or a creditor? Give your reasons.

   2) Will you borrow money for investment? Why or why not?

UNIT 10
Globalization

1. Discuss the following questions with your partner.

   1) What is globalization/globalisation? When did it start?
   2) What is the difference between "global" and "international"?
   3) Do you regard yourself as a citizen of the world as well as a citizen of China? In what ways do you behave as a citizen of each?
   4) Could you name some global corporations that you are familiar with? What influence do they have on your life?

2. For many of the world's people, globalization has not worked out as advertised while some others believe that the advantages of it outweigh the disadvantages. Read the following viewpoints about globalization. Tell your group members which of them you agree with and which you disagree with; which are advantages and which are disadvantages.

   a. Globalization has increased free trade between nations.
   b. It has increased likelihood of economic disruptions in one nation affecting all nations.
   c. Corporations have greater flexibility to operate across borders.
   d. There is a greater chance of reactions for globalization being violent in an attempt to preserve cultural heritage.
   e. Global mass media ties the world together.
   f. Control of world media by a handful of corporations will limit cultural expression.
   g. It may produce a greater risk of diseases being transported unintentionally between nations.
   h. Increased flow of communications allows vital information to be shared between individuals and corporations around the world.
   i. Transportation for goods and people can be done with greater ease and speed.
   j. The likelihood of war between developed nations may be reduced.

k. There may be decreases in environmental integrity as polluting corporations take advantage of weak regulatory rules in developing countries.

Preview: Globalization is usually understood as a process in which barriers (physical, political, economic, cultural) separating different regions of the world are reduced or removed, thereby stimulating exchanges in knowledge and goods. Globalization promotes mutual reliance. As the number of exchanges of goods and of information increases, the result is a growing interdependence between countries as they come to rely on various imported products, services, and cultural input. However, there is another side to globalization that is less savory. In the absence of barriers, globalization invites the strong to the territory of the weak, opening the door to wholesale exploitation. The following article focuses on how the strong western multinationals should respond to the challenges and opportunities brought by the new global contenders from developing nations.

Emerging Giants

By Pete Engardio

[1] Like other rural residents of southern Mississippi[1], Jamie Lucenberg, 35, faced a huge **cleanup** job last fall in the wake of Hurricane Katrina[2]. He needed a tractor fast to clear **debris** and trees from his 17-**acre** family farm, just 16 miles north of **devastated** Biloxi[3]. "We **literally** had to cut our way up and down the **blacktop** roads," recalls Lucenberg.

[2] But rather than buy an American-made John Deere[4] or New Holland[5], brands he grew up with, Lucenberg chose a **shiny** red Mahindra 5500[6] made by India's Mahindra & Mahindra Ltd.[7] "I have been around equipment all my life," says Lucenberg, who also

---

1 Mississippi /ˌmɪsɪˈsɪpɪ/ 密西西比州（美国）
2 Hurricane Katrina /ˈhʌrɪkən kəˈtriːnə/ 卡特里娜飓风，2005 年，卡特里娜飓风袭击了美国海湾地区，并导致全球能源和其他商品价格急剧上涨
3 Biloxi /bɪˈlɒksɪ/ 比洛克西，美国密西西比州东南部一城市
4 John Deere 约翰·迪尔（强鹿），美国农机品牌
5 New Holland 纽荷兰，美国农机品牌
6 Mahindra 5500 /mɑˈhɪndrə/ 印度马亨德拉公司生产的马亨德拉 5500 拖拉机
7 India's Mahindra & Mahindra Ltd. 印度马亨德拉公司

used the tractor to earn extra money clearing destroyed homes along the Gulf Coast. But for $27,000, complete with a front loader, the 54-hp Mahindra "is by far the best for the money. It has more power and heavier steel," Lucenberg says.

[3] Surprised that a company from India is penetrating a U.S. market long dominated by **venerable** names like Deere & Co.[1]? Then it's time to take a look at how globalization has come full circle. A new breed of ambitious **multinational** is rising on the world scene, presenting both challenges and opportunities for established global players.

[4] These new **contenders hail** from seemingly unlikely places, developing nations such as Brazil, China, India, Russia, and even Egypt and South Africa. They are shaking up entire industries, from farm equipment and refrigerators to aircraft and telecom services, and changing the rules of global competition.

[5] Unlike Japanese and Korean **conglomerates**, which benefited from protection and big profits at home before they took on the world, these are mostly companies that have **prevailed** in brutally competitive domestic markets, where local companies have to duke it out with homegrown rivals and Western multinationals every day. As a result, these emerging champions must make profits at price levels unheard of in the U.S. or Europe. Indian generic drugmakers, for example, often charge customers in their home market as little as 1% to 2% of what people pay in the U.S. **Cellular** outfits in North Africa, Brazil, and India offer phone service for pennies per minute. Yet these companies often thrive in such tough environments. Egyptian cellular operator Orascom[2] boasts margins of 49%; Mahindra's pretax profit rose 81% last year.

[6] What makes these upstarts global contenders? Their key advantages are access to some of the world's most dynamic growth markets and **immense** pools of low-cost resources, be they production workers, engineers, land, **petroleum**, or iron ore. But these **aspiring** giants are about much more than low cost. The best of the pack are proving as innovative and **expertly** run as any in the business, **astutely** absorbing global consumer trends and technologies and getting new products to market faster than their rivals. Globalization and the Internet are ushering in this "**seismic** change" to the competitive **landscape**, says management guru Ram Charan. Because they can tap the same managerial talent, information, and capital as Western companies, "anyone from anywhere who sets his mind to it can really restructure an industry," Charan says. "Make no mistake; this now is a global game."

---

1 Deere & Co. 美国迪尔公司，世界最大的农机设备制造商
2 Orascom /ˈɒrəskɒm/ 埃及电讯集团

[7] U.S. corporations, of course, have **weathered** waves of new rivals before. The 1960s and '70s saw the rise of Western European industrial groups such as Unilever[1], Philips[2], Siemens[3], and Volkswagen[4]. Then came Japanese giants such as Sony and Toyota[5], followed by South Korean **powerhouses** such as Hyundai[6] and Samsung in the '90s. Each time, chief executives found themselves caught off guard. The best U.S. corporations adapted and emerged stronger than before.

[8] How can Western multinationals respond? The first step is to begin respecting the new competition. That is the attitude David C. Everitt, president of Deere's $10.5 billion agricultural division, is adopting toward Mahindra. Everitt concedes the Indian rival could someday pass Deere in global unit sales. Mahindra dominates the Indian market, which is bigger even than America's, and is especially strong in the small tractors that account for two-thirds of U.S. sales. But Deere also is picking up its game by, among other things, boosting R&D in higher-end tractors for mega-farms in the U.S., Europe, and Brazil, and expanding its own production in India and elsewhere. "We are not afraid of competition," Everitt says. "It gets the juices going and helps us find ways to be better."

[9] Another strategy is to refuse to **cede** ground either at home or abroad. Last year, Whirlpool Corp[7]. agreed to pay a surprisingly high $2.8 billion to buy Maytag Corp.[8] It wanted to keep Maytag out of the hands of China's Haier[9], which is ramping up in the U.S. and had made a rival bid. Cisco[10], meanwhile, is keeping up the pressure in China, Huawei's[11] home market. Cisco continues to win large orders from Chinese corporations, has **plowed** $650 million into Chinese tech startups, and has **forged** a tieup with local Huawei rival ZTE Corp[12].

---

1 Unilever /ju(:)naɪˈlevə/ 联合利华，于 1930 年由荷兰人造黄油公司与英国利华兄弟制皂公司合并而成，是世界上最大的日用消费品制造商之一

2 Philips /ˈfɪlɪps/ 荷兰皇家飞利浦电子公司，是全球医疗保健、照明与个人优质生活领域的领导者

3 Siemens /ˈsiːmənz/ 德国西门子，世界上最大的电气工程和电子公司之一

4 Volkswagen /ˈfɔːlksˌvaːgən/ 德国大众汽车公司，世界十大汽车公司之一

5 Toyota /təʊˈjəʊtɑː/ 日本丰田汽车公司

6 Hyundai /ˈhɪndaɪ/ 韩国现代汽车株式会社

7 Whirlpool Corp. /ˈ(h)wɜːlpuːl-/ 美国惠而浦公司，全球最具规模的大型白色家电制造商

8 Maytag Corp. /ˈmeɪtæg-/ 美国美泰公司，主要从事家纺贸易

9 Haier 中国海尔集团公司，世界第四大白色家电制造商

10 Cisco /ˈsɪskəʊ/ 美国思科网络技术有限公司

11 Huawei 深圳华为技术有限公司，从事通信网络技术与产品的研究、开发、生产与销售

12 ZTE Corp. 中兴通讯，中国最大的通信设备制造业上市公司

[10] Then there's always the strategy of joining the new challengers. Nortel Networks Ltd.[1] and 3Com[2] have formed telecom equipment and design ventures with Huawei. And Navistar International Corp.[3] in Warrenville, Ill.[4], has a joint venture with Mahindra to build trucks and buses for export. "These companies can be opportunities, if you can work with them," says Harold L. Sirkin, senior vice-president at Boston Consulting Group (BCG), which recently published a study based on data collected from 3,000 companies in 12 developing nations.

[11] No matter how the big U.S. companies respond, gone is the era when they could afford to wait for an emerging market to **ripen**, then count on their ability to roll over the **unsophisticated** local players. "If you don't participate in these markets, you not only miss opportunities but also are cut out of all the innovation that comes from competing there," says University of Michigan[5] management strategist C.K. Prahalad. "Then you won't be able to **withstand** the pressure when these companies come and hit you here." Whether one chooses to **confront** or collaborate, the new multinationals are set to change the rules in industry after industry.

(1023 words)
From *Business Week*

New Words

cleanup /ˈkliːnʌp/
n. a thorough cleaning or ordering, especially after an event that creates a mess 彻底的清理或排序

debris /ˈdebriː/
n. scattered fragments; wreckage 散落的碎片；瓦砾；残骸

acre /ˈeɪkə/
n. measure of land, 4840 square yards or about 4050 square meters 英亩（等于 4840 平方码或约 4050 平方米）

devastate /ˈdevəsteɪt/
v. completely destroy (something); ruin 彻底毁坏（某事物）；毁灭；摧毁

literally /ˈlɪtərəli/
ad. really, actually; used in spoken English to emphasize that what you are saying is true, even though it seems exaggerated or

---

1 Nortel Networks Ltd.　加拿大北电网络有限公司
2 3Com　美国 3Com 公司，国际著名的、历史最悠久的数据网络公司，3 个 com 分别代表 computer- 计算机、communication- 通讯和 compatibility- 兼容
3 Navistar International Corp. /ˈnəvɪstə--/　航星国际公司，美国卡车制造商
4 Warrenville, Ill. /ˈwɒrənvɪl-/　沃伦维尔，位于美国伊利诺伊州
5 University of Michigan　密歇根大学，创建于 1817 年，是美国著名的综合性公立大学

UNIT 10 Globalization

surprising 真实地；确切地

blacktop /ˈblækˌtɑp/
n. a thick black sticky substance that becomes hard as it dries, used to cover roads; pavement（与碎石混合用以铺路面的）沥青；柏油路

shiny /ˈʃaɪni/
a. smooth and bright 发亮的；锃亮的

venerable /ˈvenərəbl/
a. very old and respected because of age, experience, historical importance etc.（因年纪、经历或曾拥有过的重要地位等而）令人尊重敬佩的；老牌的

multinational /mʌltɪˈnæʃən(ə)l/
n. company that does business in many different countries 跨国公司

contender /kənˈtendə(r)/
n. a person who tries to win something in a competition with others 竞争者；争夺者；对手

hail /heɪl/
v. originate from (a place) 来自（某地）

conglomerate /kɒnˈglɒmərɪt/
n. a large business organization consisting of several different companies that have joined together（通过合并若干企业而组建的）大公司，企业集团

prevail /prɪˈveɪl/
v. win; be greater in strength or influence; triumph 获胜，占上风；力量或影响较大；胜利

cellular /ˈseljʊlə/
n. a mobile radiotelephone that uses a network of short-range transmitters located in overlapping cells throughout a region, with a central station making connections to regular telephone lines, also called mobile telephone 蜂窝式移动电话

immense /ɪˈmens/
a. extremely large 巨大的；广大的

petroleum /pɪˈtrəʊlɪəm/
n. oil that is obtained from below the surface of the Earth and is used to make petrol and various chemical substances 石油

aspiring /əsˈpaɪərɪŋ/
a. desiring or striving for recognition or advancement; ambitious for fame, success etc. 有进取心的；有抱负的；渴望成功的

expertly /ˈekspɜːtlɪ/
ad. in a skillful manner; with readiness and accuracy 熟练地；专业地

astutely /əˈstjuːtlɪ/
ad. in a clever way; shrewdly 精明地；敏锐地

seismic /ˈsaɪzmɪk/
a. very great, serious, or important; earthshaking 极其重要的；震撼世界的

landscape /ˈlændskeɪp/
n. the general situation in which a particular activity takes place 全景；形势

weather /ˈweðə/
v. survive; come safely through (something) 平安度过（危难），经历（危难）而存活

powerhouse /ˈpaʊəhaʊs/
n. an organization or place that produces a lot of ideas and has a lot of influence 有影响力的机构或地方

cede /siːd/
v. give something such as an area of land or a right to a country or person, especially when you are forced to 割让，让与

plow /plaʊ/
v. inject into, invest or reinvest (profits) in the business that produced them 将（利润）作为资本再投资于原企业中

forge /fɔːdʒ/
v.(fig.) create (usu. a lasting relationship) by means of much hard work 〈比喻〉（靠艰苦工作）建立（通常为长期关系）

ripen /ˈraɪpən/
v. become mature 成熟

unsophisticated /ʌnsəˈfɪstɪkeɪtɪd/
a. not having a lot of knowledge or experience 知识、经验不丰富的

withstand /wɪðˈstænd/
v. endure; resist 承受住，经得住，抵住

confront /kənˈfrʌnt/
v. face with defiance or hostility 对抗；抵抗

Phrases & Expressions

in the wake of
coming after or following and resulting from something 经过……之后，在……之后

come/go/ turn full circle
turned entirely around, or sometimes to end in the same situation in which you began, even though there have been changes in the time in between 循环；周而复始

shake up
make dramatic changes to an organization in order to make it more effective 改革，变革；改组

duke it out
fight it out 打个输赢

iron ore
an ore from which iron can be extracted 铁矿石

usher in
be the start of something new 开创；开始；引进某（新）事物

put/set/turn one's mind to sth.
decide that one wants to achieve something and try very hard to do it 下定决心要做某事

catch/throw sb. off guard
surprise someone by doing something that they are not ready to deal with （乘某人不备做某事而）使某人措手不及

unit sales
a measure of the total sales that a firm earns in a given reporting period, as expressed on a per unit of output basis, a useful figure for analysts to know the average product prices and find possible margin pressure 单位产品销售额

ramp up
increase a company's operations in anticipation of increased demand 增加、扩张商业活动

joint venture
a partnership or conglomerate, formed often to share risk or expertise 合资企业

count on
rely on; depend on 依赖，依靠

cut out
squeeze out, prevent from participating 排挤出

be set to
be ready to do something; be determined to do something 准备好做某事；决定做某事

Exercises

Comprehension

1. Answer the following content questions with your partner.

   1) Why did Jamie Lucenberg buy a Mahindra 5500 rather than an American-

UNIT 10 Globalization

made John Deere or New Holland?

2) What enables those newly emerging companies from the less developed countries to compete globally?

3) What strategies can the Western multinationals apply to face the challenges and threats from the new global contenders?

4) Why did Whirlpool Corp. buy Maytag at a very high price?

5) How do the new contenders from developing nations differ from Japanese and Korean conglomerates?

6) How many waves of rivals have U.S. corporations weathered before? What were they?

7) What is Deere's attitude towards the competition from Mahindra?

2. The following are the main ideas mentioned in the passage with some points unfinished. And they are not arranged in the same order as they appear in the passage. Fill in the blanks and rearrange them properly.

> a. Western multinational companies have different strategies to respond to the emergence of these new global contenders and those who _____ themselves in the new competition turned _____ into _____ and have become even stronger.
>
> b. No matter what strategies the established western multinationals take, they have to remember the only way out of the fierce competition is to _____ and _____ it.
>
> c. The key reason of these new contenders' survival and success is that they have _____ to the dynamic growth markets and make good use of _____ _____. Additionally those best performers among them are just as _____ and _____ _____ as any well-established ones.
>
> d. These new global contenders must make profits at _____ _____ _____ unheard of in U.S. or Europe because of their _____ _____ domestic markets.
>
> e. The example that a Mississippi farmer bought a tractor made by an _____ _____ rather than an American-made brand he grew up with shows that _____ _____ _____ are bringing both challenges and opportunities to the established global players.
>
> f. These new global contenders are mostly from _____ _____ and greatly changing the present _____ _____ _____.
>
> The correct order: □→□→□→□→□→□

Critical Thinking

Work in group to discuss the following questions.

1) Globalization has various aspects which affect the world in several different ways. Tell in brief about the effects of globaliztion on the following aspects:
   - economy...
   - information...
   - culture...
   - ecology...

2) It is said that the gap between the rich and the poor will get even wider as the industrialized powers relentlessly pursue globalization as a means towards economic growth. What do you think about this view?

Vocabulary

1. Match the verbs in Column A with their synonyms in Column B. Then think of a noun or a noun phrase to make collocations with each pair of verbs. The first one has been done for you as an example.

A	B	
1) cede	a. utilize	c. cede / abandon territory
2) contend	b. endure	
3) aspire to	c. abandon	
4) boast	d. desire	
5) plow	e. initiate	
6) tap	f. compete	
7) weather	g. create	
8) usher in	h. reinvest	
9) forge	i. possess	
10) withstand	j. survive	

2. Rewrite the following sentences using the noun forms of verbs in the box. Do not change the meanings of the sentences. The first one has been done for you.

complete	penetrate	prevail	emerge
adapt	devastate	confront	cede

1) The purpose of this plan is to complete all payments before deadline.

The purpose of this plan is to ensure the completion of all payments before deadline.

2) The government may be forced to accept bank privatization by stealth as private investors are gradually penetrating the banking market.

    _____.

3) This view is well accepted by many employees while it does not prevail in all parts of the executive branch.

    _____.

4) Once new product ideas emerge, you should conduct market research to gauge their viability.

    _____.

5) To succeed, companies should do everything possible to adapt to the fast-changing global environment.

    _____.

6) Larger charitable organizations are doing a tremendous job of getting immediate relief efforts to help the Tsunami-devastated areas.

    _____.

7) We should not take a risk to confront directly with our rivals when we don't have sufficient funding to conduct another advertising campaign.

    _____.

8) Pressure from the joint venture in Russia, may lead the British oil company to cede control to either Rosneft or Gazprom, the Russian state-owned energy companies.

    _____.

3. **Rewrite each of the following sentences by replacing the italicized part with the appropriate words or phrases in the text.**

    1) Many businesses today *rely on* takeovers to acquire new products and technologies.

        _____.

    2) The increasing globalization of world trade has an *earthshaking* influence on China or even on the world.

        _____.

3) The total amount of government debt was expected to rise sharply over the following several years *after* the Korean financial and economic crisis.
   _____.

4) Gucci surprised many by buying the *long-standing and respected* label Balenciaga and announced its intention to build up its fragrance business.
   _____.

5) The business relationship between these two companies has *become mature* after 5 year's collaboration.
   _____.

6) There is an opportunity in the next ten years for a few companies — perhaps one or two in each industry — to define *the general business situation* for the next 50 years.
   _____.

7) Companies who can't work out strategy to cope with the globalization or adapt to the fast changing world will soon be *squeezed out of* the market.
   _____.

8) The board of directors announced yesterday that the company will take some actions *to make changes to* its organizational structure.
   _____.

9) With the experience of involving overseas trainers, Scouts of China *is determined to* restructure and fully revitalize its national training scheme.
   _____.

10) In the 21st century, almost all companies have to *compete with each other* on the global stage.
    _____.

Translation

1. Translate the following paragraph into Chinese.

   What makes these upstarts global contenders? Their key advantages are access to some of the world's most dynamic growth markets and immense pools of low-cost resources, be they production workers, engineers, land, petroleum, or iron ore. But these aspiring giants are about much more than low cost. The best of the pack are proving as innovative and expertly run as any in the business, astutely absorbing global consumer trends and technologies and getting new products to market faster than their rivals. Globalization and the Internet are ushering in this "seismic change" to the competitive landscape, says management guru Ram Charan. Because they can tap the same managerial talent, information, and capital as Western companies, "anyone from anywhere who sets his mind to it can really restructure an industry," Charan says. "Make no mistake; this now is a global game."

2. **Put the following two paragraphs into English, using the words and phrases given in the box below.**

emerge	contender	landscape	prevail	upstart
cede	aspiring	confront	be set to	conglomerate

在全球化的浪潮中，涌现出了来自发展中国家的许多新兴巨人。这些新竞争者不同于日韩财团，他们大多是在国内近乎白热化的竞争中脱颖而出的跨国公司。这些后起之秀雄心勃勃、抱负远大，他们的出现既对老牌公司发起了挑战，同时也给他们带来了机遇。

老牌公司该如何应对呢？首先要充分认识到新的竞争形势，然后再根据实际情况制定相应的战略。常见战略之一是在国内外市场上坚守阵地。战略之二是与新竞争者合作。但不论是对抗还是合作，新兴跨国公司都已准备好改变相关行业的游戏规则。

Mini-debate on Globalization

Globalization is the tendency of investment funds and businesses to move beyond domestic and national markets to other markets around the globe, allowing them to become interconnected with different markets. Proponents of globalization say that it helps developing nations "catch up" to industrialized nations much faster through increased employment and technological advances and Asian economies are often highlighted as examples of globalization's success. Critics of globalization say that it

weakens national sovereignty and allows rich nations to ship domestic jobs overseas where labor is much cheaper. Globalization increased the inequality between countries, especially between the rich and the poor. Is globalization the way to solve the problems existing in this world? What is the real story about globalization? It largely depends on your personal perspective. Now role-play the proponents and the critics, defending your opinions on the topic: **Economic Globalization Is an Effective Way to Tackle Poverty in a Country.** Work by the following steps:

1) Preparation. Be sure to coordinate with your partner on the following:
   - Each should select at least 2 articles;
   - Each will select at least 3 facts and 3 expert opinions that support your side;
   - Each will copy/paste essential information and citations from the selected articles to a Draft Summary;
   - Use the Draft Summary to organize and print note cards for your presentation;
   - Each will have sufficient information for a 2-to-3-minute presentation.

2) Sequence of Activities. You and your partner must also be prepared for a series of 3 Crossfires that give you the opportunity to question each other between presentations.

   Round 1
   - Team A Speaker 1: 3-minute limit (make logical points for your side);
   - Team B Speaker 1: 3-minute limit (make opposing points for your side);
   - Each side makes notes to prepare questions for the first Crossfire;
   - Timeout: 1 minute (Create the questions for the Crossfire);
   - Crossfire (between A1 & B1): 2-minute limit (use the questions you created from the Timeout).

   Round 2 (Repeat the instructions for Round 1)
   - Team A Speaker 2: 3-minute limit;
   - Team B Speaker 2: 3-minute limit;
   - Timeout: 1 minute;
   - Crossfire (between A2 & B2): 2-minute limit.

   Round 3
   - Timeout: 2 minutes (you and your partner should decide only the most

important points to present)
- A1 summary: 1 minute limit;
- B1 summary: 1 minute limit;
- Grand Crossfire (all speakers): 3-minute limit.

Round 4
- Timeout: 2 minutes (you and your partner should decide on the most important point for your side and any glaring weakness in your opponents' arguments)
- A2 Last Shot: 1 minute limit ;
- B2 Last Shot: 1 minute limit.

3) Evaluation. When you are debating in front of another group or in class, your fellow students will judge the winning side. They may keep score, which helps them to be part of the activity. You will have your turn to do this when other mini-debates are scheduled. The scoring system that follows will be used to judge the winning side:

Student Rubrics Model to Participate and Determine the Debate Winner

Debate Activities Sequence	Affirmative Score	Negative Score
Scoring (Convincing = 4; Satisfactory = 2; Little Impact = 1)		
Affirmative (Pro Issue) Speaker 1		
Negative (Con Issue) Speaker 1		
Crossfire for the Affirmative (Pro Issue)		
Crossfire for the Negative (Con Issue)		
Affirmative (Pro Issue) Speaker 2		
Negative (Con Issue) Speaker 2		
Crossfire for the Affirmative (Pro Issue)		
Crossfire for the Negative (Con Issue)		
Affirmative Speaker 1 (Pro Issue) Summary		
Negative Speaker 1 (Con Issue) Summary		
Grand Crossfire (all speakers) for the Affirmative (Pro)		

续表

Debate Activities Sequence	Affirmative Score	Negative Score
Grand Crossfire (all speakers) for the Negative (Con)		
Affirmative Speaker 2 (Pro Issue) Last Shot		
Negative Speaker 2 (Con Issue) Last Shot		
Student Evaluator: Totals		

Language Hints

Opening the statement
- Honorable judges, distinguished guests, ladies and gentleman...
- As is known to all,...has played a very important role...
- Nowadays, as you know,...is popular...
- I would like to say something first.
- We take an absolutely different position from our friends. They believe...But our position is just the contrary:...
- ...

Closing statement
- All right. That was the final question and answer and we now go to the closing statements.
- First, I'd like to thank...and my opponents for participating in this debate and making it possible.
- I want to say that even though we disagree with... on..., I really respect what they have done in this debate.
- I appreciate their efforts and wish them well. Thank you very much.
- ...

Cross-examining
- I just don't understand why our friends hold such a hostile view towards...
- If I understand you correctly, you said that...
- But didn't you say that...?
- I was wondering where you stood on the question of...
- My dear friend/my fellow debater, please give me a clear answer now.
- Do you choose to turn a blind eye to...?
- I need to remind our friend that...
- May I point it out that you have made a very serious mistake?
- That's what's wrong with you.
- Well said. But the fact is...
- You keep saying that.../As you said, ... but...
- Are you of the same opinion as I?
- Well, that may be true. But I'm afraid I can't entirely agree with you there.
- It is quite true that...But we still think that...
- I'm with you here/Yes, you are right here, but...
- But we should not always look on the negative side of things.
- ...

Investigation Report

Investigation Report

An investigation report is a report written on the instruction or commission of some people or body. It is drawn on the base of a close survey or investigation, aimed to provide facts as objectively as possible. An investigation report usually functions as source of information backing the future strategy or decision.

To write an investigation report, one should keep in mind that the findings are based on real facts; otherwise the report is of no value and may cause poor or wrong strategy to be made. It should indicate the way applied in the investigation with the expressions like:

- We carried out the survey in the aspects of...
- We interview with...
- The questionnaires were collected...

After a brief introduction and illustration, the report is organized as follows:

- Findings
- Conclusion

Some investigation reports are presented with Recommendation after Conclusion, while it is not a must.

When you are writing a business report, you should pay attention to the following tips:

- Include in your report objective and impersonal data relevant to the subject matter so as to facilitate the decision-making. Don't insert your personal viewpoints if not requested.
- Arrange detailed data in a logical order and put related findings together.
- Follow the same grammatical pattern from head to bottom so as to make the language style consistent.
- Use clear and concise language all through.
- Read through your finished report carefully and double check the accuracy of the data, figures in particular.

Study the following samples and then do the exercises according to the directions.

Sample 1: A formal report

Report on the Decline in Sales of Shanghai Branch

Location: Shanghai   Date: October 9, 2008

On your instructions, we examined the causes of the decline in sales of Shanghai Branch. We visited the office and most of their major customers there. The following are our findings.

> This section may be filled in at a later date after the draft report is delivered and discussed.

Findings

- Some of the major customers in Shanghai have closed down, and some have moved to other areas.
- Other customers are planning to move to Suzhou or Wuxi as business there is booming and they can enjoy favorable policy from the local government there.
- The Shanghai Office has not kept an up-to-date mailing list for sending circulars to existing customers who have moved, or potential customers moving in.
- The customers I visited were interested in more advanced air-conditioning systems instead of the traditional models we supply them with at present.

> Facts in bullet form are best in this section. Give the reader factual contributing factors without drawing conclusions.

Conclusions

- A more favorable after-sales mix is needed to keep our customers there.
- An up-to-date circulars list should be made.
- The supply needs adjustment as to replace a part of the present models with new ones.

> Draw your conclusions here. Be specific, cite the incident's root cause, and use your facts.

Recommendation

- A traveling sales representative needs to be positioned in Shanghai to keep contact with customers who have moved out of Shanghai but may still purchase our goods.
- Shanghai Branch needs technical support in dealing with information or data sorting.
- Replacement should be made in supply with the latest models.

Sarah Lee
CC: Mike Johnson
    (Sales Manager)

UNIT **10** Globalization

Sample 2: An informal report

To: Susan Baker, Personnel Director
From: David Brown, Personnel Relation Coordinator
Date: May 12, 2008
Subject: Flextime System

Here is the report you asked me to prepare based on the research about the possibility of practicing the flextime working system.

Procedure
1. All staffs were interviewed on their needs for various time bands. Staffs were then interviewed on their preferences for various time bands.
2. A questionnaire was issued to all staff asking them to state which time they wanted.
3. The work done by the staff was observed to see if it was necessary for all staff to be present during "core time", and to ascertain when precisely these core time are.

Findings

Staff Needs
1. The major finding from interviewing staff on their needs is that most of the working mothers need to be free from 3:30 in the afternoons. The reasons are as follows:
   - Collection of young children from school;
   - Being at home when their children arrive home from school;
   - Preparing meals for the family between the hours of 5 and 7 p.m.
2. Staff who have recently moved, or who have lived far away from the firm for some time, need extra time to arrive punctually in the morning.

Staff Preference
1. Approximately 60% of the staff interviewed prefer to arrive later in the morning. The period ranges from 30 minutes to 3 hours later.
2. 25% of the staff interviewed prefer to finish work earlier than at present. This ranges from 30 minutes to 1 hour 30 minutes.

Core Time

1. Checking on the validity, accuracy and urgency of forms, documents and applications sent to the firm requires an efficient and streamlined operation. Some members of staff need to be on hand to verify, cross-check and revise communication ready for signing and dispatch.
2. The greatest volume of telephoned requests for information and advice is between the hours of 10:00 a.m. and 3:00 p.m.
3. The least busy period is from 3 to 5 p.m., when business calls fall away, and some work is left for the following morning.

Conclusions

1. There is a conflict between the 23% of staff who need to arrive earlier in the day, and the 60% who prefer to arrive later. Most of the paperwork needs to be done earlier, to be filed, signed, and dispatched while senior staff are available, and also to catch the earlier postal collections.
2. The 15% of staff—the working mothers—who need to arrive earlier and leave earlier would help to clear the backlog of work from the previous day, but they need to be helped by extra staff.
3. There needs to be heavy discouragement of staff wishing to arrive 2 hours and more later than at present.
4. We need to test the degree of certainty about late arrivals. Some staff are obviously not sure yet when they prefer to arrive.

Recommendations

1. The following time bands can be effected:
    - 8:30 to 4:00
    - 9:00 to 4:30
    - 9:30 to 5:00
    - 10:30 to 5:00
    - 10:30 to 6:00
2. In the first three time bands, volunteers would be asked to bring the percentage up from 19% to 50%. Failing this, a compulsory rota system should be introduced in consultation with the trade union.
3. All staff must be in the premises between 10:00 am and 3:00 pm. This is the "core time" we recommend.
4. The needs of working mothers should have priority in early finishing.
5. The needs of those who live far away should have priority in late arrival time band.

UNIT 10 Globalization

1. The famous American XYZ Company dealing with central cooling systems has expanded its business into Southeast Asia, but the second yearly sales was falling, 67% less than that of the first year. The company doubts whether it is right for them to become a global company. A sales manager was asked to write an investigation report as follows. Please complete it by translating the Chinese in brackets into English.

   To: Andrew Dane, General Manager
   From: David Johnson, Sales Manager
   Date: December 25, 2008
   Subject: The Drops on the Second Yearly Sales

   Our company expanded business to Southeast Asia, _____ _____ （但是第二年的销售量在下降，比第一年减少67%）. The sales of last year were $15 mil while those of this year were $4.95 mil. Our most important markets in Southeast Asia are in Thailand, Malaysia and Singapore. _____ （我们的产品在这些国家的销售量占我公司总销售量的三分之二）. We carried out a regional survey and ascribe the drops to the following factors:

   Findings
   - The long rainy weather. _____ （今年的雨季比上一年雨季长得多）. This should be taken into consideration in the drops on sales.
   - The pressing market competition. _____ （因为有太多的竞争产品上市,今年的销售量很难与去年保持同一水平）. Take Singapore for example, there are at least 10 other major brands of central cooling systems.
   - The different consuming habits. _____ （东南亚人在购物时已习惯于将产品价格作为最重要的因素来考虑）.

   Conclusions
   - The market is slow but competition is pressing. _____ _____ （即使今年我们的销售量下降了，我们的市场占有率仍然会不错，因为我们已建立了许多分销渠道。这点是肯定无疑的）. We might get over the fierce competition as long as we could offer strong support and better after-sales service.

- However, in order to deal with the rainy season, we should develop a wider range of products to adjust to it.
- Though the sales dropped this year, _____
  （东南亚市场对整个公司来说是非常重要的，因此不能放弃）.

Recommendation
- A promotion campaign is needed.
- After-sales team should be strengthened.
- New products should be researched and developed.

2. Get the following investigation report rearranged under the three subtitles: Findings, Conclusions and Recommendations.

> Our area manager in Morlanda has reported distribution difficulties in the north of the country, an area affected by flood during the last few months. There have been 22 truck breakdowns and these have resulted in complaints about poor delivery times. On the other hand, there have been no problems with delivery times in the south. In fact, there is evidence that the warehouse there is both overstocked and overmanned. It is obvious that the major geographical differences between the north and the south were not taken into account when planning the distribution network in Morlanda. In view of this, the feasibility of warehousing more goods in the north should be considered. Another problem which the area manager has reported is difficulty in obtaining prompt payment for goods delivery. Evidence of this can be found in the annual accounts which indicate that $25,000 was owed at the end of the year. Small customers are largely to blame. In two cases, customers have gone bankrupt and this has resulted in bad debts of $45,000. The area manager concludes that this problem will continue as long as the economy is depressed. He suggests that a penalty clause should be included in all delivery contracts.

3. The committee from the Purchasing Department of QuayWest is asked to recommend a supplier for the company's new range of leisurewear. It was presented with a short list of five potential suppliers to select from; Consort Trading, Smokovska, Namlong Sportwear, Shiva Trading and Hai Xin Group. The factors considered include price, quality, delivery, and flexibility. You, Daisy Hopkins, are a secretary of the committee. Please write a report, with the help of the related information given below, to the general manager, Karl Anderson,

recommending a supplier for the company's new range of leisurewear.

- *Consort Trading:*   *offers the best deal financially; unable to guarantee garments compliant with EU standards*
- *Smokovska:*   *produces goods of an extremely high quality; charges high price*
- *Namlong Sportwear:*   *with poor standards of craftsmanship; difficult to justify paying the price quoted*
- *Shiva Trading:*   *is shown an acceptable quality level*
- *Hai Xin Group:*   *is doubtful whether the garments they produced would meet EU standards; the prices being unreasonably high*

Business Expressions

1. Match the business expressions in the box with the definitions given below and then translate expressions into Chinese.

hard currency	exchange rate	trade fair
economic sanctions	offshore manufacturing	trade surplus
global governance	free port	countervailing duty
trade barrier		

1) the foreign manufacture of goods by a domestic firm primarily for import into its home country

_____

2) the currency of a nation which may be exchanged for that of another nation without restriction, sometimes referred to as convertible currency

_____

3) a stage-setting event in which firms of several nationalities present their products or services to prospective customers in a pre-formatted setting

_____

4) an extra charge that a country places on imported goods to counter the subsidies or bounties granted to the exporters of the goods by their home governments

   _____

5) economic penalties, such as prohibiting trade, stopping financial transactions, or barring economic and military assistance, used to achieve the goal of influencing the target nation

   _____

6) the price of one currency expressed in terms of another, i.e., the number of units of one currency that may be exchanged for one unit of another currency

   _____

7) rules and institutions for managing and regulating actions or processes of global import; specifically, object of international reform efforts pursuing design of democratic transnational institutions and control over economic activity

   _____

8) a positive balance of trade, namely, the amount of goods and services that a country exports that is in excess of the amount of goods and services it imports

   _____

9) any form of governmental or operational activity or restriction that renders importation of some goods into a country difficult or impossible

   _____

10) a port or an area of a port in which imported goods can be held or processed free of customs duties before reexport

    _____

2. The following abbreviations are all related to Globalization. Write down their full forms in the spaces provided below. You may consult the dictionary for the ones you don't know.

   1) MFN   _____
   2) MNC   _____
   3) ILO   _____
   4) GATT   _____
   5) FTAA   _____

6) FDI _____
7) IMF _____
8) WTO _____
9) OECD _____
10) TBT _____
11) APEC _____
12) WB _____
13) NAFTA _____
14) MAI _____
15) INGO _____
16) TRQ _____
17) EPZ _____

3. The following statements are about Globalization. Complete each of them with the best choice from the four answers marked A, B, C and D.

1) The economist examines the impact of the 'flattening' of the globe, and argues that _____ trade, outsourcing, supply-chaining and political forces have changed the world permanently, for both better and worse.

   A. localized   B. globalized   C. domestic   D. foreign

2) Globalization in its literal sense is the process of globalizing, _____ of some things or phenomena into global ones.

   A. transformation   B. exchange   C. transfer   D. transmission

3) The term "_____" stresses the importance of international trade, relations and treaties between or among nations.

   A. industrialization   B. multinationalism
   C. multilateralism   D. internationalization

4) Globalization refers to economic _____ on a global scale, into a global economy, which blurs national boundaries.

   A. combination   B. integration
   C. restructuring   D. allies

5) In the 17th century, globalization became a business phenomenon when many _____ corporations were established.

   A. state-owned   B. foreign-funded
   C. overseas   D. multinational

6) The Dutch East India Company was the first company in the world to share risk and enable joint ownership through the issuing of _____: an important driver for globalization.

   A. shares   B. funds   C. bonds   D. securities

7) Export _____ are direct government payments or other economic inducements given to domestic producers of goods that are sold in foreign markets.

   A. subsidies   B. bonus   C. allowance   D. quotas

8) With the increase of the country's agricultural and industrial _____, there is a decline in international economic integration.

   A. restrictions   B. governance
   C. protectionism   D. barriers

9) Globalization has been facilitated by advances in technology which have reduced the costs of trade, and trade _____ rounds.

   A. negotiation B. deal   C. dispute   D. cycle

10) _____ occurs when a country sells goods internationally at prices lower than their national market.

   A. Monopolizing   B. Oligopolizing   C. Dumping   D. Boycotting

Specialized Reading

1. Read the following passage about measuring globalization and then judge whether the following statements are true (T) or false (F) or not mentioned (NM) in the passage.

   Looking specifically at economic globalization, it can be measured in different ways. These centre around the four main economic flows that characterize globalization:

   Goods and services, e.g. exports plus imports as a proportion of national income or per capita of population;

   Labor/people, e.g. net migration rates; inward or outward migration flows, weighted by population;

   Capital, e.g. inward or outward direct investment as a proportion of national income or per head of population;

   Technology, e.g. international research & development flows; proportion of populations (and rates of change thereof) using particular inventions (especially

UNIT 10 Globalization

"factor-neutral" technological advances such as the telephone, motorcar, broadband).

As globalization is not only an economic phenomenon, a multivariate approach to measuring globalization is the recent index calculated by the Swiss think tank KOF[1]. The index measures the three main dimensions of globalization: economic, social, and political. In addition to three indices measuring these dimensions, an overall index of globalization and sub-indices referring to actual economic flows, economic restrictions, data on personal contact, data on information flows, and data on cultural proximity is calculated. Data is available on a yearly basis for 122 countries, as detailed in Dreher, Gaston and Martens[2]. According to the index, the world's most globalized country is Belgium, followed by Austria, Sweden, the United Kingdom and the Netherlands. The least globalized countries according to the KOF-index are Haiti, Myanmar, the Central African Republic and Burundi. Other measures conceptualize globalization as diffusion and develop interactive procedure to capture the degree of its impact.

A.T. Kearney[3] and *Foreign Policy* magazine[4] jointly publish another Globalization Index. According to the index, Singapore, Ireland, Switzerland, the U.S., the Netherlands, Canada and Denmark are the most globalized, while Egypt, Indonesia, India and Iran are the least globalized among countries listed.

1) _____ One characteristic of globalization is its indirect investment as a proportion of national income.

2) _____ The higher the net migration rate, the lower the degree of globalization.

3) _____ Exports and imports as a proportion of national income can reflect the degree of globalization.

---

1 Swiss KOF has produced leading indicators, which is a composite of business surveys from various sectors. The recent index calculated by the Swiss think tank KOF measures the three main dimensions of globalization: economic, social, and political.

2 The KOF Index of Globalization was introduced in 2002 and is updated and described in detail by Dreher, Gaston and Martens. Dreher, Gaston and Martens have produced the most systematic and comprehensive research both measuring globalization and analyzing its impact.

3 A.T. Kearney is a global management consulting firm, focusing on strategic and operational CEO-agenda concerns. The stated mission of A.T. Kearney is to help the world's leading corporations gain and sustain competitive advantage, and achieve profound, tangible results. Its slogan is: Ideas that last.

4 *Foreign Policy* is a bimonthly American magazine founded in 1970 by Samuel P. Huntington and Warren Demian Manshel. It is published by the Carnegie Endowment.

4) _____ Cultural aspect is measured in the index of globalization of Swiss think tank.

5) _____ In addition to an overall index of globalization, there are several sub-indices of calculation.

6) _____ According to Dreher, Gaston and Martens, the United Kingdom is more globalized than Belgium.

7) _____ In terms of the globalization index published by *Foreign Policy* magazine, the most globalized countries mentioned outnumbered the least globalized countries.

8) _____ A.T. Kearney and *Foreign Policy* magazine published the globalization index on the basis of 122 countries.

2. **Read the following passage about the effects of globalization and then come up with the questions that match the corresponding answers.**

   Globalization has various aspects which affect the world in several different ways such as:

   Industrial — emergence of worldwide production markets and broader access to a range of foreign products for consumers and companies.

   Financial — emergence of worldwide financial markets and better access to external financing for corporate, national and subnational borrowers.

   Economic — realization of a global common market, based on the freedom of exchange of goods and capital.

   Political — creation of a world government which regulates the relationships among nations and guarantees the rights arising from social and economic globalization.

   Informational — increase in information flows between geographically remote locations.

   Cultural — growth of cross — cultural contacts; advent of new categories of consciousness and identities such as Globalism, which embodies cultural diffusion, the desire to consume and enjoy foreign products and ideas, adopt new technology and practices, and participate in a "world culture;" loss of languages (and corresponding loss of ideas).

   Ecological — the advent of global environmental challenges that cannot be solved without international cooperation, such as climate change, cross-boundary water and air pollution, over-fishing of the ocean, and the spread of invasive species.

Many factories are built in developing countries where they can pollute freely.

Social — increased circulation by people of all nations with fewer restrictions.

Transportation — fewer and fewer European cars on European roads each year (the same can also be said about American cars on American roads) and the death of distance through the incorporation of technology to decrease travel time.

International cultural exchange — spreading of multiculturalism, and better individual access to cultural diversity (e.g. through the export of Hollywood and Bollywood movies). However, the imported culture can easily supplant the local culture, causing reduction in diversity through hybridization or even assimilation. The most prominent form of this is Westernization; greater international travel and tourism; greater immigration, including illegal immigration; spread of local consumer products (e.g. food) to other countries (often adapted to their culture); world-wide fads and pop culture; world-wide sporting events such as FIFA World Cup and the Olympic Games; formation or development of a set of universal values.

Technical — development of a global telecommunications infrastructure and greater transborder data flow, using such technologies as the Internet, communication satellites, submarine fiber optic cable, and wireless telephones; increase in the number of standards applied globally, e.g. copyright laws, patents and world trade agreements.

Legal/Ethical — the push by many advocates for an international criminal court and international justice movements; crime importation and raising awareness of global crime-fighting efforts and cooperation and sexual awareness. Sexual awareness is often easy to only focus on the economic aspects of globalization. This term also has strong social meanings behind it. Globalization can also mean a cultural interaction between different countries. Globalization may also have social effects such as changes in sexual inequality, and to this issue bring about a greater awareness of the different (often more brutal) types of gender discrimination throughout the world. For example, women and girls in African countries have long been subjected to female circumcision — such a harmful procedure has been since exposed to the world and the practice is now decreasing in occurrence.

1) Globalization has affected the world in industrial, financial, economic, political, informational, cultural, ecological, social aspects as well as transportation, international cultural exchange, technology, legal process and ethical issues.

   Question: _____

2) Political globalization is the creation of a world government which regulates the relationships among nations and guarantees the rights arising from social and economic globalization.

   Question: _____

3) With regard to informational globalization, there will emerge an increase in information flows between geographically remote locations.

   Question: _____

4) It is the cultural globalization that will bring about the desire to consume and enjoy foreign products and ideas.

   Question: _____

5) International cooperation can help to overcome ecological problems such as climate change, cross-boundary water and air pollution, over-fishing of the ocean, and the spread of invasive species.

   Question: _____

6) The social globalization will result in an increased circulation by people of all nations with fewer restrictions.

   Question: _____

7) The side effects of the international cultural exchange are that the imported culture can easily supplant the local culture, causing reduction in diversity through hybridization or even assimilation.

   Question: _____

8) Due to the effect of globalization on legal and ethical issues, a lot can be done such as an international criminal court and international justice movements; crime importation and raising awareness of global crime-fighting efforts and cooperation and sexual awareness.

   Question: _____

3. **Discuss the following questions with your group members.**

   1) For China, globalization is often seen as a double-edged sword that brings opportunities and challenges, advantages and disadvantages. What are the positive and negative effects of globalization on China?

   2) How are you, personally, affected or influenced by globalization in your daily life? Tell with some examples.

GLOSSARY

Words	Units		Definitions
abrasive	4	a.	粗鲁的
accelerate	9	v.	加速；促进
accommodate	9	v.	允许；考虑；使适应；使符合
accordingly	6	ad.	相应地
accountable	8	a.	应负责的，有责任的；可解释的
accumulate	1	v.	（数量）逐渐增加；（质量）渐渐提高
acre	10	n.	英亩（等于 4840 平方码或约 4050 平方米）
acrimonious	1	a.	尖刻的；讥讽的；激烈的
adjust	9	v.	调整，调节，校准；使适合
ado	6	n.	纷扰；忙乱；小题大做；麻烦；困扰
aerial	1	a.	航空的；飞机的；由飞机进行的
aerospace	1	n.	航空航天工业；航空航天技术
aggravating	5	a.	令人恼怒的，使人烦恼的
aggressively	7	ad.	强有力地；坚持己见地
alas	6	int.	（表示遗憾等的惊叹声）哎呀；唉
albeit	1	conj.	即使；虽然；尽管
alliance	7	n.	联盟；联合
alongside	6	ad.	与……同时；与……共存
aloof	4	a.	冷淡的，疏远的
alpha	5	n.	〈喻〉成功者；希腊字母表的第一个字母
also-ran	5	n.	〈喻〉没有成功或无成就的人
animated	2	a.	动画的
anticipate	2	v.	期望；预料（某事物）
application	3	n.	【计算机】应用程序；应用软件
arena	2	n.	活动或斗争的场所或场面
array	2	n.	大堆；大群；大量
arrogant	7	a.	傲慢的；自大的

269

Words	Units		Definitions
aspiring	10	a.	有进取心的；有抱负的；渴望成功的
astronomical	1	a.	巨大的；庞大的
astutely	10	ad.	精明地；敏锐地
attorney	7	n.	代理人；律师
auctioneer	2	n.	拍卖人
authenticity	4	n.	真实性
baby-boomer	6	n.	（第二次世界大战后的）生育高峰期出生的人
backfire	3	v.	发生意外；产生事与愿违的结果
backlash	5	n.	（对重大事件等）强烈反应；反冲
balance	9	n.	资产负债表；资金平衡表（显示收支总差额的记录）
balloon	6	v.	大大增加；激增
ballpark	2	n.	(数额的)变动范围；变量范围
behemoth	2	n.	庞然大物
bemused	4	a.	困惑的，茫然的，不知所措的
beneficiary	9	n.	受益人
bidder	6	n.	出价人；竞标人
bigotry	6	n.	偏见；偏执的行为
bill	5	v.	宣布；贴广告；列入节目单
blacktop	10	n.	（与碎石混合用以铺路面的）沥青；柏油路
boast	9	v.	有（引以为荣的事物）
bolster	9	v.	支撑；鼓舞
bombard	1	v.	轰击，不断攻击
bond	9	n.	债券
bonus	8	n.	奖金；红利
brainbox	6	n.	〈非正式〉非常聪明的人
breach	8	n.	违反；忽视；破坏（规则、职责、契约等）
brutal	7	a.	激烈的；残酷的；令人不快又无可否认的
buffet	3	v.	反复敲打，连续猛击
by-product	9	n.	副产品
capability	3	n.	性能；功能
cartel	1	n.	卡特尔（各公司为了减少竞争、增加利润而组成的联盟），企业联盟

附录 1 Glossary

Words	Units		Definitions
categorize	4	v.	分类
cede	10	v.	割让，让与
cellular	10	n.	蜂窝式移动电话
charismatic	4	a.	有号召力的；有神授能力的
chop	6	v.	解雇；削减
cite	4	v.	引用，引证
cleanup	10	n.	彻底的清理或排序
cliché	4	n.	陈词滥调，老套
clinical	1	a.	十分客观且不带个人情感的；分析的
clip	4	n.	节选，片段
clip	9	n.	缩减
collision	7	n.	碰撞；冲突
commentator	1	n.	评论员；在新闻中报告和分析事件的广播员或作家
commute	5	v.	每天往返于家和工作单位之间
compensation	8	n.	补偿，赔偿
compile	9	v.	编辑；汇编
complacency	7	n.	自满；得意
complacent	7	a.	自满的，得意的
comprise	9	v.	由……构成；由……组成
concede	8	v.	让步
concourse	3	n.	群集场所；大厅；广场
confront	10	v.	对抗；抵抗
confront	7	v.	面对；面临
conglomerate	10	n.	（通过合并若干企业而组建的）大公司，企业集团
contender	10	n.	竞争者；争夺者；对手
contribute	9	v.	贡献；促成……
convert	3	v.	使转变
coordinate	5	v.	协调；综合；管理
corporate	9	a.	法人团体的；公司的
corruption	1	n.	腐败；贪污；贿赂；受贿
creepy	3	a.	令人生厌的，令人反感的；令人毛骨悚然的，令人不寒而栗的

Words	Units		Definitions
cum	1	prep.	兼作；和
currency	9	n.	货币，通货
cutback	9	n.	缩减，削减，减少
cutting-edge	5	a.	最领先的，最前沿的
cyberspace	2	n.	网络空间，计算机化世界
cyclical	1	a.	循环的；周期性的
debris	10	n.	散落的碎片；瓦砾；残骸
decisive	1	a.	决定性的；有明确结果的
deficit	9	n.	不足；缺乏
de-ice	5	v.	除去……上的冰
demography	6	n.	人口组成（或构成）
destined	8	a.	注定的
devastate	10	v.	彻底毁坏（某事物）；毁灭；摧毁
dip	9	n.	下降
dire	6	a.	极糟的；可怕的
disdain	4	v.	鄙视，不屑
disruption	5	n.	中断；扰乱
dissection	1	n.	剖析；仔细研究或分析
diversity	2	n.	多种多样；多样性
doom	1	v.	使……在劫难逃；注定失败
dose	7	n.	剂量
downturn	9	n.	低迷时期
drag	9	n.	阻碍；妨碍或减慢进程的事物；劣势
drill (down)	3	v.	【计算机】提取多级数据库的低层数据
dumbfound	8	v.	充满惊讶与不解；迷惑
duopoly	1	n.	两家卖主垄断市场（的局面）
dynamism	2	n.	精力，活力；干劲
elite	6	a.	（由于有权力、才能、财富等）被视为最好的或最重要的社会集团；精英；尖子
empathize	5	v.	理解；移情
empathy	5	n.	感情移入，同感；（对他人的感情、经历等的）想象力和感受
entice	3	v.	诱惑；吸引
envision	3	v.	想象；展望

附录 1　Glossary

Words	Units		Definitions
epic	1	n. / a.	描写英雄事迹的诗；史诗 / 具有史诗性质的，史诗般的
epiphany	3	n.	对事物真谛的顿悟；事物本质的突然显露
espionage	1	n.	侦探；间谍活动
evaporate	7	v.	蒸发；消失
exemplify	4	v.	例证
exhort	4	v.	恳切地、通常令人激动地劝告、建议或请求
expertly	10	ad.	熟练地；专业地
fabric	2	n.	织物
fabric	8	n.	一种复杂的基础结构
facilitator	7	n.	援助；援手
fallout	8	n.	（尤指一特殊事件预料不到的）附带影响或后果
fancy-free	6	a.	随心所欲的，无义务或约束的；无忧无虑的
fantasy	3	n.	幻想
fascinating	8	a.	迷人的，醉人的
fiasco	5	n.	彻底的失败，惨败
fiduciary	8	a.	基于信用的；信托的；受信托的
fillip	9	n.	刺激；激励，鼓励
flawed	4	a.	有缺陷的
flop	1	n.	失败
flourish	2	v.	昌盛，兴旺，繁荣
footloose	6	a.	自由自在的，行动无拘束的
forfeit	8	v.	（因做错事或为得到某事物）失去或放弃（另一事物）
forge	10	v.	〈喻〉（靠艰苦工作）建立（通常为长期关系）
forthcoming	4	a.	即将来临的
foul-mouthed	2	a.	口出恶言的，出言粗俗的
gear	2	n.	（远征、运动等需用的）设备、装备、衣物等
gloomily	2	ad.	忧愁地，沮丧地
gnawing	6	a.	折磨人的，令人痛苦的
grandeur	1	n.	伟大；壮丽；雄伟

Words	Units		Definitions
greenback	9	n.	美钞
gripping	1	a.	激动人心的；吸引人的；扣人心弦的
grudgingly	9	ad.	不情愿地，勉强地
guru	6	n.	专家；权威
hail	10	v.	来自（某地）
harassment	8	n.	烦扰；骚扰
haunt	6	v.	缠扰，烦扰
head-to-head	1	a.	短兵相接的；正面交锋的 n. 白刃战；势均力敌的比赛
heady	6	a.	易使人醉的；使人兴奋的
hijack	6	v.	〈非正式〉盗用；滥用
hike	9	n.	突然的或急剧的上升，上涨；增加
hit	2	n.	红极一时的人物或事物；成功
homegrown	9	a.	本国（或本地）制造的
hum	9	v.	活跃；忙碌
hyped-up	4	a.	被令人兴奋的事刺激的
immense	10	a.	巨大的，广大的
imminent	6	a.	邻近的；即将发生的；逼近的
imprisonment	7	n.	关押；入狱
impromptu	3	a.	事先无准备的；即兴的
inextricable	5	a.	分不开的，紧密联系的
inflation	9	n.	通货膨胀
innate	6	a.	先天的，天生的
insider	8	n.	内部的人；会员；知道内情的人；权威人士
insight	7	n.	（对复杂事情的）顿悟，猛醒
institution	6	n.	社会公共机构
intangible	6	a.	触摸不到的；无形的
integral	2	a.	构成整体所必需的
integrity	8	n.	正直，诚实
intensity	7	n.	特别强烈的程度、力量或动力；（感情的）强度
intervene	6	v.	介入；干预；调停，调解，斡旋
intractable	7	a.	难处理的

附录1　Glossary

Words	Units		Definitions
invariably	8	ad.	不变地；总是
invite	4	v.	征求；请求
irritating	6	a.	使人不愉快的，恼人的，使人烦恼的
jaw-dropping	4	a.	令人瞠目的；让人大跌眼镜的
juncture	8	n.	时刻；关键时刻
justify	6	v.	证明……正当（或有理、正确）
kiosk	3	n.	售货亭
kitschy	2	a.	（艺术、设计等）俗气、矫饰的
know-how	6	n.	〈口〉技术；实际知识，技能
landscape	10	n.	全景；形势
landscape	2	n.	全景
lapse	8	n.	错误，过失
latent	7	a.	潜在的；潜伏的，隐藏的
lawsuit	6	n.	诉讼（尤指非刑事案件）
ledger	9	n.	分类账
legacy	6	n.	遗赠，遗赠的财物；遗产
lineup	2	n.	为某目的而安排的一批事情或项目；（用于同一用途的）一批东西
lingo	3	n.	行话，术语
literally	10	ad.	真实地；确切地
long-haul	1	a.	（运送货物或旅客）长途的；远距离的
lucrative	1	a.	可获利的，赚钱的
lure	6	v.	吸引，引诱
lurk	7	v.	潜伏；埋伏
luxurious	5	a.	奢侈的；极舒适的
manipulate	3	v.	（熟练地）操作；使用；巧妙地处理
maze	5	n.	（事情等的）错综，复杂
mecca	2	n.	渴望去的地方；胜地
merchandising	2	n.	买卖（商品）；推销（商品）
meritocracy	6	n.	精英领导
mettle	7	n.	忍耐力；勇气；精神
microcosm	2	n.	缩影，具体而微者
momentum	8	n.	动力；势头

Words	Units		Definitions
monopoly	1	n.	垄断；专营服务
morale	8	n.	士气；民心
motivating	4	a.	激励的，鼓舞人的
multinational	10	n.	跨国公司
narrative	1	n.	故事；叙述
navigate	3	v.	【计算机】浏览（网站、文件、因特网等）；导航
navigation	3	n.	【计算机】浏览（网站、文件、因特网等）；导航
newsletter	4	n.	时事通讯，新闻快报
niche	2	n.	产品或服务所需的特殊领域；利基（针对企业的优势细分出来的市场）
optimize	3	v.	使尽可能完善
orientation	5	n.	培训，训练
oust	4	v.	驱逐；撵走从而取代
outcome	8	n.	结果，成果
outfit	2	n. / v.	机构；商业组织／装备；配备；供给
outfit	3	n.	全套服装
outfitter	5	n.	（专营）商店
outlay	9	n.	花费，开支（尤指有助于公司等进一步发展的）
overdo	6	v.	把……做得过分；过于夸张
ownership	8	n.	所有权；物主身份
panic	6	n.	恐慌，惊慌
pant	4	v.	喘气
paranoia	7	n.	多疑
paranoid	7	a.	多疑的
patent	6	n.	专利
peer	4	n.	同等之人，同辈
perk	2	n.	（工作、职位等带来的）好处，利益；便利；特权
perspective	8	n.	相对重要的客观评估和评价；观点，看法
persuasion	2	n.	信念；见解

附录 1 Glossary

Words	Units		Definitions
peruse	3	v.	仔细观察；仔细考虑；仔细阅读
pervasive	8	a.	无处不在的；遍布的
petroleum	10	n.	石油
pillar	9	n.	柱子，支柱；栋梁
plight	5	n.	困境
plow	10	v.	将（利润）作为资本再投资于原企业中
pocketbook	8	n.	经济来源；钱袋，皮夹
poll	2	v.	对某人作民意调查
pop	3	v.	冷不防地出现（或发生），（突然）冒出
populist	6	n.	平民主义者
post	9	v.	发布，公布，宣布（尤指财经信息或警告）
potent	1	a.	有力的；有效的
powerhouse	10	n.	有影响力的机构或地方
preach	4	v.	说教；鼓吹
precarious	8	a.	不稳定的
prevail	10	v.	获胜，占上风；力量或影响较大；胜利
proactive	5	a.	积极主动的；先发制人的
project	6	v.	预计；推断
prompt	5	v.	促使或激励（某人）做某事
prosecute	7	v.	起诉；告发
prowess	1	n.	不凡的技能
pursuant	7	a.	出自并依据……的；与……一致的；依照的
purveyor	2	n.	供应货物或提供服务的人或公司
quilting	2	n.	（被子的）绗缝；一种手工艺爱好
rank-and-file	5	a.	普通的，一般的
rating	3	n.	评定结果；评分
ration	6	v.	配给供应，定量供应
receipt	9	n.	收入；收到的数量
recession	9	n.	衰退（经济活动普遍而持续地衰败，尤指三个连续季度的国民生产总值的下降）
reinforce	8	v.	增强，加强
relentlessly	1	ad.	不停地，不松懈地；无情地，残酷地
reserved	4	a.	有所保留的；含蓄的

Words	Units		Definitions
resignation	8	n.	辞职
resolution	3	n.	分辨率
resonate	5	v.	产生共鸣；发出回响，回荡
rich-media	3	a.	富媒体的（具有动画、声音、视频和／或交互性的信息传播方法）
rife	1	a.	流行的；普遍的
ripen	10	v.	成熟
rock	1	v.	使（某人／某事物）极为不安或震惊
scandal	1	n.	丑行；使人震惊的丑恶事；丑闻
scented	2	a.	有香味的
sci-fi	3	n. & a.	〈口〉科学幻想小说（的）
scramble	5	n.	争夺；抢夺
scripted	5	a.	照稿读的
seamless	5	a.	平滑的；浑然一体的；无裂缝的；无伤痕的
second-tier	6	a.	二线的，二流的
secure	1	v.	获得
security	9	n.	有价证券；标明所有权和债权的文件；股票证书或证券
seismic	10	n.	极其重要的；震撼世界的
sensory	2	a.	感觉的，感受的
session	5	n.	（进行某活动连续的）一段时间
setback	8	n.	挫折，顿挫
shiny	10	a.	发亮的；锃亮的
shortcut	8	n.	捷径
shrine	5	n.	具有重要意义的地方
sink	8	v.	使进入低下或被毁的状况；击败或破坏
snag	8	n.	阻碍，障碍
snarl	5	n.	拥挤、阻塞的状态（尤指交通）
snowboarding	2	n.	滑板滑雪运动
soul-searching	8	n.	真挚的自我反省；深思
span	9	v.	横跨，跨越
spectacular	8	a.	引人注目的；与众不同的；轰动一时的；惊人的
sphere	4	n.	方面；领域

附录 1 Glossary

Words	Units		Definitions
spin	3	v.	使旋转
spouse	8	n.	配偶（指夫或妻）
sprint	1	n.	速度或活动的突然爆发；全速疾跑，短距离赛跑
squabble	1	v.	口角；争吵
stake	1	n.	投资；赌注
straight-talkers	4	n.	言语坦率者，直言不讳者
stream	3	v.	用计算机网络流媒体播放
stylish	2	a.	时髦的，新潮的；高雅的
sub-standard	6	a.	不够标准的，在标准以下的
subtract	9	v.	减去；减
successor	1	n.	继任者；接替的事物
sue	7	v.	控告；起诉
suit	7	n.	诉讼（尤指非刑事案件）
super-jumbo	1	n.	特大型客机
supplemental	3	a.	补充的
surge	9	v.	猛冲；激增
suspicion	1	n.	怀疑；嫌疑
sustainable	8	a.	可持续的
sustained	1	a.	持续的，持久的
synonym	6	n.	同义词
tailspin	7	n.	混乱；慌乱；失控状态
tap	7	v.	发掘，开发；自某物/某人处引出或获取（某物）
texture	3	n.	（一物体表面、物质或织物的）质地；外观；手感（如厚薄、软硬、粗细等）
thriller	3	n.	惊险电影；恐怖电影
thrive	2	n.	茁壮成长，蓬勃发展，繁荣
thrust	9	n.	猛推；推力
tolerate	1	v.	容忍，忍受
transition	3	n.	过渡，过渡时期；转变，变迁
trawl	3	v.	在……搜罗；查阅
treacherous	8	a.	变化莫测的；危险的；欺骗性的
trespassers	6	n.	非法侵入某人地界者

Words	Units		Definitions
trickle	1	v.	缓缓地流；细流
trigger	3	v.	引起；促使
triumph	1	n.	成功；胜利；得意扬扬
turkey	2	n.	火鸡
turnaround	4	n.	（经济、经营等的）彻底转变
turnover	5	n.	人事变更率，人员调整率
ubiquitous	1	a.	无处不在的；十分普遍的
unconventional	4	a.	非传统的
underestimate	4	v.	低估，看轻
understated	4	a.	表达简略的；不充分的
unfold	5	v.	（使某事物）显露，展现
unsophisticated	10	a.	知识、经验不丰富的
upswing	9	n.	增长，向上的趋势；兴隆
uptake	5	n.	理解，领会
utilization	9	n.	利用
vanish	2	v.	完全消失；不复存在；消逝
venerable	10	a.	（因年纪、经历或曾拥有过的重要地位等而）令人尊重敬佩的；老牌的
versus	1	prep.	对；对抗
visual	3	n.	画面；图像
voucher	5	n.	（代替现金的）凭单，凭证，代金券
waffly	6	a.	含糊其辞的，模棱两可的
weather	10	v.	平安度过（危难），经历（危难）而存活
whoop	4	v.	大叫，高声喊叫
withstand	10	v.	承受住，经得住，抵住
wrench	7	v.	猛扭；猛推
wry	1	a.	嘲弄的，用反语表达幽默的；不高兴的；不屑的
XML	3	abbr.	可扩展标记语言
yawning	9	a.	裂开的；距离大的
yeahhhs	4	int.	耶
yield	9	n.	（投资等的）利润；收益
zoom	3	v.	（摄影机）迅速接近被摄对象；（用变焦距镜头）推近

Phrases & Expressions

Phrases & Expressions	Units	Definitions
account for	9	占总数的数量或比例
act on	4	按照……行事
allow for	8	考虑到某种可能性；考虑到客观情况
as for	6	至于
as usual	9	照常
at one's fingertips	3	近在手边；随时可供应用；立即可以得到
at rates of	9	以……的速度
at top of one's voice	4	提高嗓门，声嘶力竭
baby boomer	2	生育高峰期出生的人
be lost on	7	不产生效果；不为注意
be set to	10	准备好做某事；决定做某事
big-box store	2	占地面积很大的大零售商店；大盒子商业中心
bottom line	8	要点，关键之处
bottom line	9	最终赢利（或亏损）；损益表底线
bounce back	1	（受挫折后）恢复元气
bring out	7	生产某物；使发挥；使显露
business cycle	6	经济周期（以衰退、财政复苏、增长、财政下跌为典型特征）
call for	6	要求；需要
call in a loan	7	讨还借款
capital goods	9	资本货物
cases in point	4	适当的例子
cast/spread one's net wide	6	想尽办法寻找，千方百计搜罗
catch up on	1	了解（已发生的事情）
catch/throw sb. off guard	10	（乘某人不备做某事而）使某人措手不及
churn out	6	大量地生产出

Phrases & Expressions	Units	Definitions
clamp down (on)	6	（对……）进行压制；（对……）强行限制；（对……）进行取缔
come across	4	使人产生某种印象
come clean	8	坦白交代，承认
come close to sth. / to doing sth.	1	几乎达到；差不多
come up with	5	提出（建议），拿出（主意）
come/go/turn full circle	10	循环；周而复始
contract rigging	1	合同欺诈
count on	10	依赖，依靠
cover up	8	掩盖；隐瞒
credit market	9	信贷市场
creep in	7	慢慢地或无声地进入
crow over	1	自鸣得意，扬扬自得
cup of tea	2	喜爱的事物
cut out	10	排挤出
cut short	9	提前缩减
do well	6	明智；做得好，进展好
dole out	1	布施；少量分配
dress up	2	穿上盛装
drop out	3	退出
duke it out	10	打个输赢
end up (with)	6	以……告终
fall apart	1	崩溃；破裂
fall back on	9	有困难时（能）求助于某人；依靠某事物
fantasy football	3	空幻足球
fight one's way	7	努力前进，克服困难前进
flow from sth.	6	来自，产生于，源于
for all intents and purposes	5	在一切重要方面；实际上；几乎完全
frontline reps	5	第一线的工作人员
get by	2	勉强维生；设法维持
give in	8	屈服，让步
go bust	6	〈俚〉破产
go round	6	（指某物的数或量）足够每人一份

附录2　Phrases & Expressions

Phrases & Expressions	Units	Definitions
go with	1	与某事同时（或同地）存在；与某事相伴而生
grind to a halt	1	（指过程）慢慢停止
in a similar vein	2	同样地
in charge	4	主管
in particular	9	特别是，尤其是
in place	3	到位的；可用的
in return for	8	以……为报答，回报，回礼
in sb's interest(s)	6	为某人的利益，对某人有好处，有利于某人
in the event of	5	如果……发生
in the long run	8	从长远看；从最终结果来看
in the shape of sb. / sth.	1	以某人 / 某事物的形式
in the short term	8	短期
in the wake of	10	经过……之后，在……之后
in... health	8	处于……身体状态
ink... with	7	与……签约
iron ore	10	铁矿石
joint venture	10	合资企业
keep... up to date	4	使……及时了解
later on	8	稍后；以后
lay the foundation for	8	为……打基础
lead by example	8	身体力行，起带头作用
let your guard down	7	放松警惕
like hell	6	拼命地
look back	8	回顾，回想
lose height	1	失去领先地位
make amends	5	补偿；赔偿；将功补（过）
make do (with)	6	凑合着对付过去；将就使用，勉强应付
make for	1	促成；有利于
make one's name	1	成名
meta data	3	诠释数据
on a tear	9	快速发展
on balance	9	总而言之

Phrases & Expressions	Units	Definitions
on record	9	（指事实、事件等）记载下来的；（尤指）正式记录的
on the go	3	〈口〉忙个不停
one way or the other	7	不是用这种方法就是用那种方法
Pacific Rim	9	太平洋圈；环太平洋国家和地区
pay homage to	4	对……表示尊敬或尊重
place/put a premium on	6	高度评价；高度重视
pluck sb. from the field	5	成功提拔；成功地重用（不知名的人）
plug into	3	与……连接
press ahead (with sth.)	1	加紧（努力）；坚决继续进行
press release	3	（通讯社或政府机构等发布的）新闻稿
prime time	3	黄金时间；全盛时期
pull back	5	退出
put on	4	装作有某事物，假装采纳某事物
put/set/turn one's mind to sth.	10	下定决心要做某事
ramp up	10	增加、扩张商业活动
rather than	4	而不是……，而非……；替代……
reach out to sb.	4	向人们表示你对他们感兴趣，愿意和他们交流
rev up	2	增加，增长；更加活跃
rise to the challenge	7	有随机应变、克服困难、完成任务等的能力
root in	4	植根于
sales volume	3	销售额
set apart from	2	使某人/某事物与众不同或优于其他的
shake up	10	改革，变革；改组
shopping mall	2	大型零售购物中心
shore up	9	支持
show up	9	（使）看得见；变得明显；显现出来
sign up	3	与……达成交易
slippery slope	8	〈英，非正式〉（恶习等）无法克制以致严重后果
soft loan	1	无条件长期低息贷款；优惠贷款
specialty retailer	2	特种商品零售商；特色零售店
spell out	8	使清楚易懂；详细解释

Phrases & Expressions	Units	Definitions
stand for	3	主张；支持
stand out	6	引人注目
stay/be true to your principles/beliefs	8	忠实于原则/信仰
step into	7	开始做某事
stock option	8	优先认股权，在规定的时间内以规定的价格买卖具体证券或商品的权利
structural unemployment	6	（指因工业改组，尤指因技术进步而非供需变化造成的）结构性失业
take advantage of	9	利用
take off in a big way	8	大规模地开始
take on	8	呈现（某种性质、样子等）；装成某事物
take pity on...	5	同情
take... to heart	4	很在乎某事，对某事看得很重
talk at	4	对……唠叨不休
throw sth away	6	浪费掉（本领）；错过（机会）
to the extreme	4	极度地，非常地
to this day	1	直到如今；甚至现在
town hall	4	市政厅
trade union	6	工会
turn one's back on	1	背弃；掉头不理睬某人
unit sales	10	单位产品销售额
ups and downs	1	盛衰；浮沉
usher in	10	开创；开始；引进某（新）事物
venture capital	7	风险投资
wink at	7	假装看不见

Activity File

Unit Three

Role A

Amazon.com, Inc.

Description

Opened its virtual doors in July 1995 by Jeff Bezos in Seattle.

Operates retail Web sites; sources and sells a range of products to its customers; provides programs that enable third parties to sell products on its Web sites; allow customers to shop for products owned by third parties using its features and technologies.

Business

Sells only on-line and is essentially an information broker; has constantly growing database of over 12 million customers in more than 160 countries; is the place to find and discover anything customers want to buy online; have earth's biggest selection of products, including millions of books, free electronic greeting cards, online auctions, videos, CDs, DVDs, toys, games, electronics, kitchenware, computers, and more.

Mission

To become the largest selection of select retail categories; to provide the best shopping experience; to convince all online customers to use Amazon as their search platform; to provides excellent customers personalize services and discount profitable prices.

Corporation objectives

Improve customer relationships; expand products and services; expand partnerships; profitability in every Amazon.com business.

Marketing Objectives

Achieve a 200% increase in sales per year for books; achieve a 250% increase in sales per year for music; achieve a 275% increase in sales per year for movies; achieve a 100% increase in sales per year for electronics & software.

Contact information

1200 12th Avenue South

Suite 1200

Seattle, WA 98144-2734

United States - Map

Phone: 206-266-1000

Fax: 206-622-2405

Web Site: http://www.amazon.com

EBay Inc.

Description

Formed as a sole proprietorship in September 1995; incorporated in California in May 1996; reincorporated in Delaware and completed the initial public offering of its common stock in September 1998; brings together millions of buyers and sellers every day on a local, national and international basis through an array of websites; provides online marketplaces for the sale of goods and services, online payments services and online communication offerings to a diverse community of individuals and businesses.

Business

Three primary businesses: the eBay Marketplaces, providing the infrastructure to enable online commerce in a variety of formats, including the traditional auction platform; Payments business, consisting of its PayPal business, enables businesses to securely, easily and quickly send and receive payments online; Communications business, consisting of its Skype business, enables VoIP calls between Skype users, as well as provides low-cost connectivity to traditional fixed-line and mobile telephones.

Competitors

Amazon.com; Google; Microsoft; Yahoo!; Collectors Universe; Sotheby's Holdings

Mission

Create the world's online marketplace by improving and expanding across three main areas: categories, formats, and geographies.

Efforts

Seeks to attract buyers and sellers to its community by offering:

Buyers: selection, value, convenience and Entertainment; Sellers: access to markets, efficient marketing and distribution costs, ability to maximize prices and opportunity to increase sales, products and services, expand partnerships.

Contact information

2145 Hamilton Avenue

San Jose, CA 95125

United States

Phone: 408-376-7400

Fax: 408-369-4855

Web Site: http://www.ebay.com